THE MAKING OF THE AUDEN CANON

The Making of the
AUDEN CANON

by Joseph Warren Beach

THE UNIVERSITY OF MINNESOTA PRESS

821.91
A899B

Acknowledgments

MY GRATEFUL acknowledgments for assistance in this study are made to the University of Minnesota Library and to the public libraries of Minneapolis and St. Paul, to many individuals in the University Library, and especially to Mrs. Janet Rhame for her helpful service in securing interlibrary loans. In this matter of interlibrary loans acknowledgments are made to the Library of Congress, the university libraries of Yale, Columbia, Pennsylvania, and Iowa, the Newberry Library of Chicago, and the public library of Cincinnati, without whose courteous help a number of rare books would have been inaccessible to me.

Most especially I wish to make acknowledgment to my good friends Professors William Van O'Connor and Leonard Unger for their unfailing interest in this undertaking and for invaluable suggestions for my study and its manner of presentation. I also wish to acknowledge my indebtedness to Mrs. O'Connor for her frequent helpfulness in locating passages in the Bible and in English classical poetry, and to my wife, Dagmar Doneghy, for her patience with the vagaries of a bookworm and her unflagging interest in my present undertaking.

J. W. B.

March 15, 1957

Table of Contents

THE MAKING OF THE AUDEN CANON

Preliminary Statement of Aims

THE following is meant to be a record of the facts in regard to W. H. Auden's procedure in making up the texts of the *Collected Poetry* (Random House, 1945) and the *Collected Shorter Poems* (Faber and Faber, 1950), in the following matters: textual alterations made in the poems as they appeared in earlier collections and/or in periodicals; excision of passages of some length in the poems reprinted; elimination of entire poems published in earlier collections and/or periodicals. Suggestions will be made as we go along as to the probable reasons for the revisions, excisions, and eliminations noted, in terms of the poet's artistic ideals and taste, and of changes in his thinking during the period covered.

My hope is that this study may not be altogether barren of results serviceable in a critique and evaluation of the work of this distinguished poet. But while my interest is certainly not confined to the technical aspects of the subject, this project does involve a large amount of factual detail, requiring close attention to textual variations. I have tried in my presentation to lighten the burden of factuality so far as is consistent with thoroughness and precision. But even so it may at times tax the patience of readers eager to reach broad critical conclusions. And accordingly, for my general conclusions, such as they are, the reader is referred particularly to Chapters 18 to 20, where they are summarized.

Most often, in reprinting a poem from an earlier volume or from a periodical, Auden reproduces it without change, thus indicating his approval of it as it stands. But the exceptions to this procedure are numerous and significant, and it is with these exceptions that this study is mainly concerned. In the following chapter, I begin with an interesting and typical example of the procedure by which a poem is made to conform to the poet's taste and views at the time the collection was made.

((1

"In Time of War": Revisions in the Commentary

IN 1937, W. H. Auden and Christopher Isherwood were commissioned by the English publishing house of Faber and Faber to write a travel book about the East. They left England in January 1938 and returned at the end of July. The Sino-Japanese War was in full swing, and the two writers spent nearly four months traveling in China, conferring with people of many races and brands of opinion and visiting several battlefronts. Early in 1939, in London and New York, was published their *Journey to a War*. The account of their travels and impressions was here given in a prose "travel diary" written apparently by Isherwood; and this was accompanied by thirty-four sonnets and a verse "Commentary" written by Auden.

Twenty-seven of these sonnets, entitled "In Time of War," together with the Commentary, make up an extended philosophical essay on the political and spiritual condition of the world at the time of writing, from the point of view of a man observing the local scene in China, but also familiar with the history of mankind from the beginning of life on the planet. We witness here the separation of man from lower animal life through development of his higher faculties. We review the phenomena of chivalry, the appearance of the democratic ideal, the search for truth, the rise of prophets and poets, the progress of civilization in the form of finance, churches, monasticism, scientific discovery, and spiritual disillusionment. Many heroic leaders and deliverers had their turn, until, as that age ended and "the last deliverer died / In bed, grown idle and unhappy," the inventors of "Fairly-Noble unifying Lies" undertook but failed to unite and pacify the world. There are pictures of the misery and helplessness of the common people, and the common soldier, in time of war, while "Austria died and China was forsaken." But in spite of all this, the poet persists in praising life itself. He acknowledges that, with the best of intentions, "the Good Place has not been," and "the life of man is never quite completed." But he insists that men do have the power of choice, they can labor in "the little workshop of love," and their destiny is in their own hands. "We have no destiny assigned us"; "Nothing is given: we must find our law."

In the Commentary we have a still broader survey of human evolution, the growth of the ideal of "human freedom," and the many setbacks that it has had: the collapse of the Roman Empire; the loss of hope in the Church accompanying the advance of scientific study; and the class struggle following on the Industrial Revolution and the setting of head and heart at odds with each other. This all culminates in the spreading power of fascist authoritarianism as exemplified in Italy, Germany, Japan, and Spain. The totalitarian propaganda is summed up in a statement in which its partisans say, *"Man can have Unity if Man will give up Freedom,"* and bid their followers:

"Leave Truth to the Police and us; we know the Good;
We build the Perfect City time shall never alter."

The poet goes on to trace the rudiments of these poisonous ideas through many historical leaders and thinkers, from Ch'in Shih Huang Ti to Bernard Bosanquet, and including Genghis Khan, Napoleon, "Plato the good, despairing of the average man," Hobbes, and Hegel. But all along, he points out, there have been great supporters of human freedom, "who never lost their faith in knowledge nor in man," and who still speak to us from the grave. They tell us how it is our own injustice that has undermined our freedom; but assure us that, with "a whole and happy conscience," and "by those who reverence it," life can be "mastered" and Unity be made "compatible with Freedom." And finally this single voice of Man is heard invoking the power within him, praying that he may outgrow his madness, may "rally the lost and trembling forces of the will,"

> *Till they construct at last a human justice,*
> *The contribution of our star, within the shadow*
> *Of which uplifting, loving, and constraining power*
> *All other reasons may rejoice and operate.*

Altogether "In Time of War" makes an eloquent and inspiriting plea for the humanistic ideal of the good life, to be built up on earth by the earnest pursuit of social justice supported by generous fellow-feeling. But it is well known that, within a very few years of its composition, Auden became a convinced adherent of the strict Christian doctrine that the good life in its fullness can never be approximated on earth save with the aid of supernatural grace, and never wholly realized save in Eternity in the City of God. And present-day readers of "In Time of War" who are not closely attentive to the text may very well take this whole work to be an anticipation of the most orthodox Christian views. Indeed, when they read these poems in the *Collected Poetry* of 1945, they will find what seems clear evidence that this is the case. For when they come to the concluding passages of the Commentary, they will find, in the last stanza, a statement very different from that quoted above from the original publication. They will read instead:

> *Till, as the contribution of our star, we follow*
> *The clear instructions of that Justice, in the shadow*
> *Of Whose uplifting, loving, and constraining power*
> *All human reasons do rejoice and operate.*

The reader will here note that, instead of *"constructing at last a human justice,"* man is adjuring himself to *"follow the clear instructions"* of a Justice not human — a Justice capitalized and thereby signalized as divine. The divinity of this Justice is further emphasized by the capitalized personal pronoun "Whose" in the following line, in place of the neutral "which," and the substitution in the final line of "human reasons" for "other reasons," where (in the revision) the human reasons of a secular or purely humanistic philosophy are opposed to the divine reasons derived from God's will. The same alterations from the original form of the poem are reproduced in the English volume that most nearly corresponds to the American *Collected Poetry*, the *Collected Shorter Poems 1930–1944*, 1950. And since this is the last poem included in that volume (though not the latest in date), and these four lines are the final lines of text, the reader may well be left with the impression that this entire set of poems was written by a man who was at the time a convinced adherent of orthodox Christian doctrine, and may proceed to read them over page by page in the light of this mistaken assumption.

This alteration of the phrasing and sense of the final stanza is the most important but not the sole revision made in the 1945 text of the Commentary. Earlier in the poem, Auden was speaking of the rise of the Christian and other churches on the ruins of the Roman Empire and what he originally wrote was: "Upon its ruins rose the Universal Churches." He was thinking, it might seem, not merely of the Christian churches, Roman Catholic, Greek Orthodox, Anglican, etc., but also of Islam, with its pretensions to universality; and there would appear to be some irony in his reference to their common and competing claims. In 1945 and 1950 this line reads: "Upon its ruins rose the Plainly Visible Churches." Here the reference would seem to be to the distinction made by St. Augustine between the visible churches of this imperfect temporal world and the true and infallible church that exists in the invisible and eternal City of God. And once again what was a neutral or slightly ironic view of ecclesiastical history was turned into a properly Christian and inoffensive rendering of the same facts.

Somewhat later in the poem Auden is referring to the great debate going on throughout the earth between the proponents of fascist authoritarianism and of humanist democracy (or socialism). It is actually going on, he says, in the Moslem world, in England, in America, Hungary, France, and "here" in China. Here "thousands believe" (in fascism) "and millions are half-way to conviction." But everywhere, too, are those religious or metaphysical fatalists who take no side in this debate.

Where others have accepted *Pascal's* wager and resolve
To take whatever happens as the will of God,
Or with *Spinoza* vote that evil is unreal.

Everyone has heard of Pascal's decision, where the balance hangs
even between unfaith and faith, to take his chance with faith,
since, if that is not truth he can lose nothing, and if it is truth he
may gain eternal life and happiness. Well, this passage as it stood
would seem to reflect unfavorably on Christian Pascal as promoting neutralism and inaction in the great debate and struggle of the
ages. And Auden, in 1945, evidently realizing that the ironic tone
of this stanza does not suit his present position, simply drops it
out of the poem. The present-day reader will not find it in either
1945 or 1950.

The other revisions are less impressive in themselves, but in the
light of those already noted may be taken as indicative of a similar
motivation. In introducing Man's final appeal in favor of a human
justice to be constructed, Auden wrote in the original: "The
Voice of Man: 'O teach me to outgrow my madness.'" In 1945
and 1950 this reads: "The Voice of Man: *'O teach us to outgrow
our madness.'*" One does not know how to account for this slight
change unless possibly on the assumption that it seemed to the
author to give to this invocation more the effect of a church
prayer addressed to the deity. But it is quite insufficient to over-
rule the clear indications of the context. What Man is here invoking is not any supernal power outside, but a strength and
wisdom within his own heart, communicated to him by the spirits
of all those dead and living ones "who never lost their faith in
knowledge nor in man," but who lived and died, and were still
living and dying, for the ideal of freedom. This voice of Man the
poet hears everywhere throughout the world, and more especially
he hears it in Shanghai, the city that was the seat of the abortive
socialist revolution as pictured by Malraux in his novel *La Condition humaine.*

And now I hear it rising round me from Shanghai,
And mingling in the distant mutter of guerilla fighting,
The voice of Man. . . .

9

Just at this point there came another stanza which the author cut out. This is a part of Man's utterance.

> It's better to be sane than mad, or liked than dreaded;
> It's better to sit down to nice meals than to nasty;
> It's better to sleep two than single; it's better
>   to be happy.

The poet was here enumerating, in homely realistic terms, some of the advantages of a peaceful and ordered world over the present state of violence and disorder. It is madness and fear that provoke wars and are bred by them. Isherwood often refers in his travel diary to Auden's suffering in health from the "nasty" diet sometimes encountered in their Chinese travels. Looking back on the poem at a later date, Auden must have felt that these details were not in harmony with the exalted and prayerful tone of this concluding passage of admonition.

Thus by the omission of two offending three-line stanzas and by the discreet rewording of several passages retained, Auden in 1945 gave to this whole set of poems, "In Time of War," a more distinctively religious cast than they had when first written in 1938 and published in 1939 — making them more admissible into what we may call the Auden canon. It is as if a pagan had been transformed into a child of grace by the magic of baptismal regeneration.

ℭ 2

Certain Peculiarities of Auden's Method

A S T H I S study proceeds, we shall come upon many instances of this process of improvement or sanctification by slight verbal alterations and the excision of dubious passages, some of them of considerable length. More striking still is the total abandonment of many poems, very often for apparently ideological reasons. And in one case, we shall find Auden reprinting in the *Collected Poetry* a long prose sermon from *The Dog beneath the Skin,* which was there a satirical parody of ecclesiastical eloquence employed in the interest of political propaganda, but which, as reproduced word for word in the canonical volume, is presented as a profound and edifying exposition of religious truth. Auden introduces this sermon with a brief note explaining the finer points of doctrine set forth in it. But otherwise he relies simply on its appearing where it does along with other edifying work to ensure our taking it as a sober religious document and not, what it was in origin, a sneering Voltairean exposé of clerical hypocrisy and time-serving under the influence of mass hysteria.

This process of turning to the purposes of sound thinking and edification work that in 1945 seemed unsound or questionable in its original form is facilitated by the comparative inaccessibility of Auden's earlier publications to the general reader, the fact that in the earlier volumes most of the poems do not have titles, but are identifiable only by their opening lines, and the almost complete darkness in which the reader is left in the *Collected Poetry* as to the date and provenance of any particular poem and the context in which it was originally conceived.

If Auden's poems were mere lyrical effusions expressive of the author's mood, or pure imaginative creations without philosophical intention, such placing of the poems in their original context would not be felt as particularly needful, or would have only a curious interest for critics tracing the poet's development and progress in craftsmanship. Nor would it be of pressing importance if the philosophical meaning were transparently clear as if rendered with the plainness, precision, and literalness of scientific prose. But that is not the case. Here we are dealing with a typical "modern" poet, who sedulously avoids the "frontal attack" on his subject, whose thought is characteristically rendered by the "oblique" or indirect method, the terms of his discourse being, not philosophical abstractions and plain statements of fact, but symbols, myths, and implications, and whose effects are complicated by the use of such rhetorical devices as irony, "ambiguity," and dramatic impersonation. As a poet of our age, he inclines to shun the sort of explanation, definition, and painstaking development of topic sentences in which young students are exercised in college courses in expository writing. His poetry is highly evocative, imaginative, "incantatory." Like others of his time, he aims at brevity and condensation rather than at diffuseness and elaboration. Clarity is with him a secondary consideration; and for the untrained or literal-minded reader he is often difficult and even obscure. So that for a reader who wishes earnestly to get at the original intent of a given poem, it is often a matter of real importance to determine the date of composition in order that it may be understood in terms of the theories, prepossessions, and attitudes prevailing with the author at the time of writing.

And here it is that Mr. Auden most signally fails to enlighten us. In the *Collected Poetry* the order in which the poems follow one another is more a cause than a cure for confusion. In Parts I and III, comprising the main body of the shorter poems and of those designated as Songs and Other Musical Pieces, a simple enough principle is followed. In each of these parts, the poems succeed one another in alphabetical order, not of titles but of first lines. "Musée des Beaux Arts" comes first because the first line,

"About suffering they were never wrong," begins with the letters Abo. "In War Time" follows next because the poem begins with the letters Abr. "The Witnesses" comes last in this first set of poems because it starts with the letters You. This apparently simple and logical system has doubtless certain advantages for author and reader. For one thing it makes it unnecessary to append an index of first lines, though someone must have compiled such an index so that poems from many different sources might be made to fall in their correct positions in the alphabetical order. But this system does not have the advantage of placing together poems that have a natural affinity in style, subject matter, or thought; nor does it give the reader any clue as to the date of composition or the place in which the poem originally appeared. The poems in Part I begin with a piece from early in 1939, follow this with a poem which made its first appearance in 1945, and end with a poem made up of two parts, one dating from 1933 and one from 1935; and in between, poems from 1930 constantly jostle those from 1941, poems from 1936 those from 1944.

Now, between 1930 and 1945 Auden changed styles and ideological positions several times, and in the end he changed them radically. And the reader is constantly passing from poems conceived in one ideology to poems conceived in some quite different ideology or philosophy. One may not be aware that he is making this transition, and may innocently interpret a poem rooted in one ideological position in terms of an opposed position. But even so, a discerning reader, though unaware of the transition, may be conscious of some discomfort in making it. In these woods he finds much to interest him and much to impress. He feels sure that they are full of game. But like anyone lost in the woods, he suspects that he is going round in circles. And if at length he begins to take account of the alphabetical system followed, he cannot fail to realize that the alphabet makes strange bedfellows.

Part III, Songs and Other Musical Pieces, follows the same system. Between Parts I and III is inserted, as Part II, "Letter to a Wound," a piece of prose taken from the volume of revolutionary poems, *The Orators*, 1932. But of this derivation the reader is

probably unaware, and he proceeds to interpret this prose composition in terms of the religious poetry of 1945.

In the second half of the *Collected Poetry*, a new system is fol-
lowed, and this is roughly, though deceptively, chronological.
Part IV consists of another prose composition, "Depravity: A
Sermon," from the relatively early volume *The Dog beneath the
Skin*. Part V is "The Quest," a sonnet sequence which first appeared in the *New Republic* in November 1940, and then in the
1941 collection entitled in England *New Year Letter* and in the
United States *The Double Man*. Part VI is the long poem "New
Year Letter," which appeared first in the *Atlantic Monthly* in
January and February 1941, and then later in that year in the
same collection with "The Quest." Part VII, I will consider in the
following paragraph. Parts VIII and IX consist of two long
poems, "The Sea and the Mirror" and "For the Time Being,"
which appeared together in 1944 in the volume entitled *For the
Time Being*.

Parts V, VI, VIII, and IX, it will be observed, comprise poems
written in the early 1940's, during the period immediately following the author's definitive conversion to orthodox Christianity,
and their arrangement corresponds to a chronological sequence
in composition, suggesting Auden's progressive confirmation in
his religious philosophy. And this might readily be taken as an
indication that Part IV (the prose sermon) and Part VII ("In
Time of War") belong to this period and reflect its religious attitudes. This impression is reinforced by the placing of "In Time
of War" *after* "The Quest" and "New Year Letter," as well as by
Auden's prefatory note to the sermon definitely signalizing it as
a serious religious treatise. But, as we have seen, the sermon was
taken over bodily from *The Dog beneath the Skin* and was written in an obviously unregenerate frame of mind; and "In Time
of War," with its Commentary, was written in 1938 and published
early in 1939, many months before the coming of the great historical catastrophe which, as I suggest in Chapter 19, completely
undermined Auden's faith in humanity and set in motion, or
greatly accelerated, the process of his conversion.

14

We have seen how in 1945 Auden tried by revision to bring the earlier composition into line with his later views. But, with "In Time of War" as with the rechristened sermon, the author's main reliance seems to have been on mere *context* to give the work an odor of sanctity which it would not have had if placed in the time-order of composition. The alphabet has been discarded as a principle of arrangement, but we have here a mystifying method similar to that operative throughout the 125-odd short poems thrown together in an unassorted heap in Part I and the thirty-eight Musical Pieces treated in the same way in Part III. The order of sequence throws no light at all on the context in which a given poem may best be understood. Instead of light, indeed, for the unwary reader, it tends to throw darkness.

In the *Collected Shorter Poems* of 1950 the alphabetical system is followed for the individual poems in Parts I and III, while *Paid on Both Sides* and "In Time of War" are assigned to Parts II and IV. And a special element of confusion is introduced by the altering of the titles of sixteen of the poems. In this British collection there is at least an index of first lines, which helps in the identification of poems from earlier volumes. But in either of these collections, it requires laborious research on the reader's part to trace any given poem to its original source. And naturally, there is nowhere a list of earlier poems of Auden's that were dropped along the way.

I do not mean to imply that this curious system of contextual obfuscation was deliberately designed by the poet to confuse and deceive his innocent readers. I am rather assuming that it indicates an extraordinary faculty he has for domesticating, within the frame of mind that at any moment possesses him, work conceived in some quite different frame of mind. It is at any rate a peculiarity of his temperament that we must not overlook if we wish to make out the probable intention of any given poem at the time it was written.

And there is something else we must have in mind. Mystification was from the start a favorite game of his imagination if not of his mind. In this matter it is indeed hard to know in any case whether the mind is simply lending itself to the suggestions of the imagination, or the imagination bodying forth the abstract constructions of the mind. As a boy Auden and his intimates played for years the game of spies and conspirators, and the delight in conspiracy gives its tone to his poetry for many years. It was perhaps this fancy for the conspiratorial that made so attractive to these young men the Marxian ideology, which seemed to require them to work underground and communicate in secret codes. This fanciful need for mystification may, too, have been intensified by the sense of guilt which, in spite of themselves, clung to their acts of rebellion against the conventional order. The intellectual pioneering of heroes and exiles was given a fillip of danger from the sense that they were under observation by secret Watchers planted by the enemy or by their own party to check up on them. Such are the "Two" in "The Witnesses," an early poem which Auden placed last in his main group of poems in 1945. They are always watching the hero from left and right and "over the garden wall." Such is the mysterious Him who figures in a piece called "Argument," included among other prose pieces in Book I of *The Orators* under the general title of "The Initiates." From Him one receives the call to secret meetings. He has something to do with our passing the frontier, or with "the establishment of a torpedo base at the head of the loch." We may at any time "meet Him alone on the narrow path, forcing a question, would show our unique knowledge." He is the mythical Leader of this band of conspirators, the imaginary embodiment of the cause to which they owe their loyalty, and one who requires of them strict discipline and tactical skill. It would not have been hard to print this piece in a *Collected Poetry*, and turn him into a sort of deity. But, as we shall see in Chapter 7, the entire book in which it appears was conceived in a frame of mind much more congenial to Marxian revolutionism than to Christian theism.

One prose piece from "The Initiates" Auden did include in the *Collected Poetry* as Part II, the "Letter to a Wound." I have no doubt that it is there intended to convey some distinctly religious message; and interpreters of Auden's thought are likely to be insensibly moved by its placing there to hear in it religious over-tones appropriate to the company it keeps. And indeed there is nothing to make this implausible. The writer of this letter has been for months suffering from a "wound" which has required his visiting a surgeon. Or rather he has been *enjoying* this path-ological condition, for he is in love with it. It is his darling. What-ever the date of its writing, this piece is an exercise in irony. The style of the supposed writer is that of a "nice" soft middle-class person addressing someone with whom he finds it comfortable to be in love, though in reality this love is debilitating self-deception, a sure sign of decadence, and essentially an expression of a death wish.* In Auden's pseudo-Freudian psychology our diseases are infallibly the symptoms of what is rotten in our hearts. And so we love and cherish them. This is a conception that will fit well into Auden's frame of reference in any one of several periods of his writing.

Another prose discourse in "The Initiates," which Auden did not see fit to reprint in 1945, is his "Address for a Prize-Day." Interpreters of Auden have pointed out that this is in style a parody of the stuffy and not too sincere sort of thing that school-masters address to their pupils on commemorative occasions. But equally penetrating and well-informed interpreters point out that the types of mentality and behavior against which the canting schoolmaster is here warning his boys are precisely those which the poet spends so much of his time warning his readers against. According to Spender, this discourse is "a destructive analysis of the golf-playing, church-going, tea-drinking, Boy Scoutish, eccen-tric middle class, in which Auden scoffs at the self-love, frustration, inhibitedness, and so on, of schoolmasters, parsons, spinsters, and gentry." And what it amounts to, Spender says, is "a kind of agnostic prayer against self-deception, the denial of life-forces by

---

* James G. Southworth definitely identifies the wound as homosexuality, the psychic illness of the Urning, and refers to the airman's suggestion that one's true ancestor may not be one's father. "His own true ancestor," says Mr. Southworth, "was his uncle, the homosexual." While the reference to the uncle as "the homosexual" may not be altogether convincing, the identi-fication of the wound is not implausible.

frustrating conventions, and on behalf of an open conspiracy of living in which love, whether social, personal, or sexual, is the stated aim of living."

Auden, that is, favors "love" and letting oneself be the carrier of the "life-forces," and opposes submission to inhibitions and "frustrating conventions." And these are indeed two complementary facets of a persistent theme in Auden's poetry. But "love" is in him one of the most elusive of terms, whose aspect and meaning changes as fast as Proteus changed when seized by Menelaus in hopes of getting him to prophesy. Love is sometimes the Freudian Eros, the great constructive force in human living. Its impulses must not be denied on penalty of sickness or lunacy. But "self-love" cuts one off from one's kind, shuts one up in a sterile dream-world, and (in the larger social order) prevents the reign of brotherhood and justice. What one must have for one's own health and the good of mankind is a "disciplined love." That is a love that thinks not in terms of a one-to-one relationship of reciprocal pleasure-giving, but the larger social relationship in which is sought not personal gratification but the good of the collective body. And in time this concept of a "disciplined [social] love" gives place to the concept of divine love (Agape as against Eros), where, I suppose, an absolute selflessness is the ideal consummation.

Well, that all seems like plain sailing, providing it is clear what are the inhibitions and "frustrating conventions" from which the creative Eros must free himself, and what is the discipline that must be exercised in order to secure the good of the social body, and just how the supernal Agape operates to make good citizens and at the same time children of grace, and whether the "disciplined love" means some limitation on the freedom of the creative Eros, and the supernal Agape some modification of the nature of this disciplined love. But the words of the poet are never so simple as the explications of the academic interpreter. Spender mentions "self-love" as something that is to be avoided; and when the Prize-Day orator lists the symptoms of "excessive love of self," he is evidently talking about what psychologists would call narcissism.

And the tone of the Prize-Day speaker would almost certainly make the schoolboy suppose that he was making veiled allusions to "self-abuse." Such veiled allusions are fairly frequent in Auden's early work, as where, in the discarded No. XXII of the 1930 *Poems*, the author recommends to his generation to "throw the bath-chairs right away, and learn to leave ourselves alone." *

But then again, the sexual implications of "self-love" may be even more widely inclusive. For in the Epilogue to *On This Island* (in a passage not retained in the *Collected Poetry*), "self-regard" is specifically given as the subject illuminated by Proust; and so it might be thought to cover the "last and worst" of the classes distinguished in the Prize-Day Address, "the perverted lovers." There is in the Address no specification of the particular sort of perversion meant; but since the text of this discourse is taken from Dante's classification of sinners in the Purgatorio, we can hardly fail to suppose there is here an allusion to what a schoolboy would infallibly think of in this connection. And the sickly, futile, seclusive, and nerveless character of many familiar types of men and women is at least *associated* with the self-love that has its physical counterpart in self-abuse and sexual "perversion." There are enough passages in Auden's poetry in which this association is more clearly made to give strong plausibility to this interpretation.†

* In the "Journal of an Airman" (again in *The Orators*) we have repeated references to mysteriously peccant hands, in connection with some secret weakness of the airman's which is perhaps suspected by his men and women friends, and which, "if the enemy ever got to hear of it," would nullify his whole work. But this apparently refers to the airman's proneness to *kleptomania*. I would not venture to guess why kleptomania was chosen — whether as a symbol of bourgeois possessiveness, or whether, in Auden's psychological system, this weakness has some association with sex, and perhaps with the airman's still more mysterious uncle, by some interpreters understood as "the homosexual."

† A number of such passages will be cited in the course of this study. The prominence of the theme of homosexuality has been noted by a considerable number of writers on Auden. These include Delmore Schwartz in his article on "The Two Audens" in the *Kenyon Review* for Winter 1939, and James G. Southworth in his volume, *Sowing the Wind*, Oxford, 1940. In his essay on Auden in that volume, Mr. Southworth plausibly interprets in this sense more than a dozen poems of Auden which remain otherwise somewhat obscure. In my discussion, I mention this theme only when the

Of course, it is possible to say that these adolescent deviations are here taken simply as symbolic counterparts of something in the psychological make-up of the unfortunate types thus distinguished. The covert suggestions, then, are simply means of giving imaginative coloring to the thought. And perhaps the only reply that can be made to this contention is that the ordinary reader will be unable to distinguish in this way between mere symbol and its factual counterpart, and will be left with a mistaken impression of what the poet means to convey.

But where then, one might ask, is the confusion? The poet is aware of the perils attending sexual deviation, and feels impelled to testify against it by describing its unpleasant effects in character and personality. In those matters he is recommending moral discipline and self-control.

But then what becomes of Auden as leader in "an open conspiracy" in favor of an uninhibited yielding to the life forces, and in opposition to "frustrating conventions"? What becomes of the Auden who wrote a jolly little ballad in which the abnormally chaste and pious Miss Gee develops a cancer instead of becoming, say, an unmarried mother? What becomes of the Auden who wrote in "Voltaire at Ferney" (in a passage not retained in 1945) that "as a rule, it was the pleasure-haters who became unjust"? Auden certainly in several places scornfully imputes sexual "perversion" to vicars, industrialists, and Cambridge intellectuals, and is in general worried about this deviation as something that makes men soft and incapable of effective action in behalf of social justice. But why is it that so often masculine friendships in his poetry are rendered in terms more suggestive of heterosexual love affairs? And why in his Prize-Day Address does he put such unexceptionably good moral advice and admonition in the mouth of a stuffy schoolmaster whose professional Sunday School manner tends to throw doubt on the sincerity of what he says?

The subject of love is indeed elusive and protean. Anybody is likely to feel and say one thing about it one day and another thing references are unmistakable and are pertinent to the special subject of my study.

the next day. But with a writer who so constantly takes the higher line, who has so much the air of a spiritual prophet and leader, our earnest expectations and hope for guidance are likely to be disappointed when he lands us in such a haze of ambiguity.

Many instances of such ambiguity will come to our attention as our study proceeds. Some of them are in poems dealing with "love." A peculiarly striking case is "Prothalamion," discussed in Chapter 14, which first appeared as a choral song in *The Dog beneath the Skin*, was passed over in 1945, but was reproduced without alteration in the *Collected Shorter Poems* of 1950 and so restored to the canon. In other cases the theme of love (or carnal "sin") is involved in a complicated pattern with political ideology. Such is "Danse Macabre," discussed in Chapter 16. It first appeared in a magazine in 1937, then (in truncated form) in the libretto of the musical *Ballad of Heroes*, and then, unabbreviated, in *Another Time*, before being reproduced in the canonical volumes. In this poem both "irreverent thinking" and "human desires" (typified by Sodom and Gomorrah) are favored by the not unsympathetic Devil but sternly condemned by the still more diabolical figure who seems to stand for a combination of Fascistic Dictatorship and Death. And the uninstructed reader is made very uncomfortable by the apparent necessity of choosing between two such unsavory characters.

In the case of both "Prothalamion" and "Danse Macabre," the difficulties may be partly resolved by an appreciation of the subtleties and complications of the ironic method; but to see all clear one must also have an understanding of Auden's psychological theories and his general philosophy at the time of writing.

In both cases it is highly significant that the ambiguity is much less disturbing, at least for the instructed reader, when the poem is read in its original context than when read in that of the collected poetry. In "Danse Macabre" as it appears in the cantata, the ambiguity is greatly reduced by the elimination of the bulk of the poem (ten stanzas out of seventeen) and the virtual identification of the Devil with his erstwhile adversary — that is, by the sacrifice of what is the main point of the original poem. But even here, for one who reads the poem in cold print, dense obscurity attaches to the conditions under which this identity is established. For the auditor this is slurred over by the musical setting; for how much of the sense of an opera libretto is ever taken in by the auditors, who generally cannot even make out more than a fifth part of the words? But it is clear enough that Auden here, like a thrifty seamstress fashioning a dress for a child out of her mother's discarded gown, is making the stuff from an old poem serve the requirements of a new lyric, with very little regard for the meaning which the words carried in the original.

But the old poem was not discarded. And the ambiguity is more strongly felt in the full text in *Another Time*, among poems largely produced in the brief period when Auden seems to have been hung up between opposing philosophies. And it is most strongly felt in 1945, when an uninstructed reader is still faced with the perplexities of 1937, and an instructed reader, while he may think he understands what the poet meant to say in 1937, cannot imagine what the poet thinks he is saying, or would be understood as saying, in 1945. For here this pagan irony follows directly on the sober depth of religious feeling in "September 1, 1939," and breathes the same air with such unexceptionally pious pieces as "Kairos and Logos," "Christmas 1940," "Autumn 1940," and "For the Time Being."

More even than "Prothalamion," "Danse Macabre" exposes the hazards a poet runs in putting old wine into new bottles.

One special source of confusion or dubiety is a seeming variation in Auden's way of conceiving the relation between the individual and society. This has recently been made the subject of a special study dealing with Auden and two of his associates embodied in a doctoral dissertation at the University of Wisconsin. According to Justin Replogle, the "Auden group," including Stephen Spender and C. Day Lewis, were at one in their conviction that there was need for a radical change and reform in the social body. But they were all essentially individualists, inclined to emphasize the enlightenment of the individual psyche, or personal "change of heart," as the necessary prerequisite of social change. In Marxism they met with a social philosophy which attributed the system of moral values approved in any given culture to material (economic) causes connected with the prevailing system of production. In this philosophy the emphasis was on the social body rather than on the individual soul as the locus of desiderated change. The program of social change comes first, and the moral improvement of the individual follows as effect follows cause. What made these three poets a group for a short period in the thirties, according to Mr. Replogle, was the need to adjust their ideas to those of the Marxist program, to which they looked as the present hope of a sick and dying world. This required some accommodation to the Marxist "reliance on external, material change" as primary. When they finally gave up this Marxist tenet (Spender in 1937, Day Lewis and Auden before 1940), according to Mr. Replogle they ceased to function as a group.

They actually constituted a group by virtue of the conflict going on in them all between the programmatic socialist materialism represented by Marx and the individualistic mysticism (non-Christian but basically religious) represented by D. H. Lawrence, whose influence is mainly stressed by Mr. Replogle.

Besides Lawrence there were numerous other influences somewhat at variance with the Marxian. One of these, I suspect, was that of Gerald Heard, to whom Auden dedicated two of his most significant early poems. Heard thinks in terms of evolutionism; but the "evolution" he stresses is not biological but a process of change going on historically in human society. It involves the replacement of the will to individual acquisition and power by a higher will, which is directed towards cooperative effort for common ends. Heard traces in human history the emergence of a "higher consciousness" which is "above the individual as the earlier form was below him." (See Chapter 9.) In the poet Auden this higher consciousness bears the name of Love, and makes one think a little, for all the world, of Emerson's Oversoul. In his early poem originally entitled "A Communist to Others," Auden bids his "comrades" have faith in a "love outside our own election" that everywhere "holds us in unseen connection."

This higher consciousness, or love that holds the comrades together in unseen connection, might imply nothing more mystical
than the sense of brotherhood that makes them one across the bar-
riers of class. Auden is here an "intellectual" addressing working
men, and he declares, in the original form of the poem, that "our
bowels yearn" for these exploited and downtrodden brothers. But
something mystic ever clings to the word love when it is invoked
by poets. And in any case this appeal to the active love of brothers
to bring about a just social order is very different from Marx
explaining in dialectic terms that it is the inevitable historic destiny of the working class to give the *coup de grace* to a decadent
bourgeoisie hopelessly caught in the toils of capitalist contradictions. It is this "higher consciousness" that made Auden a maverick within the ranks of socialism as he was a black sheep among
the flocks of academe.

This appeal to the mystical or natural power of love brings us
back to the manifold ambiguities attending on the use of this elusive term, which has so many distinct and often contradictory,
though interlocking, meanings that it promises a field day for the
semasiologists whenever they get around to it. And this again has
its bearing on the conflict referred to between the Marxian way
of interpreting the class struggle and the several rival ways that
are followed by Auden and his associates. With Auden it is clear
that both the individual and society as a body are stricken with
mortal illness; but it is never quite clear how far the personal
pathology derives from the social or the social from the personal.
In many cases we see society and the individual going their parallel ways towards insanity and dissolution, subject to the same
death-wish. But in the case of individual citizens at least, a personal psychology appears to be operating independently of what
is going on in the economic and political order. It is here that we
have to reckon with the peculiar psychosomatic doctrine taken
over it has been suggested from John Layard and Homer Lane,
which rather sweepingly holds that all physical disease originates
in psychical disturbances. The classical exponent of this doctrine
in imaginative literature is Dr. Krokowski in *The Magic Mountain*;

but there this extreme psychological position is balanced by the materialist extreme represented by Dr. Behrens, and the dialectic opposition of the two views is somehow figuratively resolved in the spiritualist seances that follow. In Auden there is no dialectical opposition and no fanciful resolution as in Mann's romance. Dr. Krokowski reigns in the full solemnity of his ghostly character.

Dr. Krokowski, it will be remembered, finds love somewhere at the root of all illness, and while, in his genteel euphemism, he fails to make it very clear just what he means by this term, it is presumable that what he has in mind is the sexual drive. In Auden, similarly, it would appear to be the repression of sexual impulse that is held largely responsible for the diseases prevalent among the bourgeoisie and all those subject to their cultural influence. (One says: repression of natural impulse, but it is never quite clear where the so-called unnatural sex impulses come into the picture.) Now, this type of psychological explanation of sickness is not something native to the Marxist theory of the class struggle and the contradictions of the capitalist economy. And the poetic analogy between personal sickness, insanity, and dissolution and the sickness, insanity, and dissolution of the social body, while imaginatively colorful and suggestive, does not contribute to a clear understanding of either the personal or the social situation. It is true that socialists used to consider that the sacredness of marriage and the sinfulness of sexual irregularities were bourgeois superstitions, product of an ideology born of a particular economic situation. But this is something quite different from holding that quinzy and cancer and tuberculosis and all varieties of insanity are to be traced to the sexual controls mandatory in the Hebrew and Christian codes.

And then, of course, as we have seen, the term love is by no means limited in Auden to the sexual drive; there is Eros and Agape, and "disciplined love," and simple altruism or super-ego. And there is the love "outside our own election" that "holds us in unseen connection." It is not always easy to determine where one of these leaves off and another begins, or how far they may be taken as overlapping. And it is still less easy to see just how these personal and "psychological" powers are to be brought into the Marxian picture of impersonal and "materialistic" forces released by the system of production and determining the cultural pattern of any given social order.

In general the ambiguities tend to thicken as the poet passes from one position to another, and the same text, with terms and images conformable to a given mental set, is reproduced in an apparently quite different connection, on a different stage, and by an adjustment of lighting, made to serve a different mental set and ideological intention. Thus in *The Dog beneath the Skin* we find instances of poems in which, as originally conceived, the regenerative power of love is shown in operation with no apparent reference to a social-political order that might favor this healing process, but which are now adjusted to an ideological frame of reference in which the social-political order is given large credit for the spiritual regeneration of the disorganized lovers. This is particularly pertinent to the conflict referred to between the programmatic Marxian social theory of human relations and the more personal, subjective and quasi-religious theory of which Mr. Replogle makes Lawrence the typical exponent.

In the case of these three choral poems, the conflict was temporarily resolved by a mystic marriage of convenience between the personal-psychological and the socialist-materialist systems, by which the miseries and degradations of self-regarding love were seemingly to find their cure under the more favorable conditions of a collectivist society. It is not probable that the precise terms of this marriage contract were understood by many of those present at performances of the propagandist musical show, or even many of those who could read the drama at their leisure in cold print. But they could all have a sense that the revolutionary program was here supported by considerations more spiritual and elevating than in the party manifestos of Marx and Engels. The dominant partner in this strategic union was certainly the personal-psychological doctrine sponsored by the august figure of Love. The act of choice which the young men were called on to make, in order to decide their fate and save themselves from spiritual futility and ruin, while it was, in one view, the choice of a political party and cause to fight for, was at the same time a personal moral choice; it amounted to a conversion, and it meant, first of all, that they must "look into their hearts" and see.

Two of these choruses were reproduced in the canonical collections, and here the ambiguities were considerably lightened. For now, under the new dispensation, the platform marriage of convenience has been annulled. The Marxist partner has been put away, and the personal-psychological partner can now return to his celibate independence, in which the voluntary change of heart is spontaneous and unaffected by the pressures of historical dialectic. Or rather, perhaps, these originally high-minded and mystical poems may now be given the benefit of positively Christian associations. It might even be supposed that a new and more sacred union has been consummated, and in this case one to which the old objections cannot be raised. For while in this case too the individual soul or conscience must fall back, for sanction and support, upon an abstract theoretical system quite beyond himself — in this case theological — it has always been an article of Christian faith that the truth is to be found by looking in one's heart. So that while these old poems, under their new titles "The Witnesses" and "I Shall Be Enchanted," are still not rendered in the traditional style of religious writing, and do perhaps retain some faint vestiges of paganism, they can, with an exercise of good will, be more readily fitted into the new religious frame of reference, and seem more at home there than in that of Marxian ideology.

But even so, in their new setting, and rubbing elbows with much altogether reputable company, they may not be understood in their fullness by a reader unfamiliar with Auden's earlier modes of thought; they may still need, for final clarification, some explication in terms of their original intent and the contexts in which they have already figured. They still come before us in somewhat questionable shape.

We must not, of course, hold this poet responsible for the maze of meanings traditionally attached to the word love, or for the unavoidable complexities and contradictions encountered by us all in the effort to organize our knowledge and bring sense and consistency into our theoretical constructions. And I suppose we must not expect a poet to express himself with the logical coherence and precision of a prose philosopher. Some allowance must be made for picturesqueness of expression, for the prophetic mode of utterance, and the poet's natural fondness for figurative and mythological formulations. The reader must judge for himself in the end how far the obscurities so often encountered in the poetic texts are inherent in the subject-matter as it presents itself to any speculative mind with a certain range of awareness, and how far they are assignable to the special idiosyncrasy of this writer's thinking process. All verbalizing, if not all human thinking, is dogged by ambiguity, which seems to deepen as we carry further the effort at abstraction in the formulation of "truth."

In any case, this haze of ambiguity that blurs the outlines of so much of Auden's writing would not greatly matter, it might even be an artistic asset if his poetry were taken as purely an expression of the life experience in its diversity, without any doctrinal intention. Spender tells us that it was Auden's theory in the early days that "a poet must have no opinions, no decided views which he seeks to put across in his poetry." It was also his theory that "a poet must be clinical, dispassionate about life." And Spender feels in Auden's work a certain cold impersonality that is a reflection of this clinical dispassionateness. But a writer's statements as to what he should avoid in his work are often no more than a warning to himself against what he unconsciously feels to be his own propensities. Auden may have thought that he was avoiding the didactic and instructional; but the reader constantly feels the heavy pressure of his disposition to teach and admonish, and is often saddened by his uncertainty as to just what it is that Auden is teaching and admonishing him about. Auden may have thought, too, that he was being dispassionate in his clinical method; but he is always crying, "Wolf, wolf!" and generally manages to convey to the reader something of the personal anxiety with which he is ridden and which he seems to be working off in his poetic fables.

28

These general remarks I have set at the beginning of my study in order that the reader may be aware from the start of certain difficulties he may often encounter in his effort to get at the intent of Auden's poetry at the time of writing. We may now turn to particular cases where revisions were made in individual poems in preparing them for inclusion in the *Collected Poetry*.

𝕮 3

Further Significant Verbal Alterations

THE excision of stanzas from poems retained and the
entire suppression of important early poems is much more revealing in Auden than the mere verbal alteration of the text. But I
have noted a number of poems in which significant verbal revisions serve the same purpose of giving the piece a more acceptable
religious or ideological tone, and others in which verbal alterations, as well as the elimination of stanzas, serve to reduce the
autobiographical element and tone down the partisan personal reference to adversaries in the ideological battles of the thirties.

Thus in the piece entitled in 1945 "I Shall Be Enchanted,"
which is a chorus salvaged from Auden and Isherwood's play,
The Dog beneath the Skin, or, Who is Francis? (1935). This
poem is addressed throughout to "love," and directs this personified sentiment, or spirit, to guide the questing traveler by adapting
itself to all the "legends" of the several countries, enabling him
everywhere to find "the common phrase / Required to please /
The guardians there." But in the end, when the pilgrim has grown
weary of legends, and is brandishing his "reluctant sword" over
the very neck of love, he will be amazed to find that love is still
just "what he wanted," and is "faithful . . . but disenchanted /
Your simplest love." In this poem Auden made two main textual
revisions. Love is capitalized throughout, presumably to identify
it with the Freudian Eros, "Builder of Cities," as he calls it in his
later poem "In Memory of Sigmund Freud." It has been shown
by Professor Monroe K. Spears that, in Auden's later symbolism,
the distinction is constantly made between the natural Eros and

the supernal Agape; and that, while Eros is still respected as the life force, it is found wanting to man's deeper spiritual needs, and must be supplemented by the divine Agape, informed as that is by the divine Logos. In the natural order, however, Eros is not to be disparaged. It is a great power, and rightly guided, benign. Hence it rates the capital letter.

This, I take it, was the poet's thought when he made the revision. In 1935 he may not have had in mind the supernal Agape, but was simply celebrating the benignity of Eros. The poet in 1945 wished to locate the secular Eros on a higher level of thought. But in doing so it was necessary to stress the distinction. Hence the still more significant revision found in the concluding line, where "your simplest love" gives way to "your *finite* love." This serves to distinguish the mere human and profane sentiment from that which religion inspires, and brings the early, unregenerate poem within the canon of 1945.

Another revision of similar intent is found in a poem numbered XVII among Songs and Other Musical Pieces, beginning "Not, Father, further do prolong." This is reprinted from *The Orators: An English Study* (1932), where it is the final one of "Six Odes." Some of the alterations in phrasing in this poem were obviously intended to make sense out of passages that in the original made none. Thus in the second stanza, which originally read:

> Against your direct light, displayed,
>   Regardant, absolute,
> In person stubborn and oblique
>   Our maddened set we foot.

This dislocation of words perhaps resulted from a mere typesetter's blunder, though it does serve also in the original to secure the rhyme. In 1945 Auden corrects the last line to read: "We set our maddened foot."

But more significant for Auden's thought is the later capitalizing of the pronoun "your" wherever it appears in the poem — "Your direct light," "Your accusations," etc. Now, this involves a rather fine point in regard to Auden's attitude toward theology. So far as I can see, Auden was at no time an atheist in the extrem-

31

est sense of that word. In all his early writing he was, as it were, officially obliged to be anti–Church-religion by his position as leader of the opposition along the whole line of ideological controversy. But that did not require him to deny the presence of a spiritual power operative in the universe or refrain, as a poet, from personifying the moral law to which men owe allegiance.

In his brilliant and provocative essay on "Changes of Attitude and Rhetoric in Auden's Poetry" (the *Southern Review*), Randall Jarrell has indicated the lines of division between the party of the left (the We's) and the party of established tradition (the They's). He indicates how shrewdly (even if instinctively) the We's made their choice of slogans, principles, sentiments, and authorities to espouse, so as to put themselves in the right and their opponents in the wrong. They often picked their antecedents among highly respectable writers; and in the spiritual world they repudiated not so much religion itself as the dogmas of the Church. Their ideology was a highly composite and synthetic structure. They were rationalists and mystics in the same breath. It is agreed by all the most perspicuous interpreters of Auden (Hoggart, Spears, Jarrell) that he was in all periods of his writing a strenuous and militant moralist; and he seems to have held all along that there is in the world what we might call an Ethical Absolute, as in this poem — "your direct light, regardant, absolute."

This poem was probably written at a very early date, and while the author was master in a boarding school. Though apparently first published in 1932, it appears in the same volume with five other odes, one of which is dated 1927, and another carries the title "January 1, 1931." In all of the other poems written between 1930 and 1939, so far as I have noted, there is very little if any direct appeal to the deity, as He is conceived of in Christian or even broadly theistic systems. And this is the more remarkable considering the themes the author is treating. One seeming exception is in the soliloquy of Michael Ransom, the leading character in *The Ascent of F6* (Auden and Isherwood's play, 1936). Here, after the climber's conference with the abbot on the slopes of the mountain, Ransom does invoke his Ethical Absolute, which he identifies with the evolutionary force so frequently present in Auden's speculations: "You who are the history and creator of all these forms in which we are condemned to suffer, to whom the necessary is also the just." To this life principle he does appeal, and asks him to "show men, show each of us upon this mortal star the danger that under His hand is swiftly palpitating."

The danger in question, against which he warns his fellow climber, is that of falling into corruption; and the corruption is precisely that of the enemy party — the hypocritical party of the establishment — with their loud-speakers and posing and photographing and ceremonial banqueting. By his character's appeal to the personified You and Him, Auden has skillfully managed to undermine "Their" position by the assumption of "Their" slogans, according to the strategy that Mr. Jarrell has described. Michael Ransom is a divided spirit; and since he is the product and (albeit reluctant) tool of the Old Gang, it is dramatically proper that he should in his vocabulary draw upon their mythology.

One might also put a theological construction on the "watcher in the dark" invoked by the chorus in *Paid on Both Sides* ("Can speak of trouble, pressure on men"), whose "sudden hand" humbles great pride, and in the light of whose bright day men come to realize that they have been vile. But the case is made less clear when we associate this watcher in the dark with the Him of the prose "Argument" and the mysterious "Two" who figure in "The Witnesses" (both referred to in the preceding chapter, and the latter discussed at length in Chapter 13). These fanciful allegorical creations of the boys' play-world of spies and counterspies are not to be taken too seriously in a consideration of Auden's theology. The "watcher in the dark" has a more solemn sound, to suit the tone of primitive mythology in this Anglo-Saxon style chorus; it testifies chiefly to the young poet's facility in projecting his imagination into a variety of poetic worlds.

When Auden in this period speaks *in propria persona*, the abstraction to which he appeals is "love," as in the Prologue to *On*

This Island (1936).* And this love, lower case, has not yet taken on the quality of the Christian Agape which becomes the dominant figure in his later poetry. It is still the "disciplined love," the sociable love of one's fellows, which in his earlier period he opposes to the mere self-indulgent and unsociable "pleasure principle." The Prologue in which he invokes this love (dating from 1932) is full of references to the evolutionary process out of which has come Man's "possible dream" of a better world. As late as the collection of 1940 (*Another Time*) he is publishing poems in which the law of love is preferred to the judge's law, the priest's law, the law that is simply "the wisdom of old" or "the loud angry crowd." Everyone in his ignorance identifies law with some other word. We all share in this ignorance; but we lovers insist on identifying it with love. (*Another Time*, No. II; *Collected Poetry*, "Law Like Love.") It may be noted in passing that, in reprinting the Prologue to *On This Island*, the poet raises the rank of "love" by capitalizing it; but in reprinting "Law Like Love" he leaves this personage in the ranks of lower case.

In the very early poem we are here discussing (Song No. XVII) Auden does directly address his deity, or Ethical Absolute, as "Father." But his feeling-attitude toward this paternal image does not move him when first writing to capitalize the pronouns referring to what is perhaps an ideal abstraction rather than the personal Creator of Christian theology. Indeed we cannot even be certain that his capitalizing of "father" was by authorial intention. In *The Orators* the opening *words* of *all* the odes are capitalized to suit an editorial standard of typographical elegance — "WHAT SIREN zooming," "THOUGH AWARE of our rank," "NOT, FATHER, further do prolong." We cannot be certain that Auden did not write, "Not, father, further," as well as "your direct light," "your accusations," etc. At any rate, when in 1945 this poem was brought into the canon, capitals were in all cases supplied, and any suggestion of non-Christian thought done away with.

* This volume was published in London under the title *Look, Stranger!*, Faber and Faber, 1936. My references are all to the American edition, *On This Island*, Random House, 1937, but I use the date of first publication of this collection, 1936.

There is still another possibility in regard to this poem, which I would not myself have ventured to raise. But it has been raised by Mr. Spears in his *Sewanee* article on "Late Auden: The Satirist as Lunatic Clergyman." Mr. Spears is illustrating the variety of masks assumed by the poet to give lightness and pungency to his satiric or ironic effects, and in this case the device perhaps derived from Blake's *Songs of Experience*, where "the childlike images prove, at second glance, to have loaded double meanings." One such device is the assumption of the mask of the popular lyric, where "the innocent form is made to convey an unexpected and ominously contrasting matter, as in the ballad 'Let me tell you a little story.'" I shall return to this poem later, in Chapter 8. Mr. Spears continues: "A variation is Auden's occasional employment of the prayer, as in the well-known 'Petition' and 'Not, Father, further do prolong'; here again a shock effect is obtained through ominously charging a conventionally innocent form." Mr. Spears' observation is acute and illuminating with regard to the subtlety and originality of Auden's technique. The perverse twists of the heart, as seen by a psychological modern, are certainly rendered in terms not traditionally found in our prayer books, and especially, in "Petition," with a satirical realism going a little queerly with the solemn confessional tone of prayer. And, judging by the context, Mr. Spears seems to be saying that the form of prayer, and so, presumably, its theological assumptions, are, in this very early Auden, a sort of dramatic mask. If this is his intention, he may be suggesting that the address to the Father in the poem we have been discussing does not necessarily imply that Auden was assuming the reality of the Christian deity.

Another curious and complicating feature of "Petition" (No. XXX in *Poems* 1930) is that the Lord, if it is "the Lord" that is here in question, is addressed under the form of "Sir," not used in prayers in the English service. But this may be taken as a further refinement of poetical technique, or imaginative conception, whether the Lord addressed is the deity of the Church or a personification of an Ethical Absolute. This is not the only instance of Auden's personifying an ethical abstraction as the lord of the manor and addressing it (or him) accordingly. This very form of address is used in Ode II of *The Orators* (not reprinted in 1945) in a petition to the "heart of the heartless world" to favor the healthy growth of the boys in Sedbergh School.

> Give you leave for that, sir, well in them, flow,
> Deep in their wheel-pits may they know you foaming
> and feel you warm.

There is no suggestion that this personified life force is to be associated with any theological being, abstract or personal. In the original version of "Not All the Candidates Pass," published in an anthology in 1933, the "Lords of Limit" are similarly called upon by the poet for the guidance of his schoolboy pupils, and addressed in the plural as "gentlemen," corresponding to the "sir" of the earlier "petitions." They are imagined in the plural, as I point out in Chapter 5, because they are identifiable with the Two watchers in "The Witnesses," and they are likened to gamekeepers who stand with guns to warn off trespassers from forbidden territory. These "gentlemen," like the Two, are watching, or limiting the path of the young adventurer from Left and Right. Again, as I shall show in Chapter 9, the frame of reference is secular and "humanistic" rather than religious, and the ethical abstraction to which the poet is making his appeal is the "higher consciousness" of men, the collective conscience, whose evolution is described by Gerald Heard in several books which had their strong influence on the thinking of Auden in this early period.

It is in this general frame of reference, almost certainly secular, that we should read the ode from *The Orators*. And it is this which gives its significance to the revised spelling by which the later Auden gave to the personage there addressed a more unmistakably theological character.

Other revisions made for the *Collected Poetry* had various presumable motivations. The poem entitled "January 1, 1931" is the first of "Six Odes" from *The Orators*. It records a dream in which the poet reviews the "losses" suffered by Our party of progressive spirits during the year 1930. (Interpretations in detail are admittedly speculative.) Among their "losses" was the death of D. H.

Lawrence (March 2, 1930). Another was symbolized by the emergence of an undressed German from the lake reeds, presumably an enemy spy, leading "Stephen" to say: "Destroy this temple" (Mark 14:58). Somewhere the scene shifts to Germany (?), and the poet says that the temple (it) did fall: "The Jewess fled Southwards." "Christopher" in Europe appears to be following the rise of fascism; and (everywhere?) selfish people sought escape in picture palaces and grew degenerate. Many pretenders to wisdom came forward as "healers." The poem ends with the voice of a beggar asking for more definite news about East Europe, hoping for some champion to arise to throw "the bully of Corinth in the sanded circle" (Hitler?).

This poem is an intimate rendering of the spirit and tone of a small clique of literary men who see themselves as radical social reformers; and the most important of them are mentioned by their first names — Wystan (Auden himself), Stephen (Spender), and Christopher (Isherwood). In his dream Auden heard a voice saying, "Wystan, Stephen, Christopher, all of you, / Read of your losses." From the high plateau of his position in 1945, Auden naturally looks down with some irony and regret on the mistaken ideology of these young men, and with some humor upon their bold pretensions to the prophetic function — conscious, perhaps, of personal character traits in them which did not altogether match their pretensions. He evidently considers it more discreet, and in better taste, to cut out the naive and painfully personal references. And so for this line he substitutes, somewhat darkly: "And heard a voice saying — 'Subjects, Objects, all of you.'" And this system of revision is carried through the poem. Instead of "Christopher stood, his face grown lined with wincing," he now writes, "Maverick stood." Instead of "Stephen signalled from the sand dunes," "Pretzel signalled." Those in the know will recognize the code names, while the uninitiated reader will be amused by the colorful sobriquets.

A similar system is followed when the references are to persons less heartily admired, as not being members of our gang. The lines which originally read:

> Of all the healers, Granny in mittens, the Mop, the
>   white surgeon,
>   And loony Layard,

now appear as:

> Granny in mittens, the Judge, the bucolic doctor,
>   And the suave archdeacon.

This toning down of personal reference was clearly made in the interest of good taste after the fighting passions had cooled. As for the excision of the phrase "of all the healers," this was presumably made for improvement of the meter.

But while the poem was indeed a radical manifesto, there was really nothing in it fundamentally inconsistent with Auden's lifelong views. The sixth and seventh stanzas, while esoteric in their symbolism, are conventionally moralistic in tone. The abhorrence of fascism could not offend the poet in any period of his writing. With the proper cleaning up, there was no reason why the poem should not be admitted to the canon.

It would be unduly tedious and time-consuming to list all the slight verbal changes made by Auden in his poems when reprinting them from earlier collections or from periodicals. Most of them have no appreciable significance in relation to Auden's thought or even in relation to his esthetic ideals, except as showing that he was consciously concerned to tidy up his work in small matters of rhetorical propriety or precision in imagery. I am accordingly relegating to a note (see p. 257) some data in regard to such revisions, including remarks on Auden's dealings in revision with the matter of punctuation, where critical interest approaches the vanishing point. Auden's dealings with punctuation do indeed express something in his temperament and his attitude toward conventions in general and rhetorical conventions in particular. But they would perhaps enlighten us more in regard to the preferences of editors than in regard to the poet's.

I will confine myself here to illustrations from two poems in which verbal alterations are appreciable in amount and have some real artistic significance. And in particular they bring us face to face with the famous problem of "difficulty" and "communication" in modern poetry — a problem of more than usual urgency in the case of Auden because of what I have called the element of mystification in his writing.

"It's So Dull Here" is the title given to a piece first published in *New Verse* in June 1934, where it was called simply "Poem," and then reprinted in *On This Island* as No. XXIII, before it was reprinted again in the *Collected Poetry*. This poem of sixteen blank-verse lines calls up the picture of a "village of the heart," with its rural Hall, and the grand old couple who loved us all when we were children, but now invaded by a trunk road, "thin cafés," and touristy people, with their "identical and townee smartness," to whom one must now "look for comfort" though strangers. It is as it stands an intriguing composition; but I had never been able to penetrate its symbolism until I came on it in its earliest periodical form. In the six central lines as they appear in the original the author gives us the key to each of his symbols. Where now we read

> one of the new
> Trunk roads passes the very door already,
> And the thin cafés spring up over night,

we have in the original, "trunk roads of *fear*," and "*greed's* thin cafés." In the two following lines are explained the symbols of "sham ornamentation" and "the strident swimming pool." The sham ornamentation is that of the *feelings*; the strident swimming pool is that of the *senses* and *thoughts*. We need not detail the alteration in the following lines, which does not affect the sense, but merely serves to adjust the old text to the new version.

Thus we come to understand that the poet's theme here is nothing so simple as the invasion of the country home by the vulgar smartness and superficiality of tourism and the town. These are all symbols of a deeper trouble and corruption in the spirit; and we recognize a complex of motives common enough in Auden. Even the comfortable homeyness which is thus disturbed stands for a self-centered insularity that is suspect. Fear and greed are, in the modern world, taking possession of our souls, together with

39

falsity of sentiment and selfish indulgence in the unsocial pleasures of the senses and the mind.

But now when Auden took a good look at this piece before including it in his early collection of poems, he was evidently impressed with the bald explicitness with which the intention of his symbols was spelt out for the reader, as if he were writing old-fashioned allegory. He was moved to cut off all the explanatory labels and leave the images to speak for themselves. The result *was* "purer" poetry. But one wonders how many readers now can actually make out what the poet is driving at. This is a rather crucial instance of the choice that so often confronted Auden between improving a poem imaginatively or leaving it in a form less satisfying to his poetic ideal but decidedly more satisfying as a statement of what he meant. What he meant was to make the comfy "village of the heart" a symbol of the selfish individualism that threatened to undermine the social structure, or actually characterized the social structure whose dominant motives were fear, greed, emotional thinness, sensuality, and the indulgence of private (as opposed to truly social) feelings and thoughts. This was, of course, in 1934, an integral part of his socialist ideology. In 1945 selfish individualism was still something to be deprecated by a Christian, but it was no longer conceived in the framework of a collectivist ideal. And as the poem appears, even in 1936, so much of the original intention has disappeared that the reader is left wondering just why this leader of the avant-garde is making so much fuss about the urbanization of a country village. And when he encounters it in 1945, he is aware of nothing more soul-stirring than the author's revulsion from modern innovations and the innocuous recommendation of neighborly love and service.

In this case, the poet has killed two birds with one stone: he has improved the poem as a work of art, and he has purged it of any meaning that could give offense to anyone. And if it still remains a riddle to the simple reader, that is not a matter that need give too much concern to a "modern" poet.

Other interesting examples of fairly extensive textual revision are three of the sonnets of the sequence "In Time of War," published first in periodicals in 1936 and 1938, then (as revised) in *Journey to a War* (1939), and finally (without further revision) in the collections of 1945 and 1950. In the case of two of these, I will leave the details for a note (see p. 260), and merely observe that each time the original poem was made more understandable by being given a title. Sonnet XII, "And the age ended, and the last deliverer died," appeared in the June–July 1936 number of *New Verse* under the illuminating title "The Economic Man." Sonnet XXI, "The life of man is never quite completed," appeared, along with four others, in the *New Republic* for December 7, 1938, as well as (by itself) in John Lehmann's anthology, *New Writing* (fall 1938), under the equally illuminating title "Exiles."

Sonnet XVIII, "Far from the heart of culture he was used," appeared in the same number of the *New Republic*, as well as in the British *New Statesman and Nation* (July 2) and the *Living Age* (September), under the title "Chinese Soldier." The passage replaced later in revision directly commends this obscure anonymous youth (this "unknown soldier") to the respectful attention of the poet's Western readers.

> Professors of Europe, hostess, citizen,
> Respect this boy. Unknown to your reporters
> He turned to dust in China that your daughters . . .

well, that they be not "disgraced before the dogs." In preparing this sonnet for book publication in *Journey to a War*, Auden presumably did not fancy the chatty and condescending tone in which he addresses professor, hostess, and citizen, or the flatness with which he advises them to respect the boy, or the personal reference to himself and his friend as reporters. (Perhaps the rhyming of "reporters" and "daughters" recalled too vividly Eliot's burlesque passage,

> O the moon shone bright on Mrs. Porter
> And on her daughter
> They wash their feet in soda water.)

What he substitutes for all these light touches is subtler, more realistic, and more distinctive.

> He neither knew nor chose the Good, but taught us
> And added meaning like a comma, when
> He turned to dust in China . . .

It is true that, in leaving out the title, following his system for the entire sequence, Auden leaves us guessing at the reference as he so generally does in this whole series. Indeed, wherever we run down the original of one of these sonnets, we realize that far the most significant of all his revisions is the simple omission of the titles.* In the later series of sonnets, "The Quest," in many ways closely parallel to this "In Time of War," the titles are given,† and they have much light to throw on the intention of the several poems and of the series as a whole. We are left to speculate on Auden's reasons for suppressing the titles in this earlier sequence. But whatever his reasons, there is no doubt as to the effect. Over and over again the reader is put to great pains to identify the character or type referred to in a given sonnet or even to make out the general theme of the poem. One does not see how the imaginative effect of these poems would be impaired by giving them titles, provided the titles given suited the subject and intention of the poem. The case is exactly the opposite with many untitled poems from the earlier volumes to which in 1945 the poet gave fancy, often facetious, titles which suited neither the tone of the poem nor the philosophical associations which it originally carried, and actually failed to do justice to the poetic quality of the composition. One may not share the current popular objection to "obscurity" in modern poetry, where the obscurity is inherent in the natural subtlety and complexity of the poetic conception, or results from the "oblique," the symbolic, or dramatic method of presentation, from the use of irony, or from the writer's wish

* In the case of No. XIV, "Yes, we are going to suffer, now; the sky," we have, not precisely the original of this poem, but an earlier poem which served as a rough draft for both this and the following sonnet, "Engines bear them through the sky: they're free." And here we know that the original title, perhaps for them both, was that of this earlier canceled poem, "Air Raid." Reference will be made to this in the Supplementary Notes.

† The titles are given in *The Double Man* and the *Collected Poetry*, but in the (possibly earlier) *New Year Letter* the sonnets have numbers but no titles.

42

to avoid baldness and diffuseness of exposition. But one may fairly object to a poet's playing impish tricks with his own work, or failing to give to the reader such help as a title may give when it is actually an organic part of the creative act. This may not unfairly be placed under the head of mystification. And we cannot fail to note that the difficulty under which the reader labors because of the want of titles for the sonnets of "In Time of War" may contribute to a state of mind in which he will more readily fall in with the religious interpretation put upon them by Auden in his 1945 revisions of the Commentary.

ℭ 4

Passages Eliminated for Ideological Reasons

MUCH more drastic than these verbal emendations is the sort of revision that consists in leaving out of a poem that is retained passages of appreciable length running anywhere from four to twenty-eight lines. Of this sort of revision I have noted a considerable number of striking instances.

In some cases, it is fairly easy to make out the probable reason for the excisions made by Auden in 1945. Thus in the poem entitled "Consider," taken over from No. XXIX of *Poems* 1930, beginning "Consider this and in our time." This is one of many poems in which Auden warns his compatriots against a spiritual malady which he and his associates regarded as a threat to the soundness of English society. It has its psychological origins, and its effects moral, societal, political. This view involves "the doctrine that physical disease is invariably teleological, a mode of expression of the Id, caused by a sense of guilt." And this, according to Isherwood, "was an important part of the psycho-analytical philosophy taught in Berlin by John Layard, a disciple of the 'healer' Homer Lane, and deriving ultimately from Groddeck and Freud." (I am quoting from Monroe K. Spears, "The Dominant Symbols in Auden's Poetry," *Sewanee Review*, summer 1951.) In this doctrine the death wish seems to have been closely associated with the "pleasure principle."

In "Consider," Auden is warning "seekers after happiness, all who follow / The convolutions of your simple wish," that "it is later than you think." A great number of those in Great Britain, he says, are approaching the state when they are likely to "disin-

44

tegrate on an instant in the explosion of mania / Or lapse forever into a classic fatigue." The "Supreme Antagonist" is marshaling his cohorts of various types; he has started a rumor which is destined to scatter the people, "seized with immeasurable neurotic dread." The Supreme Antagonist is presumably Death himself, as he appears in Auden's early Marxist play, *The Dance of Death* (discussed in Chapter 12). It is the bourgeoisie who are the special victims of, and collaborators with, Death. As the announcer says at the beginning of the play: "We present to you this evening a picture of the decline of a class, of how its members dream of a new life, but secretly desire the old, for there is death inside them."

And this brings us to the portion of the poem "Consider" that Auden found it desirable to suppress in his 1945 collection. It refers to certain particularly influential representatives of the bourgeoisie for whom "the game is up," and who will not long escape their doom. There is the financier, who will not longer need his typist and his "boy," and there are the decadent academics and clergy,

> Who, thinking, pace in slippers on the lawns
> Of College Quad or Cathedral Close.

They are, he says, "born nurses" — that is, fomenters of psychic illness: they wear shorts, "sleep with people," and play fives.

However extravagant and confused the terms in which the youthful psychologist expressed himself, the mature poet may have found much of essential truth in this poem as a whole. And apart from this particular passage, there is nothing unmistakably Marxian in its text. But the association not merely of the financier, but even the university scholar and the clergyman, with sexual irregularity and the soft life must have seemed to him in later years an outrage to decency and a violation of the rules of fair play. What he could save he did, but this he could do only by cutting out the diseased tissue.

Somewhat similar may have been his reasons for cutting out two stanzas of "As We Like It," which was No. XXXI, the Epilogue, in *On This Island*, beginning "Certainly our city — with its

45

byres of poverty down to / The river's edge." This poem was a double-barreled weapon of socialist propaganda, moralized on the same psychological pattern as the other. On the one hand the poet denounces the "betrayers," the forces of hatred and fear, "the conscience-stricken, the weapon-making." On the other hand he recites the names of wise teachers who have convinced "us" of our vanity and pointed the way to "the really better world." These last included the explorer Nansen, the medical missionary Schweitzer, the psychologists Freud and Groddeck; they included Lawrence, who "revealed the sensations hidden by shame," and Kafka, who recorded "the sense of guilt," and Proust with his study of the vice of "self-regard."

Auden in 1945 was still pleased to see in print this curious amalgam of Freud and Marx, with Lord knows what fantastically jarring notions drawn from literary sex-psychology and from plain humanitarian ethics. But when it came to naming the various irreconcilable apostles of this synthetic creed, acknowledging the begetters of his fantasy, the mature Auden seems to have found this too much for him; and the two telltale stanzas had to go. The thing looked much better as sheer imaginative writing than as sober philosophy documented with footnotes upon sources.

The situation is somewhat similar with certain other poems from the early time from which even longer passages were eliminated in the 1945 revision. One of these was from *On This Island*, the poem later given the title "A Summer Night 1933" (No. II: "Out on the lawn I lie in bed"). From this poem the 1945 volume omits the fifth, tenth, eleventh, and twelfth of the original sixteen stanzas, or one-fourth of the whole poem. In this poem Auden is reviewing the happy times when he used to sit on calm evenings "equal with colleagues in a ring," when "Fear gave his watch no look." As the moon "climbs the European sky," he thinks of all those he loved, who did not care to know what violence was done in Poland (Tennyson: "Shall I weep if a Poland fall, Shall I shriek if a Hungary fail?"), "what doubtful act allows / Our freedom in this English house." And then he looks forward anxiously to the time when the high waters will retreat and expose the "stranded monster" of the political deep, depriving these friends of their luxurious privacy, and he calls upon them to summon all their strength to meet the stiuation.

In the first of the omitted stanzas, he speaks of the eyes in which he is glad to look every day and have his look returned, and which he will find with him when in the morning he wakes with the birds and the sun. In the series of three stanzas in a row, he refers to the intrusion of the hungry multitude outside upon his dream of private loves; and he traces everywhere "intentions not our own" in people able to achieve what they themselves might have accomplished if they had put their hands to the task. And finally he says there is "little strength remaining" in all they have loved. All that they have loved he would gladly give up for a bit of useful action on their own part, including

> The Oxford colleges, Big Ben
> And all the birds in Wicken Fen.

"Sweet city with her dreaming spires"! Oxford and Parliament, the young radical indicates, have failed to meet the challenge of the time. And it is easy to see why the reformed poet did not wish to retain these slurs upon the reverend educational and legislative institutions.

It is a little less easy to see why, along with this, he should have suppressed his reference to his own set of loving friends, indifferent to the political and social situation and priding themselves simply on their "metaphysical distress" and their casual charities ("our kindness to ten persons"). When it comes to the earlier stanza on the passionate friendships of young men, he may well have wished not to preserve this record of intimacies conceived a little too much in terms of erotic love.

The process of authorial expurgation did not always wait until 1945, but was sometimes practiced in much earlier volumes where considerable passages were dropped from the original version of a poem. Thus in the poem which appears in 1945 as "1929" and is No. XVI in the 1930 and 1933 editions of *Poems*, "It was Easter as I walked in the public gardens." This poem comprises four sec-

47

tions, the fourth beginning "It is time for the destruction of error." The texts of the first three sections are identical in 1930, 1933, and 1945, except for the correction in 1945 of a misprint in the earlier publications. But from the fourth section, the 1933 edition drops out two passages of ten and six lines respectively. Throughout the whole poem the process of decay and deadening in the social body is shown as accompanied by a parallel process in the private life of lovers; and the two parallel processes are brought together definitely in the concluding stanza of the fourth section, where the poet declares that the salvation of society requires "death, death of the grain,* our death, / Death of the old gang."

It is in the passages excised in 1933 that we have the most dreary picture of the futility and decadence of the two lovers (adolescents or youths) smothered under the wet blanket of sexual repressions and public conformity to an outworn social code, "Conformity with the orthodox bone, / With organized fear, the articulated skeleton" (these lines retained in the final approved version). Nothing in our literature can compare with the vividness of Auden's characterization of lusty youth struggling with the moral problem of sexual impulse — "verbal fumbling and muscle mumbling," "sebaceous belly, swollen skull, / Exchanging hats and calling dear." These sample images from the first of the omitted passages; and from the second, this image of indoor life as a symbol of forced unhealthy introspectiveness: "living together in wretched weather / In a doorless room in a leaking house."

Here, as so often with Auden's expurgations, one can see why discretion may have led him (even in his revolutionary days) to leave to obscurity much brilliantly imaginative writing. What is harder to understand is how he could have reconciled himself, after his conversion, to the exhibition of certain poems even in their expurgated form.

* Compare André Gide, "Si le grain ne meurt."

₵5

Passages Eliminated for Reasons Less Clear

IN THE case of half a dozen poems from which one or more stanzas were omitted in revision, we enter a dubious border region where our speculations as to the author's reasons are more hazardous. There may be "ideological" reasons which we do not penetrate, or there may be reasons of artistry which are not clear to the naked eye. Whether or not the poem was actually improved by the excision of these passages, it happens almost invariably that their absence from it in the present form means a loss of something that throws fuller light on the author's original intention, the way he conceived his theme when he first gave it verbal expression, or the personal circumstances or state of mind out of which the poem came to expression.* Even where we may agree with the poet that the composition is improved artistically by the sacrifice of the passages in question, the final result is likely to be a slight thickening of that mist of ambiguity that clings so persistently to his artistic activity and makes it so difficult to follow the evolution of his thought.

Perhaps the most startling instance of this is in the poem which is probably the most widely known of all his work. This is in the *Collected Poetry* entitled "September 1, 1939." It had first appeared in the *New Republic* for October 18, 1939, was reprinted in his volume *Another Time*, published in 1940, and has been given wide currency in Untermeyer's and Oscar Williams's an-

---

* For the sake of continuity I will leave for a note (see page 264) certain instances of excisions clearly made to relieve the dullness of a poem perfunctorily written or make an interesting poem more effective.

49

thologies since the appearance of the 1945 collection. It was written after Auden's coming to live in the United States, and was provoked by the outbreak of the Second World War. It was eagerly looked to for a statement of the famous poet's reaction to that catastrophic event. It is one of the poems in which he most distinctly makes his break with the old Marxian ideology. And at the same time it gives the really classical and lucid version of the ethico-psychological theory adumbrated in several of the earlier poems already discussed.

The Second World War marked the culmination of the morbid process "that has driven a culture mad." In the person of Hitler, the private malady, somehow begotten in the mind of a boy sent unwillingly to the Austrian *Realschule* at Linz, took shape as the public malady of Statism, Imperialism, Dictatorship of the Führer, and now the September night is offended by "the unmentionable odour of death." In a New York bar the private malady is exhibited by all those self-deceiving men betrayed by Eros and the death wish, lost in "an euphoric dream" — men who crave what they cannot have, "not universal love / But to be loved alone." In the eighth stanza the poet makes his perfectly clear and specific statement as to the essential identity of the two "lies" —

> The romantic lie in the brain
> Of the sensual man in the street
> And the lie of Authority.

He goes on to declare that

> There is no such thing as the State
> And no one exists alone,

And he reaches the unexceptionable conclusion that "we must love one another or die."

Now, it is precisely this culminating eighth stanza that Auden cuts out of his poem on revision.*

---

* This rejected stanza is kept in Louis Untermeyer's *Modern British Poetry*, 1950 ed., and his *Modern American and British Poetry*, 1955, and in all three of Williams's anthologies, *A Little Treasury of Modern Poetry*, 1946, *A Little Treasury of American Poetry*, 1948, and the *New Pocket Anthology of American Verse*, 1955. In the last of the three Williams anthologies there is a deplorable misprint. The final line of the stanza there,

So far as one can make out, there is nothing whatever in this poem, nor in the omitted stanza, that might not meet the approval of the mature Auden. The emphasis is all directed against fascist statism rather than in favor of the old Marxian dream of "Collective Man." Indeed, "Collective Man" is here *identified with* the abhorred statism; and the love for one another that we must have or die is directly opposed, in the manner of all his Christian writing, to the self-regarding Freudian Eros. The social order here recommended is *individualism cum Agape.* There is no better statement of Auden's political and psychological position as exhibited in much of his subsequent writing; and this poem may be cited as marking the moment in which he distinctly showed himself a reformed thinker, at least in political theory, for his religious conversion seems to have followed on this and to have been consummated somewhat later. This eighth stanza marks the crux of the whole matter. And yet, for inscrutable reasons, he chose to cut it out of the 1945 version, and to keep it out in the 1950 version.

The only possible reason one can think of is that the statement is not made here in specifically and unmistakably religious terms. But that applies equally to the parts of the poem retained and to many earlier poems admitted to the canon. Or is it possible that, on reflection, the author feared he might be misunderstood when he declared, "There is no such thing as the State," or when he referred to "the lie of Authority"? Did he fear that this first statement might be mistaken for theoretical anarchism, and that the "lie of Authority" might put him under the suspicion of antinomianism? Such misgivings have not generally been characteristic of Auden's free-wheeling mind. But it seems just possible that he was afflicted by them in the anxious years when he was meditating his great about-face.

And then again there is the possibility that he was moved by purely artistic considerations. Perhaps, as in other cases noted, he

instead of "We must love one another or die," reads, "We must love one another *and* die," which makes no sense at all in this context. In Williams's other anthologies, the correct reading is given.

felt that he had here expressed himself in too bald and abstract a style, and preferred to sacrifice what was for many of his readers his most enlightening statement, in favor of an ideal of poetic purity.

Another case in which we are left floundering is that of a very early poem, "The Exiles." This is Ode No. III from *The Orators*, beginning with the line "What siren zooming is sounding our coming?" It is conceived in terms suggesting at first sight life in a boys' school; but the images used are all symbolic of some manner of life associated with the word "exile," which occurs in the opening stanza, and which, in the plural, was later adopted by Auden for the title.

The word "exile" is not generally used by Auden to signify persons compelled to leave their country for political reasons. It is sometimes applied to those voluntary exiles (like Joyce, or the exiles in St. John Perse) who leave home upon some quest for truth or to make themselves completely independent of home ties and the prevailing climate of opinion. One thinks of Auden and MacNeice going to Iceland, of Auden expatriating himself to America. One thinks of the English writers and artists living abroad in Spender's poem "The Exiles." Sometimes, however, these isolate spirits are not regarded as resolute independents, but as lost souls like the characters in *The Age of Anxiety*. Of these Richard Hoggart writes: "In one sense all four were exiles; not artistic or intellectual exiles, but the ordinary exiles who 'lost a world they never understood' ('Loss is their shadow-wife, anxiety receives them. . . .' Auden added in this poem, written a few years earlier and sometimes called 'Exiles.')" He is referring to Sonnet XXI from "In Time of War," originally entitled "Exiles."

This much earlier poem is one of the most difficult of Auden's to interpret; and it is with considerable diffidence that I offer my interpretation. I believe that these exiles are of the second kind — the lost ones. And I think, on second thought, that the place where they are lodged, looked after, and entertained is even more like a sanitarium than a boys' school. Their coming was heralded by a "siren zooming." They are inmates of an institution, and are,

I think, those referred to in "Consider" as destined to "lapse forever into a classic fatigue." This would explain their being taken on walks, being given picnics in July and innocuous entertainments at Christmas. It would fit in with the "slight despair" they feel at "what [they] are." But the very alienation from which these patients suffer is not so much literal as symbolic of a lethargic state of mind and soul which the poet finds characteristic of a large part of the population in his day. These people are only half alive. They "live and somehow love," though they "only master / The sad posture." In the artificial security of the sanitarium they are relieved from the fears that would otherwise beset them. Living in groups, they can forget "the gun in the drawer," and not think of self-defense or suicide. It is only occasionally that they are recalled to a sense of their ineffectualness — recalled "By music on water / To lack of stature / Saying Alas / To less and less." Or sometimes walking down streets looking into shop windows, something about "the fate of ships / And the tide-wind" will "touch the old wound." And finally in a London room they will "hear in a corner / The Pffwung of burner / Accepting dearth / The shadow of death." Here enters, if not suicide, the familiar Audenesque figure of the death wish.

It is in the rejected stanzas (tenth to thirteenth) that the image of a mental institution is strongest. They are there "for [their] health," and need not fear "the fiend in the furze or the face at the manse." They have been given pacifying drugs, and their hands may show the symptoms of Parkinson's disease without their actually displaying any emotion: "Proof against shock / Our hands can shake." They are destined to "lose our colour / With scurf on collar / Peering through glasses / At our own glosses" (their own crazy reading of the facts). And so on.

Altogether we have here the dreariest picture of a human condition imaginable, only to be matched by clinical reports from an "asylum," and a most vivid symbolizing of lives in which the vital spirit has been withered away by some insidious spiritual malady. And the most harrowingly convincing touches are to be found in the four rejected stanzas. So that one cannot conceive why they *were* rejected, unless indeed the author, on consideration, found them too realistic, too specifically technical, for the purposes of poetic symbolism.

A poem of about the same period, or a little earlier, "Not All the Candidates Pass," has, we find, gone through two stages in revision. It appeared first in 1933 in *New Country*, an anthology edited by Michael Roberts, along with early versions of other poems of Auden to which we shall have occasion to refer in later chapters. It was Part II of a long poem entitled "A Happy New Year." It was reprinted in *On This Island* as No. X, "Now from my window-sill I watch the night," and in the *Collected Poetry* under its present title. In each reprinting it underwent considerable reduction in length and other minor revisions and corrections. One of these was in the last line of the ninth stanza where the "isolated personal life," identical in the two earliest versions, is changed in 1945 to the "isolated dishonest life."

This may seem a very slight and insignificant alteration; but in reality it is eloquent of the way the author's preoccupations at a later period come in to give a quite different coloring to the original thought. This poem was written while Auden was in the full flush of his Marxian feeling about English society. Part I of "A Happy New Year," as we shall see in a later chapter, is a high-spirited burlesque of bourgeois leadership in all departments of state, business, finance, religion, literature, and learning. This was never, I believe, reprinted. And in the same number of *New Country* were featured several other poems of Auden, impregnated with Marxian propaganda, which were either dropped out later or heavily expurgated. One of these, entitled "A Communist to Others," appeared in much reduced form in *On This Island* as No. XIV, "Brothers, who when the sirens roar," only to be suppressed entirely in 1945.

In the poem we are now considering, the poet is saying that the heart submits to the discipline of the Lords of Limit "when we have fallen apart / Into the isolated personal life." Auden often uses the image of an island to symbolize the selfish isolation of the individual who should ideally be united with others in the social collectivity. The isolated personal life comes under the same condemnation as those whose comfortable "village of the heart" has been invaded by the fear, greed, sensuality, and false sentiment of the town. It is in terms of this moralized ideology that we must read the phrase as it was in the original. When Auden in 1945 made this alteration, he was long past the time when he was recommending the social collectivity as an ideal pattern or directing his fire against "individualism." He was rather defending the individual against the pressures of the mass. When he replaced "personal" by "dishonest," he was probably thinking of the celibate or bachelor life as in some sense dishonest. At any rate we shall shortly see how in a poem of 1941 ("At the Grave of Henry James") he refers to the "dishonest path" of the "bachelor mind." It is not possible to determine whether he has in mind the special temptations to which young men are subject when they do not have natural relations with the other sex, or simply to the self-centered character of the celibate life. At any rate, he is clearly not thinking in terms of the social community as conceived by socialists, but in terms of personal Christian ethics. But this consideration does not seem to have been present in the original poem, and the altered phrasing introduces an ambiguity not evidently intended there.

I do not mean to imply that this poem is propagandistic or even political except in the sense that the poet is vividly aware of the troublous state of the world and has in mind the possible revolutionary violence to come in which his pupils may be involved. It is rather moralistic in a way that would be acceptable to anyone concerned with the shaping of character in the young. It shows the poet in the very sympathetic role of schoolmaster seriously and tenderly reflecting on the present character of the boys entrusted to his charge, and upon the world conditions that may determine the further favorable or unfavorable development of their character. He is watching the night from his window, apparently in the early spring when "the ice is loosened," but in a dark period of history. Some "starving visionary" (Marx?) has anticipated the day when there will be bloody "carnival within our gates," and the boys' "bodies kicked about the streets," and his meditations have a background of "prophecy" and of a state of the world symbolized by "China's drum."

Most of the poem is in the form of a "petition" addressed to the "Lords of Limit, training dark and light / And setting a tabu 'twixt left and right." These symbolic figures are conceived in a manner similar to the watchers in "The Witnesses," the final poem of Part I in the *Collected Poems*, but written at about the same time as the present piece. They are also akin to the symbolic figure in "Petition," which was No. XXX in *Poems* 1930. And as that figure was addressed as "sir," these Lords of Limit are addressed in one of the rejected stanzas as "gentlemen." They are mythological but not theological creations of the poet's fancy. They seem to represent the basic material realities, the ineluctable conditions, to which the growing boy must adjust himself, being as they are "oldest of masters, whom the schoolboy fears." And in the tabu they set " 'twixt left and right" they recall the Two who perpetually watch the hero "on [his] left and on [his] right," as well as, in the early poem "The Walking Tour," the "line with left and right / An altered gradient at another rate." The general meaning would appear to be that the line is narrow, "straight is the way," between opposing perils which the seeker after truth must follow if he is not to come to ruin.* Later in this poem the Lords of Limit are compared to gamekeepers, with guns, perpetually set at doors, on ridges, by copse or bridge, "whose presences endear / Our peace to us with a perpetual threat." †

The poet's chief prayer to these presences is not to be too strict in their treatment of the boys in his school, or even of the little town itself and the guardians of town and school. In the three stanzas omitted in *On This Island* he asks the imagined watchers to let their town stay small, to preserve their Provost, Piermaster,

---

* But it is also probable that left and right have political implications and reflect the leftist leanings of the author.

† Mr. Replogle opines that the gamekeepers here are reminders of Lawrence's *Lady Chatterley's Lover* and his recommendation of sexual normality and freedom.

Police, and to watch over "the Lindens, Ferntower, Westoe, and this Pen," and will all these to "be very very patient, gentlemen."

In 1945 two more stanzas were dropped. Here the poet prays the Lords of Limit to give his pupils "spontaneous skill" at various workshop exercises, and refers to their boyish lumpishness and frailty — "awkward, pasty, feeling the draught" — but also to their manly promise in that they "have health and skill and beauty on the brain." (Some commentators find that this obsession with health and skill and beauty is, contrariwise, a symptom not of manliness but of effeminacy, related to the boys' physical awkwardness and delicacy, and pointing to homosexuality. This might suggest a probable reason for discarding these stanzas.) The clocks strike ten; the teacher hears the voices that he loves coming up the stair for tea. They are players of badminton, and he names them individually.

In none of the stanzas rejected in 1936 or 1945 was there any treasonable matter. But they were, I suppose, more intimate and personal than the author considered appropriate when the successive revisions were made. They have their pleasing light to throw on details of the poet's life at the time of writing, on his feeling of affection for the boys, the town and the school, and the grave seriousness with which he took his responsibilities. They help to make us understand the warmth and moral earnestness that underlay his revolutionary convictions. They do perhaps somewhat obscure the simple lines of the poetic composition and interrupt its forward progress. He was doubtless right in judging that it was a better poem without them. But their absence leaves him a shade more remote and questionable as the man behind the voice.

"Voltaire at Ferney" makes a special case. This is one of the finest and most thoughtful poems in Auden's later manner. In the period when he was probably persuaded of the insufficiency of Voltaire's unbelieving approach to life, Auden was still wishing to do justice to the old fighter's lifelong "holy war" against "the false and the unfair" in church and state. There is some pathos in his reflections upon those who might have been effective allies in his crusade — D'Alembert, Pascal ("a great enemy"), dull Diderot, and Rousseau, who, "he'd always known, would blubber and give in." Even nature seemed against the lonely old man, and evil forces were rampant all over Europe. But "he must go on working."

In *Another Time*, as in the version published in *Poetry* in June 1939, this poem included a stanza eliminated from the later collections. Voltaire is thinking of women and of Lust, "one of the great teachers." He thinks of the warming earthy love of Emilie and Pimpette. And the stanza ends with a psychological observation that might have been made by Auden at any time during the later thirties: "As a rule / It was the pleasure-haters who became unjust."

On artistic grounds this stanza, surely, did not deserve to be scrapped. It adds a highly significant note to the, on the whole, sympathetic picture of the old fighter for liberty and justice. And all along Auden had been a favorer of Eros, given to pointing out the harm following on the repression of wholesome natural instincts. It is true, however, that by 1945 he was impressed with the insufficiency of Eros — even its viciousness when not supplemented by the divine Agape. And in his settled Christian state of mind the illegitimacy of Voltaire's amours may have seriously offended his religious sense. It seems possible that he came to feel that this not explicitly orthodox or satirical presentation of Voltaire's sex life might be a cause of stumbling to those weak in the faith, and that as a serious exponent of religion he was bound to suppress it. Among all his revisions, this is perhaps the one where the conscience of the artist made its heaviest sacrifice to the conscience of the religious moralist.*

* In addition to the omission of a stanza, in 1945 three minor verbal alterations were made in the poem as it appeared in *Poetry* and *Another Time*. In the opening line, "Perfectly happy now, he looked at his estate," the first word is changed to "Almost." In the first line of the last stanza, "So, like a sentinel, he could not sleep," etc., the first word is changed to "Yet" and the comma dropped. In the fifth line of the first stanza, "Some of the trees he'd planted were progressing well" (*Poetry*), the text of *Another Time* is defective, and the word "planted" appears as "plan ed" with one type space unoccupied. By some accident the "t" had fallen out. In 1945 the printers, evidently working with this text, did their best to make sense out of it, and the line appears: "Some of the trees he'd planned." The con-

This is the most convenient place to consider one of Auden's finest poems, from which considerable passages were eliminated, "At the Grave of Henry James." This is a work of crucial importance in relation to his turning from what I have called his humanist to his Christian philosophy. It was apparently written in the spring of 1941, after the snow had melted in the Cambridge graveyard, and was published in the *Partisan Review* for July and August. It was during this year that Auden was making clear in prose articles that he had definitely taken the step of espousing the Christian faith in which he was brought up as a boy. My reason for discussing this poem is the fact that, along with other minor revisions, some of them occasioned, we must suppose, by carelessness in preparing copy or reading proof for the *Partisan*, the author chose to cut out four important stanzas of the original version. The poet is appealing to the spirit of a revered master —"poet of the difficult, dear addicted artist . . . great and talkative man . . . master of nuance and scruple" — asking him to come to his assistance, teach him discipline, distinction, and proportion, save him from irrevelance and "the vanity of our calling," and severely edit his "loose impromptu song." But more than that, he is asking him to "pray for him and for all writers living or dead." And the context abundantly shows that the poet has in mind not merely his artistic but his spiritual salvation, as amid all the violence of war and the riot of mere animal life, the day of judgment approaches.

He alludes to many of James's stories, but has most vividly in mind "The Beast in the Jungle," and it is this that he echoes where he speaks of the time approaching when

> Out from the jungle of an undistinguished moment
> The flexible shadow springs.

Just at this point comes the first of the omitted stanzas, where he asks what but the honour of a great house (with its cradles and

text plainly calls for "planted." But "planned" makes some sort of sense, and in 1950, the printers, evidently working with the 1945 text, had nothing to do but perpetuate the error. In the line "He'd led the other children in a holy war," the word "led" is obviously a correction for "had" in the *Poetry* version.

tombs) "may persuade . . . the bachelor mind to doubt / Its dishonest path." Here and in the lines that follow contrasting the impulses to "withness" (living with others) and Withoutness (living apart from others), he still seems to be thinking of "The Beast in the Jungle," and of Marcher, the self-centered protagonist of that tale. Marcher lived for years in perpetual fear of some doom that was hanging over him, waiting to spring upon him, but did not have the heart or the insight to recognize the preciousness of a woman's love when it was put in his way, and after her death, while visiting her tomb, he receives the full impact of his belated recognition. The doom that threatened him all along had been the realization of his own inadequacy to meet the challenge of life and love. This was the beast that had lurked in "the jungle of his life," and that now with its leaping "settled" him. James's image of the tiger's spring was linked in Auden's thought, as it was in Eliot's, with Blake's image of the tiger "burning bright in the forest of the night." Blake's tiger did not spring as James's did. The tiger's spring appears several times in the poetry of both Eliot and Auden. And I think it reasonable to suppose that the unfortunate "bachelor mind" referred to in the discarded stanza somehow links together in Auden's thinking the three names of Marcher and James and himself, and that it is also linked by association with the *affaire fatale* of marriage referred to in the stanza shortly after this which was not discarded.

James was for Auden an example to himself of an author who ignored the outward and superficial, the accidental aspects of things ("the obvious"), and stuck to his central spiritual concerns. He is evidently thinking of the relatively unimportant problems of political organization which had occupied so much of his own thought and writing. And James can teach him not to "riot with irrelevance" — to "fumble no more / In the old limp pocket of the minor exhibition." (Here, as throughout the poem, Auden is paying James the compliment of writing in the famous periphrastic and figurative manner of "the great and talkative man.")

For the most part, Auden is speaking of James as a master of the art of writing, but all the time he is making the literary art a symbol of the higher spiritual art of living. In the next of the discarded stanzas he speaks of the Cambridge graveyard as an orchard in which the arrangement of the bones suggests how "our lives conceal a pattern which shows / A tendency to execute formative movements." And a little later, in two successive stanzas not retained, he speaks of himself as a creature "descended / From an ancient line of respectable fish" (referring to his evolutionary origin), who, between two glacial epochs, is engaged in "weaving / His conscience on [earth's] calm." He shows himself in fear of the Hereafter, and unable to "imagine the rising Rome" (the heavenly City of God), or to "guess from what shore / The signal will flash" (announcing the day of judgment). And so, in the concluding stanzas which were retained, he can ask his revered master to "make intercession / For the treason of all clerks," and prepare his spirit to meet "the author / And giver of all good things."

He may have had in mind here the passages recorded in the three synoptic gospels in which Jesus warns his disciples of the necessity of being perpetually in readiness for the coming of the Lord in the last day. Thus in Matthew: "But of that day and hour knoweth no man, no, nor the angels of heaven, but my Father only . . . Watch therefore; for ye know not what hour your Lord doth come." Etc. In his phrase "the treason of all clerks," Auden is obviously alluding to the famous book by Julien Benda, *La Trahison des clercs*, first published in Paris in 1927, translated by Richard Aldington and published in 1928 in England under the title *The Great Betrayal*, and in the United States as *The Treason of the Intellectuals*.*

Benda's contention is that learned men should confine their attention to purely "transcendental" or "spiritual" values, and should not yield to the political passions, such as nationalism, that have been rampant among writers in his day, as in the case of Treitschke, Ostwalt, Brunetière, Barrès, Lemaître, Péguy, Maurras, d'Annunzio, and Kipling. He was writing before the triumph of fascism in Germany and Spain and the widespread espousal of so-

* Now available in a cheap edition, with introduction by Herbert Read, published by the Beacon Press, Boston, 1955.

cialism in the West. But Auden, following his conversion, is clearly applying Benda's rigorous test to his own preoccupation, throughout the thirties, with such unspiritual matters as social and political organization and the mere constructing of "a human justice." He is in effect in this poem abjuring most of his previous activities as a poet, and makes one think of Chaucer's supposed deathbed repudiation of all his secular works, and Petrarch's anxious dialogue with St. Augustine on the subject of his humanistic (unreligious) works.

Auden may have had several reasons for cutting out the four stanzas. Some of them may have been purely artistic reasons. Stanza 17 of the original, about the bones in the "orchard," rather bogs down in figures of speech that are scarcely firm enough to support the weight of the thought. And the same thing might be said of the abstract word "withness" and the corresponding "Without," suggesting the jargon of semantics and psychology, in characterization of "the bachelor mind." Again, Auden may have wished to play down until the concluding stanzas the emphasis on the spiritual meaning that underlies his appeal to the literary craftsmanship of his Master. He may have wished to keep as long as possible to the "objective correlative" furnished by the Master's craftsmanship, and so cut out the earlier references to the dishonest path followed by the bachelor mind, to the fish's progeny weaving his conscience upon earth's calm, to the dreaded Hereafter, the unimaginable City of God, and the signal that would flash for the unannounced coming of the Lord.

But there was also, I fancy, a personal reason which might as such be regarded as involving artistic considerations. Auden, in 1945, wished to make his poem more impersonal than it was in its original form, and he accordingly cut out most items that might have a reference to himself personally not as an artist but as a soul to be saved. This meant dropping stanza 12, with its reference to the bachelor mind, stanza 24, with its reference to the weaving of his conscience upon earth's calm, and stanza 25, with its reference to his dread of the Hereafter and his inability to guess from what shore the signal would flash. Stanza 24 brings in another phrase which may be taken as referring to himself. The descendant of an ancient line of respectable fish is characterized as having "a certain *méchant* charm." This might conceivably refer to the "respectable fish" in general. But it sounds so much like the way Auden's friends would speak of him, and so much like one of his earlier poses, that it was probably meant to be an ironic characterization of himself. And one can quite understand both how he might have written it that way in 1941 and how he might have wished to cancel it in 1945.

Altogether, as so often with Auden's expurgations, while we may be sorry to see something go that is so interestingly revelatory, we have to acknowledge the rightness of his instinct in running his blue pencil through it. At any rate, the author must be judge as to the degree of self-revelation he will put into his work. There is certainly a limit to what we can expect from a poet in the way of public confession of his errors. And in this case there can be no possible question of disingenuousness or ambiguity as to the author's intention in the poem. The interval between its writing and its admission to the canon shows, so far as we are aware, no change in his position; and there was no occasion for emendation or expurgation in order to bring it in line with later views. The reader is always curious about the most intimate thoughts and feelings of a poet. But the poet's obligation is solely to the integrity of his poetical conception.*

---

* At the last moment, too late for adequate discussion here, I have noted Auden's excision of the next to the last stanza of "Oxford," beginning, "And all the lanes of his wish twist down to the grave." The reference is to Eros Paidagogos, the life-and-death wish that is represented throughout the poem as, in Oxford and in life generally, opposed to the peaceful spirit of Nature. This stanza, present in the original as published in the *Listener*, Feb. 9, 1938, is perhaps the most striking and explicit rendering of the idea, so common in Auden, which links together the "Freudian Eros" with the decadent death-wish; and one is at a loss to explain his elimination of it in *Another Time* and the later collections.

ℭ6

Poems Eliminated for Ideological Reasons

AND now we come finally to those early poems that were eliminated in their entirety, and first those that were seemingly rejected on philosophical or ideological considerations.

In the case of the lyrical pieces eliminated from the early volume of *Poems*, we have to distinguish between those included in both the first edition of 1930 and the second edition of 1933, and those included in either one of these but not in the other.* In 1933 seven new poems replaced an equal number not retained from 1930. So far as I can make out from the list of opening lines in the first edition as given in the bibliography published in *New Verse* for May 1937, none of these seven poems was reprinted in either the 1945 or the 1950 collection. It would seem that in 1933 Auden had already passed judgment, most likely on purely artistic grounds, upon the seven poems he replaced, and that in 1945 he did not have the heart to review his earlier verdict.

The 1930 *Poems* is a rather rare item in the United States. And even rarer than this is the little orange paper volume of Auden's *Poems* privately printed by Stephen Spender on his own press in 1928, whose opening lines are listed in the *New Verse* bibliography. From this volume four lyrical pieces were continued in

---

* I refer to the second edition as dated 1933 because it is explicitly so dated in my own copy: "First published in September MCMXXX by Faber and Faber Limited . . . second edition November MCMXXXIII." In the *New Verse* bibliography, it is listed as dated 1932. In his bibliography published in *Thought*, summer 1955, Mr. Clancy agrees with my dating of the two editions. I am assuming that the *New Verse* dating of the second edition is an error.

both editions of the published *Poems*, and also what became a chorus in *Paid on Both Sides*, which they both printed entire. This is the famous poem beginning with the line "To throw away the key and walk away." This leaves seventeen poems from this privately printed brochure which Auden dropped out in his earliest published volume and never again restored to favor. We may think of them as poems relegated by the author to the rank of juvenilia. They all date from as early as 1928 (Auden's twenty-first year). They would of course have their interest in a broader study of Auden's development, but would not presumably have capital importance in the present study. One of them, however, was published in an earlier version in *Oxford Poetry* for 1927, and again in the 1928 revision by Christopher Isherwood in an essay in *New Verse* for November 1937, and I shall have something to say about it in my first appendix, along with a dozen still earlier poems printed by Isherwood or published in anthologies.

There remain for our consideration here the twenty-three pieces (exclusive of *Paid on Both Sides*) that are common to the two published editions of the *Poems*, and the seven that appeared in 1933 but not in 1930. Or rather, we are concerned with the two poems from among these thirty that were rejected in 1945. In the case of one of these, the reasons for rejection are not too clear, and it will be discussed in the notes (see p. 265). With the other, it is more obvious why Auden should have "scrapped" it. This is No. XXII in both editions of the *Poems*, beginning with the line "Get there if you can and see the land you once were proud to own." This piece was included in Auden's later collection of *Poems* (1934), together with the entire contents of *Poems 1933*, of *The Orators*, and *The Dance of Death*. But it is easy to see why in 1945 it was Enemy Number One among Auden's early productions. It is the most slam-bang fighting manifesto in the gang warfare between his own party of Oxford radicals and assorted types representing the decadent bourgeoisie.

The poem opens with five stanzas vividly describing the industrial ruin that everywhere confronted one in England in the time of the great depression. The poet then pays his compliments to various exemplars of the accompanying moral decadence. There are the cigarette-chain-smoking Sunday lads on motorcycles, and the more upper-class pleasure-seekers who had been "our boon companions" — those "who have betrayed us nicely while we took them to our rooms." The boon companions then shade off without transition into the writers who have debauched us. I cannot identify all of these; but they include Plato, Pascal, Baudelaire, Freud, Flaubert, and the Baron, whom I take to be Proust's homosexual, pro-German Baron Charlus. The young intellectuals were attracted by the logic of these writers, and by their "loaded sideboards." There were also the "big business men," who arranged summer camps to entertain and enslave them; and there was the prestige of a perfect pater and mater, who, when their sons "asked the way to heaven," directed them the way to the "padded room." Then are listed the champions and inspirers of "our" party, who had been killed off by censorship and abuse — D. H. Lawrence "brought down by smut-hounds," William Blake, "who went dotty as he sang," Homer Lane the "healer," who "was killed in action by the Twickenham Baptist gang." Then the poet goes on to describe the growing terror throughout the countryside, the imminence of bloody proletarian revolt; and bids his disciples "shut up talking" and get ready for action — "Throw the bathchairs right away, and learn to leave ourselves alone" — or else, if they don't want to live, they had "better start to die."

With this poem, it may be noted, the process of expurgation had begun much earlier, in 1933, when two stanzas were dropped out of the 1930 version. These served to interpret the reference to the parents' way of conditioning their children toward madness, showing the unsavory dreariness of the life to which these youths were reduced by the repressive prescriptions of their elders. They had to give up the "larks" they were so eager for when they "found it wasn't done." And so their leisure is occupied with telling dirty stories.

> So we sit at table talking, pornographic as we dine,
> Each the good old topic, meaningless as an electric sign.

Even as early as 1933 Auden must have thought it indiscreet to point up too vividly the psychological theory of corruption by sexual repression.

This is one of the most colorful and enlivening of all Auden's writings. It was the early Auden, the poet who bespelled a generation of readers liking to see poets full steam up in whatever cause, and all boyish readers who loved to see the spirit of Westerns brought into the adventures of the mind, and, under the study lamp, to imagine themselves engaged in the half-sham battles of ideology. There is nothing in the substance of this poem that is not paralleled in dozens of other poems of the early thirties that Auden *did* find suitable for perpetuation. Only, the expression is so bald and brash as to be shocking to him in his maturity. There are writers here listed among the agents of corruption who are elsewhere classed among his partisans and teachers. His attitudes are so exaggerated, his antireligious bias so marked, his condemnations and comminations so sweeping, his political alarmism so extreme, his references to sexual abuses so indiscreet, that the author could hardly have done other than look upon this as an example of his juvenilia too distasteful to be longer exposed to public gaze.

One might think that by 1936 the young author would have worked off enough steam to make all that he wrote acceptable to him nine years later when the censorship began to operate seriously. But many poems collected in *On This Island* were written some years earlier than the date of publication of that volume. Three of the poems rejected by Auden in 1945 appeared in anthologies in the same year with the second edition of the 1930 *Poems*, and still another in a periodical anthology two years later. Indeed there are more major poems from *On This Island* suppressed on ideological grounds than from *Poems* 1933, though it was apparently in 1933 that he was writing his baldest political propaganda.

The first of these suppressed poems is No. XIV, "Brothers, who when the sirens roar." The original of this appeared in the avant-garde anthology *New Country*, edited by Michael Roberts and published in 1933 at the Hogarth Press by Leonard and Virginia

Woolf. In this form it bears the title "A Communist to Others," and in the first line, instead of "brothers," we have the more unmistakably Marxian form of address, "comrades." In revising this for *On This Island* the poet cut it down by half a dozen stanzas, but left it pretty much the same radical partisan propaganda as he found it in its earlier form. He begins with direct address to the office, shop, and factory proletarians who had been reduced to passive nonentities by their fear of the bosses. He admits that his set "cannot put on airs" with their humble comrades since they share their fears; but he promises the speedy downfall of "those who in every county town / For centuries have done you down." He then enumerates and directly addresses the several groups of reactionaries. There are the aristocratic youths with their Grecian figures, who "stand / In spotless flannels or with hand / Expert on trigger." He assures them that they are not really favorites of the Lady they are wooing (the Future). He then addresses the "dare-devil mystic," who tells

> The starving that their one salvation
> Is personal regeneration
> By fasting, prayer and contemplation.

(*On This Island* has "their one starvation," an obvious misprint for "their one salvation," the form in the original.) This mystic he calls a coward and assures him that his "dream of Heaven" is the same as "any bounder's," since he hopes to corner "all that the rich can here afford . . . while the world flounders." Next comes the humorous "wise man," for whom "our misery's a rumour, / And slightly funny." He is actually no better than the boss's stooge, and has watched without concern the invasion of people's minds by the "great malignant / Cambridge ulcer."

The Cambridge ulcer consists of the army of intellectuals and liberals from the rival university, who are "swarmy with friendship but of all / There are none falser." These are presumably the same set as those in the earlier poem "who have betrayed us nicely while we took them to our rooms." They are "a host of columbines and pathics," who, coming from the stronghold of mathematical science, can prove by figures "that wealth and power are

68

merely / Mental pictures." Upon them, in robust Elizabethan style of invective, he calls down every dread disease — on them and their daughters — their bankers and brokers, their "professors, agents, magic-makers, / Their poets and apostles."

Mr. Spears points out that, in his characteristic satirical masquerading, Auden has here, as in his "Letter to Lord Byron," striven "to attain lightness through adopting the *persona* of an earlier poet." In this case it is Burns, whose stanzaic form he has adopted (the rime coulée, or tailed rhyme) for conveying his vigorous invective. But however much of Burns's form and manner Auden has here taken over, it is obviously his own sentiments that he is conveying, or at any rate the sentiments that went with his role as leader of the young rebels. Auden, it seems, was always projecting himself in one role or another, even when most sincere. It is this trait in him that Isherwood hits off sympathetically in *Lions and Shadows* when he speaks of Weston's "conception of himself as a lunatic clergyman." And he speaks again, in connection with the theories of Homer Lane, of Weston's "zest and ease" in assimilating new ideas, "adding to them a touch of extravagance which was peculiarly his own."

In the stanzas cut out in 1936, there are animadversions upon double-dealing employers, and upon schoolmasters who, instead of using the whip like their predecessors, play upon their pupils' "self-adulation" to make "a weakened generation / Completely neuter." Two stanzas are addressed to the sunset poets who fly to islands in their private seas and spend their time in "endless petting." He tells them they could "help us" if they pleased and were not afraid that we are more than they could face. He ends up with an address to the "comrades" — "brothers for whom our bowels yearn" — assuring them that they are bound by invisible ties of a love "outside our own election."

Like the earlier piece from the 1930 *Poems*, this one, even in its revised form, is unredeemed (for later reading) by being a counterblast to fascist statism. It is straight Marxist propaganda, based on the concept of class struggle, and not excluding an antireligious bias. The only improvement over the earlier poem is in the ab-

sence of abuse for individual adversaries. And that was not enough
to save it in the eyes of the author in 1945.

The next one of the important poems in this volume rejected in
1945 is No. XV, "The chimneys are smoking, the crocus is out in
the border." This poem appeared in the same number of *New
Country* with "A Communist to Others," under the title "Poem."
In the original form, it begins with two lines very much in the
manner of Gerard Manley Hopkins, "Me, March, you do with
your movements master and rock / With wing-whirl, whale-
wallow, silent budding of cell." The third line is the same as in
On This Island except that here, instead of the political orator, it
is "the communist orator" who lands at the pier. From this point
on the two versions are practically the same except in two places.
The stanza in 1936 beginning "We ride on a turning globe, we
stand on a star," takes the place of two stanzas in the original
dealing with the strategic separation of the lovers. In the third
stanza, instead of "the contest of the Whites with the Reds," we
have in the original, "the contest of the Whites with *our* Reds,"
which explicitly identifies the two lovers with the leftist or revolutionary party in this ideological conflict.

In this poem, in 1950 entitled "Two Worlds," the necessary
separation of the lovers is symbolic of the division of society into
"two worlds" because, for the time being, their natural and desiderated unity has been disturbed by ideological strife. Over the
lovers, as over the whole community of men, hovers "the white
death" in the form of a cruel hawk. In some of Auden's poetry,
the hawk specifically represents fascism; but here it seems to stand
more broadly for a kind of inhuman malignness in things. What
the hawk desires is strife and death for mortals, whose "kindness"
is hidden from its eyes. It is watching the "handsome couple" below, imagining them "estranged by a mistake," quarreling and
dying, perhaps by their own hands. In the same way it is gleefully
watching, on the larger scene, "the contest of the Whites with
the Reds for the carried thing," not understanding that each of
us is intrusted with a portion of a whole which needs to be assembled by love like a puzzle picture from its many separate pieces.

At present the two parties are at war and watching each other with jealousy and suspicion. The speaker's "darling" is advised to walk off "lightly" so as not to attract the attention of the hawk; and he indicates that since they cannot, any more than those seeking social unity, take "that route that is straightest," they must choose "the crooked" way. Meantime, since the millions earnestly "wish to be one," let us all join in a dance —

> the boatmen, virgins, camera-men and us
> Round goal-post, wind-gauge, pylon or bobbing buoy.

At the same time our joy must "hide underground," like an insect or camouflaged cruiser — we must "for fear of death sham dead."

This is authentic Auden. The imagery throughout is vivid and colorful. But it is drawn from so many levels of reference, it pulls in so many directions at the same time, that the reader cannot fail to be bewildered and distracted. Unless, indeed, the reader is one of the initiates and knows the code. And even so it is hard to conceive how the social conspirators came to be at the same moment dancing in their "joy abounding" and going about their conspiratorial errands in camouflage, or tunneling underground. Still more difficult to realize is the parellelism between the public and the private lives of the conspirators. On the one hand the separation of the lovers would appear to be on grounds of conventional morality; on the other, they would seem to be secret agents of the same hidden power, who must not be seen together lest their political association be exposed.

It is possible that Auden was moved to discard this poem because he realized that the symbolism was not well enough managed to produce an effective imaginative whole. It seems even more likely, however, that in 1945 he did not wish to reproduce this picture of a young man who fancied himself engaged in political strategy in the warfare between Whites and Reds. And still less, perhaps, did he wish to feature a real or fancied love affair in which so much of camouflage was called for.

Curiously enough, however, this poem was restored to the canon in 1950; and that presents a problem which we shall have to face in a later chapter.

71

The third one of the important rejected poems in this volume is No. XVII, "Here on the cropped grass of the narrow ridge I stand." This is conceived in rather milder terms, but still has certain offensive passages. In its structure it follows somewhat Wordsworth's pattern in "Tintern Abbey." The poet recalls the time when the Malvern Hills were for him the benign, innocent setting for private happiness. But now this place and Britain as a whole have "no innocence at all." It is all the very mood of "isolation" and "fear." He has private reasons, he says, for insisting on having the truth. There has been a "boom in sorrow"; Gross Hunger has taken on "more hands every month," and business has "shivered in a banker's winter." Escapist people seek distraction and comfort in Gaumont theaters, with their pictured "noble robbers," and in churches. From "cathedrals, / Luxury liners laden with souls," one hears "the high thin rare continuous worship / Of the self-absorbed."

The poet now reviews, in European history, the period of "empires stiff in their brocaded glory," and that of monasticism thriving in "ages of disorder," when the noblest were assailed by "angel assassins." In this poem he refers to the fascist ideal of "the central state" symbolized by the cruising hawk. He hears the totalitarian propaganda spread abroad in every dialect of "the common language of collective lying." He states baldly that "the major cause of our collapse / Was a distortion of the human plastic by luxury produced." No civilization has risen higher in logical precision of thought and in "the vigours of the instrument." What is lacking is the "disciplined love which alone could have employed these engines." We have been "denying the liberty we knew to be our destiny." We are not properly tragic, for "falseness made farcical our death." The writer is finally recalled by the priory chimes to the need to keep "my will effective and my nerves in order." After apposite quotations from Wilfred Owen and Katherine Mansfield, he concludes that no one today is justified in being idle,

> For men are changed by what they do;
> And through loss and danger the hands of the unlucky
> Love one another.

This poem is not at all explicitly Marxian except in the assumption of political collapse as historically inevitable; and it *is* redeemed by its warning against fascist propaganda. It employs the psychological formula so common in Auden's poetry in the thirties. And it concludes in a vein that must have been acceptable to the poet in 1945, except perhaps in its summons to political action. But the poet himself knew what in his own mind had lain back of this more discreet discourse, and he would not admit it to the canon. Not in 1945. We shall see later that, in 1950, it was restored, albeit with certain expurgations.

This poem, it is interesting to note, was written three years before its publication in *On This Island* and appeared first in the *New Oxford Outlook* for November 1933 under the title "The Malverns," which title it bears in 1950. It was reproduced faithfully in *On This Island* except for minute alterations in punctuation, the use of italics for the speech of the thunder and the bones of war, and the omission of one whole stanza of eleven lines. In this excised stanza the author speaks of his guilty feeling at the thought of his futility in action; he refers to the Nottinghamshire mines where a much-quoted author "received / His first perceptions of the human flame" (presumably D. H. Lawrence); he also refers satirically to those he and his friends had taken for leaders: "the loony airman" (possibly T. E. Lawrence?), and "the little runt with Chaplains and a stock" (whom I have not identified). He says they had been bidden to trust their instincts, and had done so. They are bloody instincts and they come

> Like corrupt clergymen filthy from their holes
> Deformed and imbecile.

In his *Poems* (1930 and 1933), Auden had already paid his respects to D. H. Lawrence, who died in 1930, "brought down by smut-hounds." Now in 1936, T. E. Lawrence ("Private Shaw") was in his grave, and no longer a fair target for satire. As for "the little runt with Chaplains and a stock" and the "corrupt clergymen filthy from their holes," the poet must have thought these references too invidious to meet his later, more exigent standard of decorum.

And then, finally, there is No. XXX, "August for the people and their favourite islands." This poem was addressed to Christopher Isherwood and originally published in *New Verse*, October–November 1935, under the title "To a Writer on his Birthday." There is little here to give offense (ideologically) to the mature Auden. The two stanzas devoted to an account of what in his day has become of the virtues — Courage, Truth, Love, Reason, Freedom, Justice — and recording the triumph of the vices — Greed, Calculation, Mediocrity, "Smartness" (in furs), and Power — these stanzas loaded with sententious epigram, would pass for satire in any period from Juvenal to Eliot. And satire is one of the most respectable of genres. It is only in their setting that they may seem objectionable — and in the poet's consciousness of the implications they held for him at the time of writing.

He begins by recalling to his friend the pleasant days they spent together on the Isle of Wight, amused by the spectacle of pleasure-seeking frivolity. They were still "half-boys," products of "the stuccoed suburb and expensive school," their romantic hopes still "set on the spies' career." Then, five summers later, they are watching "the Baltic from a balcony." And now the password is love. It was love they trusted to "tame . . . with his trainer's look . . . a dragon who had closed the works / While the starved city fed it with the Jews." They are now somewhat shy of conventional society — "the golf-house quick one and the rector's tea." They are aware of the warnings and the lies roared by the wireless; and for them it is now "impossible / Among the well-shaped cosily to fit."

Here follow the stanzas of satire in which he sees

> Slim Truth dismissed without a character,
> And gaga Falsehood highly recommended

and then

> Freedom by Power shockingly maltreated
> And Justice exiled till Saint Geoffrey's Day.

They can no longer complacently accept "the colours and the consolations," no longer ignore "the squalid shadow of academy

74

and garden." They realize that action is urgent and its nature clear. His birthday wish to his friend is that they may both have "nearer insight to resist / The expanding fear, the savaging disaster." And he ends with a vision of how

> all sway forward on the dangerous flood
> Of history, that never sleeps or dies
> And, held one moment, burns the hand.

Well! between 1936 and 1945, history had indeed shown itself a more dangerous flood than any poet or statesman could have anticipated. And the thirty-eight-year-old poet need not have been reluctant to acknowledge the poet of twenty-nine because he had entertained this prophetic vision and had wished for his friend "nearer insight to resist / The expanding fear, the savaging disaster." He need not have blushed to think of these earnest young men who were unable to accept "the colours and the consolations" and were convinced that some action on their part was urgently called for. What may have made him blush was their youthful certainty that the nature of the action called for was clear, the presumptuousness with which they set themselves up as being in possession of the truth hidden from others, and the impatient scorn with which they looked down upon those who by age, experience, and knowledge of the world were at least as likely as themselves to have a clear view of historical truth. His tone in this poem is less abusive and bumptious than in the other poems rejected from this volume. But his opinions here were made of the same stuff as in the others, and without being explicit about it, he was grounding them on the same premises. And while the young poet did here pay his respects to the personal virtues which are essential to the health of the social body, it must have seemed shallow to him to count so much more on social machinery for making life good than upon spiritual inspiration. For "out of the heart are the issues of life." While this poem was not so obviously objectionable as the others, he must have felt that it was tarred with the same brush.

The loss to poetry with the scrapping of this piece is not perhaps so great as in the case of several of the others discussed in this chapter. But it is some loss; for this is an agreeable composition, and there is a distinct charm in its evocation of those early days of friendly companionship between gifted intellectuals in boyhood and youth. In establishing the canon of his works, as we shall see later, Auden sacrificed as many poems to his ideals for good writing as he did to his notions of true doctrine. But the sacrifice that he made to true doctrine was not light, and it did mean more of a loss to imaginative literature than what he gave up, for the most part wisely, in the interests of an artistic ideal.

But the loss to poetry was not for good. Five years later Auden was more indulgent in his judgment on this poem, and in the *Collected Shorter Poems* it appeared under the title "Birthday Poem," along with "The chimneys are smoking, the crocus is out in the border," and "Here on the cropped grass of the narrow ridge I stand" ("The Malverns").

C 7

The Orators: Poems Discarded and Poems Retained

FROM *The Orators: An English Study* (1932) more poems were discarded in 1945 than from any other volume of Auden's poems except the plays. But during the thirties this volume of poetry and prose in its entirety had a large part to play in establishing the prestige and influence of Auden, being included in the collected *Poems* 1934 (another printing 1935), along with *The Dance of Death, Paid on Both Sides,* and the lyrics from *Poems* 1933. And *The Orators* calls for special consideration both for what was kept and what was rejected in 1945. It is made up of three approximately equal parts. Book I, "The Initiates," comprises four prose pieces, including "Address for a Prize-Day," "Argument," and "Letter to a Wound." There has been some account of these in our second chapter, and we have noted that "Letter to a Wound" was included in the *Collected Poetry* as Part II. Book II of *The Orators* is "Journal of an Airman." It consists of miscellaneous disjointed notes in prose, with eight pieces in verse scattered among the prose notes. Part III consists of "Six Odes." The prose and poetry in this volume includes one poem written presumably in 1927, and other compositions dating presumably from the early thirties but not included in the 1930 (1933) *Poems.* The odes are mostly longer and are written in more elaborate meters than the lyrics in *Poems,* befitting their ode-like character. There are also, in verse, a Prologue and an Epilogue.

Virtually everything between these covers is devoted to the poet's double program of freeing men's minds from their chains and at the same time promoting the discipline of character, especially among the Initiates — those enlisted in the struggle to make men over and save them from the decadence that was undermining English society. This double program it was very difficult to carry through without causing in the reader considerable bewilderment and confusion. For the chains from which the poet would free men's minds are those imposed upon them by a bourgeois order ridden with neuroses; these neuroses are the result of fears and inhibitions deriving from a false view of human nature and its needs; these inhibitions themselves represent, for the old decadent order, a necessary discipline of character parallel to that recommended by the exponents of the new revolutionary order; and while the new men claim that theirs is a healthful discipline for life and their opponents' a diseased discipline for death, it is not always too clear just how they differ, for the two parties seem to be equally down on such vices as lust and greed and sloth.

There is, to be sure, a theoretical and functional difference. For "We" claim that our "hearts" are "pure," that our guide is love, and not . . . well, law or convention or whatever binding force prevails in the bourgeois world. Our behavior flows naturally out of our unperverted hearts and is not turned into diseased channels by repression. But it is none too easy for the reader to distinguish between the old repressions and the new disciplinary controls. And the matter is not made any clearer by our frequent uncertainty as to whether in a given case the poet is speaking with sober directness or with an undercutting tone of irony or parody.

There is little overt Marxian propaganda, and what there is is written in code and not understandable by the uninitiated reader. Even the alerted reader finds it almost impossible to distinguish here between the moral and the political doctrine. For in the mind of the poet the two were inseparably associated. The social and political iniquity of the capitalist economy had its roots in a moral decadence suggested by the phrase "the isolated personal life." This is exhibited in the dominance of greed, sensuality, sentimentality, intellectual obscurantism, and above all by a fear born of guilt and breeder of disease and madness in individuals and of violence and oppression in the social body.

Moreover, in this volume, almost everything is rendered in fanciful terms of plot and counterplot, training for conflict, guarding the frontiers, and preparing for defense and attack. The adolescent's game of spies and counterspies, of the underground movement and the coming war, furnishes most of the metaphors; and most of the rest are furnished by the Homer Lane theory of disease and neurosis. And in both cases it is not easy to judge how much of this is strictly metaphor and how much is meant to be taken for factual and "scientific." It is not even fully clear whether the revolutionary violence anticipated is of the sort involving actual fighting and bloodshed, or is conceived of as convulsions taking place in the minds and souls of men in the process of making themselves over — "glaciers calving."

Auden's reasons for rejecting this or that poem were often doubtless artistic, and in some cases they were artistic and ideological at the same time. And in each case we must have both possibilities in mind. This whole body of work is, as Spender observes, high-spirited and often full of a rollicking humor. It is written with the high excitement of a poet who has discovered his power over the word, the metaphor, and the telling image; and who, in addition to that, has just come into possession of a set of ideas — metaphysical, scientific, psychological, and ethical — upon which he may employ his poetic gift for word, metaphor, and image. This makes a potent, heady brew; and nowhere in Auden is the poet's intoxication more lively and infectious. We cannot say these are wild and whirling words; for it is clear enough that the poet knows pretty well what he means to say. But the reader is seldom as clear about this as the poet; for the poet speaks constantly in riddles. Mystification is throughout a large part of the fun; it is also a means of bridging the gap between the two sides of his program and reconciling attitudes which to the sober mind often seem irreconcilable.

"Journal of an Airman" gives us the reflections of a pilot struggling to make himself fit for service against the Enemy. It is here that mystification reigns supreme, especially in the prose notes, which are all more or less in code. I do not pretend to have figured out a third of the meanings that here go in playful disguise like ladies and cavaliers at a masked ball. The writer's being an airman implies, I suppose, that he is a high flier, one who has taken seriously Emerson's injunction to "hitch your wagon to a star."

He also takes seriously the need to discipline oneself, and is considerably worried over certain weaknesses that threaten to undermine his effectiveness in the great cause. A friend well versed in Yiddish informs me that in that dialect the word *Luftmensch* (literally airman) is commonly used in a pejorative sense, signifying something like a person with his head in the clouds, and that this use of the word would be familiar to non-Jewish Germans. It is not impossible that Auden may have heard it so used during his stay in Germany, and that he means to suggest that in his philosophic airman (albeit "one of ours") there is a strain of weakening unrealism that needs correcting. This would not be out of keeping with the complexities of attitude to which this poet is subject by virtue of his inveterate penchant for irony. This airman, though enlisted in the cause of progress and the classless society, is presumably, like Auden and his partisans, by origin a member of the decadent upper classes; and he must be vigilantly on guard against the vices to which he is subject by inheritance and training.

The great cause is, of course, revolutionary. Among other things he has developed the Mendelian theory that we are likely to be the heirs not of our fathers but of our uncles or great-grandfathers. This makes it easier for us to break the chains that bind us to our ostensible fathers, who stand for smugness, conservatism, hypocrisy, and repression. The Enemy is not actually a foreign power or even perhaps a wrong-headed political party; it is rather the crusted ideas that weaken our morale — all that is associated with the "bourgeois" mentality.

Some element of mystification, or at least of obscurity, attaches to most of the eight poems that are interspersed among the prose.

The Orators: DISCARDED AND RETAINED

Of these Auden has retained the two that are unquestionably the best — those beginning "We have brought you, they said, a map of the country" ("Have a Good Time"), and "There are some birds in these valleys" ("The Decoys"). The latter is ostensibly a poem on the way that decoy doves bring about the shooting of "the real unlucky dove." We may assume that the fowler in ambush (who is also the "madman keeper" creeping through the brushwood) stands for the Enemy, and that the real unlucky dove is the man who is taken in by the Enemy's deceptive lure. Whatever the Enemy signified to the Airman in 1932, the symbolism would equally well apply to some other totally different Enemy in 1945. And this is true in the same way of "Have a Good Time," as the other poem was so lamentably rechristened in 1945. This is written in the same sestina form that Auden uses later in the four parts of "Kairos and Logos," and most triumphantly in "Paysage Moralisé," which is perhaps the finest poem of the early thirties. I will not guarantee my interpretation of this poem. But I think that the "they" who bring "him" a map of the country, and get him a settled job at the derelict vats, are again the Enemy, trying to reduce him to their own condition of stodginess and anxiety, always remembering to wind up the clock at weekends, and fearfully staying away from the woods ("Whatever you do don't go to the wood"). And if I read the poem rightly, they failed in the end. For this braver spirit does finally penetrate the wood and "finds consummation" there, so that for the first time he "sees" the country. In any case, the recurrent images of the vats, the wood, the country, the bathing in the bay, and the weakly "love" that "brings tears to his eyes," give to this poem an unmistakable "incantatory" charm (to borrow a word from Mr. Hoggart). And here again the symbolism is flexible enough to suit the book of a later Auden with a different Enemy. And indeed the very moral of the poem still holds good for the later Auden, who was as much opposed to stodginess and anxiety in '45 or in '55 as he was in '32. And if we conceive the enemy as standing for conformity, that is no bar to the acceptance of the poem. We must realize that when Auden announced his conversion to orthodoxy, that was, in his "liberal" set, a positive act of *non-conformity*.

Six of the poems in the Journal were discarded, and, generally, for good esthetic reasons. In "After the death of their proud master," we have pictured the feeble epigones who first excuse themselves for their weakness by inventing horrific legends, and then in the next generation become the petted victims of the nursery and modern comforts, and "denying legends, believe weakness pride." There is a moral made to the later poet's hand; and he could have had nothing against this piece except that it lacks subtlety and shapeliness. The next lyric, "Well, Milder, if that's the way you're feeling," is full of obscurity not to be penetrated unless someone can bring us the lost key.* But the poet seems to be exposing the shallowness of a life made up of slight material improvements, with "plenty of beauty and nothing private," and in which no serious decisions or choices are made. Auden must have judged that the correctness of the sentiments in this composition could not make up for its hopeless obscurity.

Still more obscure is the piece of verse beginning "I'm afraid it sounds more like a fairy story." And here one doesn't know whether it is the author or the person who is speaking in the poem that is responsible for this obscurity. One feels sure there was a story behind this monologue or dialogue, and something spicy at that, and some moral connected with the incoherence of the man who took gas in the dentist's chair. It is perhaps the inevitable decay and breakdown of the bourgeois mentality that is being represented here. The thing is full of innuendoes and false starts and belated efforts to cover up indiscretions. No doubt in Auden's set

---

* The name Milder probably comes from an anonymous ballad, "The Cutty Wren," which Auden has published as No. 209 in his *Oxford Book of Light Verse* (1938). This old poem begins each stanza with some variant of the question, "O where are you going, says Milder to Malder," and was, as Mr. Hoggart has pointed out, a sort of model for Auden's Epilogue to *The Orators*, "O where are you going, said reader to rider." Auden was acquainted with this old "folk poem" some years before he made his Oxford compilation; it had already been published, between two poems of Spender's, in the same number of *New Verse*, for October–November 1935, which featured Auden's long poem, "To a Writer on His Birthday," discussed in Chapter 6.

in 1932 it all made sense. There are proper names that may not be purely fictitious. Our curiosity is roused, and we are faintly amused by the futility of the speaker or speakers. But we cannot long maintain an interest in the futility of persons we don't know when we don't even know what they are being futile about. Auden was evidently having a good time when he wrote, but in 1945 he was no longer amused.

In two of the rejected poems we come nearer to the revolutionary theme in its political or fighting aspect. They both picture the emotions of the sworn conspirators as what we may call their D-day approaches. One thinks of the young revolutionary in *The Princess Casamassima* who has been chosen to assassinate a great personage. In "The draw was at five. Did you see the result?" men have been chosen by lot for some decisive secret expedition. Their final arrangements and preparations are being made quietly. "I shall hide the housekey under the mat" recalls the earlier "To throw away the key and walk away." The piquancy of the situation lies in the apparent keeping up of the customary way of life, concerned with trifles. "The stranger here sees nothing out of the common." But they have been bidden to assemble when the moon is full; that time has come, and the high excitement of the situation is packed into two rarely emotional lines:

O charged-to-the-full-in-secret slow-beating heart,
To-night is full-moon.

Of course we are to understand this all as symbolic of the courage and stanchness of anyone called upon to face the guns in the great ideological showdown, determined to "steel the will" and "keep perfect to the last the long-kept vow." This is an excellent representation of how Auden and his intimates must have felt about themselves in their heroic moods. But in spite of the secrecy and mystery of it all ("the two dance-leaders chosen quietly by lot"), an older poet must have shrunk from the boyish touch of cloak-and-dagger melodrama.

The other side of the picture is given in "Last day but ten / It's moving again." Here we have a conspirator that has not the guts for his commando role. As the days run down from ten to the "last day of all," the mysterious "it" grows more and more fear-some, until in the end he thinks he'll run; but instead of this,

> Last day of all
> It's here and I fall.

Another interpretation, which may be taken either as an alternative to the first or as consistent with it but giving it a deeper significance, is as follows: The "it" which is such a threat to the man's peace of mind as he feels it moving in him is some neurotic obsession under which he suffers; it is a manifestation of the psychical entity which, in Groddeck's psychology, under the name of the It, "lives" the life of each one of us and determines for us the issues of life and death. It constitutes some weakness in the airman which he must master if he is to serve the good cause, but which, if he cannot master it, will be his own undoing.

The whole little story is conducted on the pattern of a children's counting game, and is not the less effective for that. It compels condensation and strictness of form. Here is a poem that, one presumes to say, might well have been kept whatever meaning we read in it.

The last one of the discarded poems from the Journal is "Beethameer, Beethameer, bully of Britain." This is a head-on satirical attack on the low-brow popular newspapers whose exploitation brought great fortunes and peerages to two famous brothers. It is easy to guess what names are faintly disguised under the forms Beethameer and Heathcliffe, and the poet pulls no punches in describing the poisonous pap-for-babes served up to a decadent bourgeoisie by these highly successful journalists. "I," says Heathcliffe, "advertise idiocy, uplift, and fear." But an older and soberer Auden must have realized that he has not quite the fine hand of H. L. Mencken for this sort of thing. Good taste and Christian charity, if not the English libel laws, would all be against its republication.

Of the six odes, Auden retained four, with some revisions and excisions. We have seen by what means three of these were made acceptable: in Chapter 3, "January 1, 1931" (Ode I) and Song

No. XVII (Ode VI); in Chapter 5, "The Exiles" (Ode III). There remains Ode V, reprinted as "Which Side Am I Supposed to Be On?" beginning "Though aware of our rank and alert to obey orders." This I have not discussed since it is reprinted without the least alteration except for slight changes in punctuation and in the capitalizing of personified abstractions. But it does call for some consideration if only to make out how it could have been so entirely acceptable in 1945.

And here I must confess that a close reading of this poem, first in the *Collected Poetry* and then in *The Orators*, leaves me in considerable doubt as to the meaning it was meant to convey whether to the initiates when it first appeared in 1932 or to those who read it now in the 1945 collection. It might seem to be the sort of thing that Auden could fancy himself addressing in all seriousness to his pupils in his boys' school. There is relatively little suggestion of that parody of masters' sprightly rhetorical histrionism which made us suspect irony on the author's part in "Address for a Prize-Day" and lent a troublesome air of ambiguity to that whole performance. And yet there are attitudes taken in the Ode which, in certain moods, Auden would have been the first to stigmatize as sentimental, reactionary, or "bourgeois." If we do take the poem as entirely serious, it is a good example of the faculty this poet has of reading himself imaginatively into points of view extremely various if not positively irreconcilable.

Let us say, then, that in this Ode Auden was pursuing that part of his program concerned with positive moral discipline, rather than the other part devoted to freeing men's minds from their chains and to that end satirically exposing the weakness and self-deception of those who would rivet their chains tighter.

The schoolmaster-poet addresses his pupils as if they were soldier recruits under military training making ready to defend "our" order against the menace of a foreign enemy. He goes with them to parade in the Cathedral square, to receive the bishop's blessing, and to stand with the "wine-dark conquerors" shouting themselves hoarse over the defeat of their adversaries, who had "fought against God." Among their enemies are the deadly sins,

Wrath, Envy, Gluttony, Greed, Sloth (Acedia), and Lust. These adversaries are not to be despised, for they think that the Lord is on their side; they are as brave as we are; and they will not betray secrets "though kept without sleep." But they are not to be trusted, and you must not think of fraternizing across the lines as happened once on Christmas Eve. The day of decision is at hand. All leaves are canceled tonight, for

> We entrain at once for the North; we shall see
>   in the morning
> The headlands we're doomed to attack.

The whole force of this speech to his pupils, or military recruits, is to make them good soldiers in "our" cause, put them in training, and make them ready to fight the enemy without any question that "we" are right or even reflection upon the issues at stake. And every boyish instinct is flattered by the stage setup of perilous frontiers, secret agents, spartan camp life, and attacks upon romantic headlands. It is a rousing call to heroic action, and incidentally a solemn lesson in moral self-control.

This is the interpretation one naturally puts upon the poem as one reads it in the *Collected Poetry*. But as one goes back and reads it in its original context, along with many other highly ironical productions of the early and middle thirties, disturbing doubts begin to insinuate themselves. Reading critically, one is aware of certain confusions, which at first one is inclined to refer to the exigencies of the allegory. The enemy is notable for bold and cunning leaders. But these represent such weakening vices as greed and sloth and lust. And it is difficult to make this consistent with the faith and courage and perfect discipline of the actual army we are facing. These are surely not the decadent representatives of a society honeycombed with neuroses and possessed by a death wish. The confusion entailed by the allegory grows worse when we try to identify this enemy with the one more often pictured and satirized in this volume, whose great fault is the disposition to repress natural impulses and fall into the diseases that follow upon such repression.

And there is still another item that tends to deepen the confusion. It is, so to speak, imported into this poem from other work of Auden's in which it is more central and pertinent. It is the idea that Fear (often conceived of as a reflex of our sense of guilt) is a prime cause of war. And here in this poem we learn that it is Fear that makes our enemy strong.

> What have we all been doing to have made from Fear
> That laconic war-bitten captain addressing them now?

The captain goes on to rouse his cohorts to a keener mood with the realization that the weaker they are the harder they must fight. If they are destined to lose the battle, they will "lie down beside / The Lord we have loved." In short, Fear is the very father of militarism. But we are all involved in this guilt, and the whole purpose of the address to his pupils is to instill in them a healthy fear of the other side in the conflict.

Allegory is indeed a tricky genre, and the simpler it is the less likely to land in such confusions. But this poet's mind is far too complicated, he is too inclined to see every aspect of the truth, for securing the best effects in this mode.

But then, as one goes on reading this and other pieces of the period, one begins to ask whether it is indeed the allegorical mode that is responsible for these confusions, and whether, for that matter, these were actually confusions in the poem as originally conceived. One reads again the passage in which the schoolmaster summons his pupils to parade in the Cathedral square, to receive the blessings of the bishop and shout themselves hoarse in triumph over an enemy who "fought against God." We begin to wonder if the poet is here speaking with his tongue in his cheek. We are reminded of the note of irony that in those days generally attached to his references to parading scouts, to cathedrals and bishops' blessings, and the exultant shouts of "wine-dark conquerors." We remember the sermon of the Vicar in *The Dog beneath the Skin* hysterically working up the boys' fighting spirit against the particular enemy that was at that moment the convenient target of militaristic nationalism. We note how consistently the youthful recruits are discouraged from asking any questions as to the precise nature of the war for which they are drafted. "Go to sleep,

Sonny!" "The quarrel was before your time, the aggressor / No one you know." There is no use speculating about the old and better days when the tall white gods landed here and established our civilization and our feast days. (Might they, by any chance, be those very hosts beyond the border against whom we are fighting?)

The young recruit is characterized as altogether a product of the present social set-up, by his mother taught to pray for "our Daddy far away fighting." He is not to ask questions. He has the names of his ancestors to live up to, and that is enough. He has simply to keep in training. We begin to realize that this is precisely the attitude against which Our party is in revolt. We remember how in *Paid on Both Sides*, it was the mothers' influence that kept up the perpetual deadly feud and led to the ruin of both adversaries: "His mother and her mother won." One of the characters in that charade observes how badly they had been instructed by their fathers. "They taught us war, / To scamper after darlings," to "find ourselves / The easy conquerors of empty bays." We remember the sneer in *Poems* XXII, "Perfect pater, marvellous mater. Knock the critic down who dares —" These passages are from poems closely contemporary with the ode. As for the deadly sins as represented in the leaders of the enemy, we remember how in "Danse Macabre" (some five years later) it is ugliest Fascism who sets out to exterminate sin and the Devil and along with them the human race. In that case we are practically driven into the arms of the Devil in our abhorrence of his adversary; and in the ode we begin to be a trifle uncertain where our sympathies are supposed to lie.

Then we read the mysterious passage dealing with those among the enemy whom we seem to recognize as former friends, and especially "that girl who rode off on her bicycle one fine summer evening," and is now on the other side. If we are acquainted with Edward Upward's *Journey to the Border* or Rex Warner's *The Wild Goose Chase*, we realize that these deserters from our side may perhaps be those very enlightened ones among us who went on heroic quests "across the frontier," who felt the impulse to "throw away the key and walk away," and made themselves "exiles" from our backward parochial way of life, and that the enemy they joined may actually be "Our" party — not the party of mealy-mouthed schoolmasters and canting bishops, of snuffling neurotics and munitions makers, but the party of Us Initiates who seek a new and better order of society. And we begin to be invaded by the rather dizzying suspicion that irony reigns throughout this piece, which is meant to be taken in a sense completely opposite to what it bears on its face.

In that case, it would be understood by the discerning reader in 1932 that, in this ode, everything is to be read in reverse. The enemy here is the party of enlightenment, of life and progress; the schoolmaster and his well disciplined pupils stand for the party of bourgeois reaction, of conventional piety, conventional morality, and the neurotic death-wish. And the trainer of youth, the professional educator in a bourgeois economy, is strengthening his pupils for resistance to attack by the threatening army of revolution. In doing so, he realizes that he must not underestimate the strength of the enemy; they have brilliant leaders, they believe they are fighting for the right; and they are certainly brave, though, as the speaker notes, "Our newspapers mention their bravery / In inverted commas," as if it were not the genuine article.

If this interpretation is correct, the poet Auden, in publicly addressing an ode to his pupils, is in effect parodying himself, in his function as patriotic and moralistic schoolmaster. It has been observed by Mr. Replogle that Auden, in the daring exercise of his irony, is capable of turning it on himself and his own party, though I do not think Mr. Replogle has cited this particular piece as an example of Auden's virtuosity in this kind. I have heard it suggested that, when Auden speaks of his pupils, he does not seriously have in mind those whom he teaches in school, but is metaphorically and jocularly referring to his friends and associates in the avant-garde.

If the reader finds himself unable to entertain this Alice-through-the-Looking-Glass view of the ode, there is still another alternative. It is just possible that the two parties in this conflict are not meant to be specifically identified as the parties of reaction and enlightenment, but are simply any parties or countries which, by virtue of their situation across the border from one another, are bound to come to blows, and who find it necessary, on one side and the other, to keep themselves in fighting trim and be ready at any moment to attack or resist. In that case, the poem is still ironic and satirical, but the object of the satire is not some particular ideology but the universal nationalism that breeds militarism and the universal militarism that breeds nationalism, and along with these the sort of morale-building hypocrisy to which all parties resort in order to justify their militant posture. All wars, we are often told, are defensive wars. And Lord Bacon, observing that for a nation to maintain its strength it must frequently wage war, advises governments to be ever ready with good moral reasons for taking up arms. Two such moral reasons are urged by the schoolmaster in the ode: one is the sinfulness and corruption of the enemy, and the other is the need for a boy to play the man and live up to the names of his heroic forbears.

But whether the enemy here is simply enemy in the abstract, the people beyond the border, or whether he is indeed the party of progress and revolution, it would seem (on the suggested interpretation) that Auden in 1932 was not actually writing this ode for the eyes and edification of his schoolboys, but for the eyes and understanding of — say — Edward Upward (who in that same year "shocked" his friends by announcing his adhesion to the Communist party), of Rex Warner, Stephen Spender, Day Lewis, Christopher Isherwood, and others in the know. For them it was, presumably, a transparent hoax, a take-off on the schoolmaster as defender of the bourgeois faith; and even the shuddering references to Envy and Lust and Sloth were perhaps part of the fun.

But if this interpretation, in either alternative form, is correct, the further question arises; how much of the irony implicit in the poem in 1932 may be understood as present and intended in the same poem as it appears in the *Collected Poetry* in 1945? The poet in giving up socialism and espousing Christianity did not, as we know, give up his sense of humor or cease to be critical of mass ideas and attitudes, though he does tend now to attack them from different points of view, under different names, and judge them by a different set of standards. It may not be "bourgeois" ideals as seen from the Marxist point of view, or the neurotic death-wish as it prevails in modern society according to the Audenesque psychology, that draws his fire. But there is still the vulgarity, the materialism, mediocrity, and spiritual emptiness that attend on a crassly mechanistic philosophy; and these often have an appearance not unlike that formerly shown by the corrupt and decadent society of our fathers as conceived by the socialist reformer.

It will be noted that in 1945 the ode is no longer designated as an address delivered by a schoolmaster to his pupils. The words "To My Pupils" no longer appear in the title, which now reads "Which Side Am I Supposed to Be On?" Though it may still be intended by the author as in some measure a parody of the schoolmasterly manner in admonition, it does not refer specifically to the poet as schoolmaster. It is the official voice of the community preparing youth for resistance to the enemy. And the poet in 1945 may indeed have been ironically aware of the cavalier manner in which the questions of youth were turned aside. "Theirs not to reason why; theirs but to do and die." It may be that in 1945 the poet would not wish to have the two parties labeled specifically, the one as the party of reaction, the other the party of progress, of the visionary hope beyond the border. It is not unlikely that his attitude toward the speaker in the poem is somewhat mixed. He can deprecate the tendency to stir up warlike impulses in the young and at the same time approve of the character-training, the disciplinary process, which involves a warning against the seven deadly sins, and a reminder that these sins (which are the enemy incarnate) are often accompanied by manly virtues not to be neglected. He may still wish to lay his emphasis on neurotic fear as the cause of disastrous conflicts in the world. In short, the poem can still serve for edification and confirmation, at the same time that the critical spirit warns against doctrinaire extremes. And the poem is indeed on any interpretation an impressive and colorful performance, fresh and tangy, rich in imaginative appeal, and at every turn provocative of thought. And one must agree with the poet that it is well worth preserving on artistic grounds.

Still, I must confess that this way of regarding the poem as it is found in its later setting is far from satisfying me. As it is read in its earlier setting there are too many ironic implications and associated attitudes, and all closely bound together in an organic whole, making up a consistent ideological pattern, and one which could hardly have been congenial to the poet in 1945. If it is taken in the sense indicated in the last paragraph, too much of the original intention must be tacitly dropped out of account to leave the poem what it was and give it the force and significance it had when it was conceived and written in the first flush of reckless creativity. With the ironies largely faded out, it would indeed be more suitable for inclusion in the canon than many other poems and prose pieces here reviewed. But can it possibly have the verve and brilliancy, the imaginative and intellectual provocativeness, it had for discerning readers of *The Orators?* The words are the same, but I have an uneasy feeling that in their sum they do not carry the same meaning. If this feeling is well grounded, it illustrates the considerable loss necessarily suffered by any work of art when, after an interval of years, it is expected to fit into a radically altered pattern of philosophical attitudes.

I have been reluctant to subject the reader to such a lengthy set of speculations in regard to the meaning of a single poem, but have seen no way of avoiding this in view of the obvious difficulties of the subject. If I have been as much as half right in my hypothetical reconstructions of meaning and intention, one must be impressed with the element of ambiguity attaching to the subject for a reader reasonably well acquainted with the changing course of Auden's thought. If I have gone altogether astray in my interpretations, this in itself testifies to the ambiguity, if not in the work objectively considered, then at least in the impact of the work on a reader approaching it in good faith.

There remain the two odes which Auden did *not* reproduce in

1945. These are a real loss to English literature, as savory examples of youthful high spirits, ingenious and enterprising play with words, virtuosity in the handling of verse forms — in short, the "first fine careless rapture" of craftsmanship discovering itself. One of these odes is written in honor of a victorious school rugby team, and the other is to congratulate a literary friend and his wife on the birth of a son. The first (Ode II) is addressed to "the captain of Sedbergh School XV, Spring, 1927." It is written in rough and ready tail-rhymed stanzas, crowded with Anglo-Saxon alliterative lines ("And watching weak from hospital ward," "Dark fearers, dreading December's harm"); with epithets on both Anglo-Saxon and Homeric models; with words fresh from a teenager's scientific reading — ohms, sensitized nodes, ducts, "the torsion, the tension, the list"; with images from the jungle ("panther's pad") and modern warfare ("when aligned like a squadron they flew downfield"); and with good old English colloquial terms of abuse ("purse-proud, swank-limbed, cock-wit"). The spirit of the whole piece is unexceptionably wholesome. The victors are congratulated and individually named and praised; the losers commiserated on their defeat, which, however, they rather deserved because of their class-conscious pride. The poet suggests that the life force will not favor lazy pride, and he prays this great benign power to do everything to cultivate healthy growth, skill, and discipline in our team.

It is true that this work is distinctly earlier than that of the first volume of *Poems*. It is perfectly direct and free from mystification. The author has not developed his special set of symbolic images, his stage décor of underground conspiracy and of friend and foe facing one another across the frontier. There is little suggestion of the fine points in ethics and ideology that dominate the thirties. Philosophically it is hardly more than a recommendation of athletic sports and work bench training for developing the capacities of the young. As poetry it is extremely promising, and even good. But it does not bear the special "marks" of the later Auden. And he is perfectly justified in relegating it to the category of juvenilia.

The other discarded ode (No. IV, "to John Warner, Son of Rex and Frances Warner") dates pretty certainly from as late as 1930, allowing time for this couple, married in 1929, to produce a son. It is as lively and rollicking as the earlier ode; but albeit written with high good humor, it is also the work of a poet with blood in his eye. The birth of this promising male baby, "hurdler, high-jumper, hope of our side," is the occasion for a great deal of abusive ridicule of English society as it stands in all classes. There are the spiritless, downtrodden members of the proletariat, "poofs and ponces, / All of them dunces"; the "upper class," always wondering whether it is safe to fall in love, to make a purchase, or risk a kiss, whose women "go out of their mind" because the men are "kind to their women, indeed too kind"; there are the military and the clergy, "Cods the curate," "Ballocks the rector" (consult Webster, NED, or Ernest Hemingway). The humorous point of the poem is that a prudish and decadent England is in need of a savior, someone "who will teach us how to behave"; and that for this they will have to look to little John Warner, that bundle of healthy instincts. He represents the life force itself, and will be particularly helpful to shy, blushing couples secretly learning to dance in an upstairs studio. If they will heed him, he'll teach them "deportment and coordination." He will be able to fix up "each unhappy Joseph and repressed Diana," and "take away their rugs" from all imaginary invalids.

In the political world there are giants that might be looked to for help, including MacDonald, Baldwin, Briand, President Hoover, Mussolini, Pilsudski, and Hitler; but they are all too noisy, and

> We're getting a little tired of boys,
> Of the ninny, the mawmet and the false alarm.

There are also invidious allusions to Professor Jeans and Bishop Barnes, and to "the Simonites, the Mosleyites and the I.L.P."

The poem concludes with an Envoi in a more elaborate and elegant stanzaic form, in which the poet sends to the happy parents the greeting of himself and his chum Derek, describes the occupations of people in Scottish Helensburgh (where he was

94

then schoolmastering), and brings the curtain down on couples passing up the hill after nightfall, when "love has its license."

This is indeed an exhilarating performance in the Skeltonian manner. But the political bias begins to show, ponces and pathics are too much in evidence, and there are too many slurs on John Bull in general and on many reverend characters in particular to suit Auden's book in 1945.

Oh yes! but he did find three little stanzas here that merited preservation. They will be found in the *Collected Poetry* under the title "Like Us." They begin with the lines "These had stopped seeking / But went on speaking." In their original context they applied to politicos like MacDonald and Baldwin, Hoover and Hitler. But taken out of their context they imply no invidious reflections upon persons great in the political world. They apply simply to those who have given up "seeking" for the truth, who in their mental laziness provoke war, and go to sleep "on the burning heap."

It remains to notice the Prologue and the Epilogue, two very fine poems which were retained in 1945. The Prologue, "By landscape once reminded of his mother's figure," now bears the title "Adolescence"; the Epilogue, "O where are you going? said reader to rider," is Song No. XXV. The first one pictures the mother-inspired boy setting out to be brave. He becomes indeed a prophet and defender of his countrymen. But we know from the Bible that "no prophet is accepted in his own country." And that was the case here. For he "receives odd welcome from the country he so defended." He is abused as a coward. And even the mother-image rejects him: "The giantess shuffles nearer, cries 'Deceiver.'" We are reminded how, in *Paid on Both Sides*, the deadly feud went on even after the intermarriage of the two houses. "His mother and her mother won." The endemic character of obscurantism and the perils of setting up prophet are acceptable themes in any stages of the poet's writing.

And so is the theme of the Epilogue. This shows dramatically, in a haunting ballad interchange, how the constant warnings against the dangers of "seeking" finally reach their culmination in

95

incapacitating horror. It takes close reading to determine whether the rider, the follower of "the path to the pass," finally succumbs to the universal fear, or whether he resists and overcomes the infection of his cowardly fellows. It seems most likely that he does resist and overcome, for the final line assures us that "he left them there . . . he left them there."

These two poems, along with "Have a Good Time" in the "Journal of an Airman," are the purest Auden of the early thirties to be found in *The Orators*, and one cannot but applaud the sureness of taste with which they were chosen for perpetuation.

And these three poems, indeed all nine of the pieces salvaged from *The Orators*, illustrate the surprising adjustability of Auden's work written from the point of view of a given ideology to the requirements of a quite different ideology involving a quite different point of view. This readjustment of the old work to the requirements of the new situation is made possible by the author's preoccupation in all periods of his writing with certain persistent themes and ideals. Throughout his career he was deeply drawn to the theme of a man who goes on heroic quest beyond the borders of his sleepy parish, undergoes the perils of adventure in strange lands, or makes himself an exile among his own people by the espousal of ideas strange and abhorrent to them. He becomes a prophet not honored in his own country, though he is actually its defender against unrecognized dangers, and "receives an odd welcome from the country he so defended." And so we have the Prologue to *The Orators* ("Adolescence"). Again, the poet is equally drawn to the related theme of brave men banded together in secret in a crusade that requires them to work underground until the day of open conflict, and who must be in perfect training to meet the attack of an Enemy that is not to be despised or trusted. And so we have the ode "To My Pupils" ("Which Side Am I Supposed to Be On?") There is the theme of temptations put in one's way by those who would divert you from your quest for truth and "consummation," who would appease you with a settled job and easy love, and frighten you by childish fear of the wood. And so we have, in the Airman's notes, "We have brought you, they said, the map of the country" ("Have a Good Time") and the Epilogue, "O where are you going, said reader to rider." Auden is ever impressed with the dangers, even for the hero and the innocent, of being deceived by the false lure, and made the victim of false causes, like the real unlucky dove. And so we have "The Decoys." All along Auden was fascinated by the opposition between health and disease, the need to be hard and fit and in training, and the constant danger of falling into sickness or even madness. And so in ode after ode we have him celebrating athletic prowess and military discipline with the zeal of a track-team trainer and a top sergeant whipping his recruits into shape.

All of these themes recur in much later poems though with altered emphasis. Thus the themes of the pilgrimage and the deceptive lure make the subject of the twenty sonnets of *The Quest* published in the *New Republic* in 1940 and republished in *The Double Man* before they appeared in the *Collected Poetry*. Only here the temptations come from a different direction, not from the bourgeois and believing right but from the proletarian materialist left ("Others had swerved off to the left before"). Here the questing heroes are betrayed, as Meredith puts it, by "what is false within," and they go, as Auden puts it, the "Negative Way toward the Dry." They ask the wrong, the merely temporal questions, and will not listen to "the Word which was / From the beginning." (Epilogue to *The Double Man*, in *Collected Poetry* "Autumn 1940.")

Some of these themes are a trifle romantic in the way they are conceived, but in underlying sentiment they are unexceptionably reputable under any ideological system. It is true that, in *The Orators*, they are all oriented by reference to Marxian objectives and assumptions, and here and there the revolutionary bias was betrayed in sallies that would certainly be disturbing to the official defenders of Church and State and current morality. But on the whole the moral tone, though unconventional, was eminently sound, and the work could be readily assimilated to the body of later writing inspired by more correct formulations of truth. Auden was always ready to employ the terminology of a doctrinal

97

system to which he did not subscribe. Isherwood tells how, as a college youth, he would note the ailments of his friends — asthma or quinsy — and identify the inner spiritual malady of which these outward maladies were symptoms. When asked how one could prevent the onset of these diseases, he would airily reply that only a pure heart could ensure one's health. And in his ode to his pupils he can name the mortal sins as readily as any Schoolman, and blandly identify them with the captains in the Enemy forces.

And thus it was that, because there was a core of soundness in him from the start, Auden, when he had come to the age of reason and sobriety, could recover many poems from his headstrong youth, conceived in contumacy and error, and make them serve in the end for edification. Most of them could be made to serve just as they stand without an iota's change. Others required the pruning hook here and there to rid them of wrong associations. A considerable number still trailed the old smell of sulphur and had best be forgotten. And there were naturally others that proved on examination to have been written in haste and unable to stand the Horatian test of seven years' cooling off before pub-lication.

ℭ 8

Light Verse, Including the Three Jolly Ballads

BESIDES those already discussed there are some half-dozen-odd poems discarded for a variety of reasons hard to bring under a single heading, but in general classifiable as artistic.* Some of these will be discussed in the Supplementary Notes (see p. 265). In this section we shall consider certain poems either discarded or retained that may be characterized as "light verse," the term employed by Auden in his learned and valuable compilation known as *The Oxford Book of Light Verse* (first published in 1938) and by Oscar Williams in the "Little Treasury of Light Verse," which forms Part II of his *Little Treasury of Modern Poetry* (Scribner's, 1946).

Most striking and numerous in this class are the poems discarded, and some of those retained, after publication in *Another Time* (1940). This volume was a catch-all for poems written since the 1936 *On This Island* and not included in *Journey to a War*. This was a period of transition for Auden in his thinking and style. It is from this volume and *The Double Man* of the following year that Jarrell takes most of his examples of the "rhetoric" that he dislikes in Auden's later work. (What would he have done

---

* I am not considering here the numerous lyrics from his plays, poems from *Letters from Iceland*, from the Notes to "New Year Letter" in *The Double Man*, which Auden did not see fit to reproduce in the *Collected Poetry*; nor poems in magazines and anthologies never collected; nor very early poems or juvenilia. These will be discussed in later chapters or in the appendixes.

if he had had *The Age of Anxiety* to draw upon, let alone "The Sea and the Mirror" and "For the Time Being"?) *Another Time* includes poems as remarkable as "The Unknown Citizen," "Spain 1937," "In Memory of W. B. Yeats," "September 1, 1939," and "In Memory of Sigmund Freud." But it also includes a number of poems almost altogether devoid of imaginative quality, such as "Heavy Date," and others in which the burlesque or cabaret style is in the ascendant. These have their interest and their smartness, but neither the "high seriousness" of our classical poetry, nor even the "modesty of nature" that is the saving grace of many a minor poet. And they sometimes show that disposition so common among British writers of this century to treat as subjects for comedy situations which the French reserve for the Grand Guignol, in the exploitation of which psychologists may be inclined to suspect a trace of sadism or necrophilia.

Auden classes these as "lighter poems," and gives them a section to themselves in *Another Time*. Some of them seem to have been written during the period when he was preparing his *Oxford Book of Light Verse*. Such verse, as he explains in his Introduction, is most likely to be produced by a poet who is in close touch with his audience, and less likely when "his interests and perceptions are not readily acceptable to society, or his audience is a highly specialized one." This last is a very apt description of Auden and his group in their relation to the general reading public; and Auden clearly felt the need to come into closer touch with this audience. He had from the beginning a considerable gift for spirited, jocular writing, as in some of the poems in *The Orators* and others published in magazines but never included in his books. But, as we shall see in later chapters, his preoccupation with light verse was at its height at a period when he was writing plays with a strong propagandist intention, where it was especially important that he should speak in a language readily understood by the man in the street. He distinguishes in the Introduction to his anthology three kinds of poetry in which light verse may be used — first, "poetry written for performance, to be spoken or sung before an audience," second, poetry "having for its subject-matter the everyday social life of its period or the experiences of the author as an ordinary human being (e.g. the poems of Chaucer, Pope, Byron)," and third, nonsense poetry, such as nursery rhymes and the verse of Edward Lear.

We are most concerned in this study with poetry of the first class, which Auden produced in abundance in his plays. In some of this he made a point of bringing the manner of the popular ballad to the exposition of serious social and psychological theories. But he was also interested in turning out still lighter verse, which could be sung by cabaret performers, and enjoyed without any worry over its ideological or ethical implications. A number of such poems were published in periodicals but never reprinted in book collections. Four of them were published in *Another Time*, of which two were reprinted in the 1945 collection, and the others left behind.

These were included in the section of "Lighter Poems," under the special heading "Four Cabaret Songs for Miss Hedli Anderson." The first of these is entitled "O Tell Me the Truth about Love," and begins "Some say that Love's a little boy / And some say he's a bird." This lyric has none of the pretensions to deep psychological seriousness, and none of the savagery, of the "Three Ballads." It is indeed an admirable cabaret song if well set and well rendered by a gifted singer or *diseuse*. It expresses the bepuzzlement all the world feels about "this thing called love" — asking how it is to be defined, where it is to be found, what it feels like, and how you are to recognize it "when it comes." Mr. Auden need not have been ashamed to admit it among his Songs and Other Musical Pieces. But he was doubtless right in finally determining that it did not quite meet the rigorous demands of his serious muse.

The same decision was still better justified in the case of the other cabaret song that he discarded, "Calypso," which begins, "Driver, drive faster and make a good run / Down the Springfield line under the shining sun." This is the utterance of a woman hurrying to town to meet her lover.

> If he's not there to meet me when I get to town,
> I'll stand on the pavement with the tears rolling down.

But tears or no tears, she knows that she is happily in love, and can afford to pity "the poor fat old banker in the sun-parlor car," who "has no one to love him except his cigar." And she ends by putting in terms of airy burlesque what is a frequent moral of Auden's serious poetry:

> For love's more important and powerful than
> Even a priest or a politician.

Of the other two cabaret songs, approved for publication in 1945, one ("Funeral Blues") is Song No. XXX, "Stop all the clocks, cut off the telephone." This I discuss in Chapter 15, where I note that it is made up of two stanzas of a funeral song in *The Ascent of F6* and three stanzas added so as to turn it into a true popular lyric and true Auden at the same time. The other ("Johnny") is Song No. XXII, "O the valley in the summer where I and my John." It has all the lilt and sentiment of an old sad song of the people, and very little of anything specifically Audenesque.

It is not easy to say why these two were approved and the other two dismissed. It's just a case of "one shall be taken, and the other shall be left."

But much more challenging to the critical sense are the "Three Ballads" which form a special group among the "lighter poems" in *Another Time*. All three of these develop psychological theories more or less legitimately derived from Freudian sources (though with a difference), and treated with sober seriousness by Auden in much of his poetry. Here they are treated in the burlesque manner. "James Honeyman" was not republished in the later collections; "Miss Gee" and "Victor" were republished, with considerable revision, from their original form in *New Writing*, fall, 1937. The revisions made in the poems kept are curious and highly provocative of critical speculation; and the three taken together (retained or abandoned) raise esthetic problems of urgent significance.

"Miss Gee" is the story of a poor, ugly, sanctimonious, and

greatly inhibited old maid, who prays the Lord not to lead her into temptation but to "make me a good girl, please." She is obviously in love with the Vicar of Saint Aloysius, who pursues her in her dreams in the form of a bull "with lowered horn." The long repression of her sexual impulses results in her developing cancer of the liver instead of begetting a child. The doctor is genuinely dismayed when he finds that he has a case of malignant tumor on his hands. He proceeds to cut his patient up amid the laughter of the medical students. In the end they wheel her off to the anatomy department, hang her up, and "a couple of Oxford Groupers / Carefully dissected her knee."

What we might call the manifest content of this surgical nightmare was probably furnished by an actual operation attended by Isherwood while he was a medical student, and duly communicated to his friend. An account of this is given by Isherwood in *Lions and Shadows*. It was an operation for removal of sarcoma of the femur, and involved the amputation of the leg of an eleven-year-old girl. It was the first operation witnessed by the young literary man, and he did not enjoy it. In his account there is no mention of the students' laughing, or of the surgeon's cutting the patient in half, of the Oxford Groupers (what would they be doing in a London operating room?), or of their hanging the dead woman up to dissect her knee. These are all embellishments of Auden's. But what may have suggested this final touch was the fact that one of the students was given the dead girl's leg for dissection in his spare time.

There was one special embellishment of Isherwood's that had been used by him and Auden in their play, *The Dog beneath the Skin*, published two years before Auden's ballad. Isherwood remarks, of the operation he attended, that the "cooks" (the nurses and dressers in their white uniforms) "took their positions round the table. But now they were no longer cooks; they were acolytes and minor priests. This was a religious ceremony." There was a sister in her "sacrificial robes," and of course the surgeon as high priest in his "black rubber gloves of office," who "pronounced the opening words." In *The Dog beneath the Skin* the imagery of a religious ceremony is elaborately developed. A "voluntary" is played on a harmonium; there is a "processional"; a prayer is intoned by the officiating priest (the surgeon), with responses by his acolytes, and the materialist credo of medical science is chanted in unison by all present.

At the critical moment in the play the lights go out. The surgeon bungles the case. He cuts the mesenteric, and is very angry with the nurse for allowing the patient to die.

It was natural, I suppose, for amateurs in pseudo-Freudian psychology to make a farce of medical science. This is Dr. Krokowski versus Dr. Behrens. But I doubt that Dr. Krokowski would allow himself to show so much gleeful humor over the gruesome details of a surgical operation.

It is interesting to note the revisions made in this poem between the early form published in *New Writing* and that of *Another Time*, which latter is virtually identical with the version of 1945. Most of the alterations are in immaterial matters of punctuation or wording: "her clothes" for "the clothes"; "and rang" for "she rang"; "laid her on the table" for "put her on the table." But there were two stanzas entirely omitted, and (what is rarer in Auden's revision) four stanzas added to take the place of one omitted. In the case of one of the stanzas omitted, the motive for its excision may have been a belated respect for the cloth, for it refers to the way the Vicar in the pulpit "took away the breath" of Miss Gee, as he preached on the text: "The Wages of Sin is Death." Another omitted stanza represents Dr. Thomas as announcing to Miss Gee that she has a cancer and will soon be dead. But current medical ethics hardly makes it plausible that he should have made this blunt communication. And the purposes of storytelling are better served by having his diagnosis revealed in the doctor's conversation with his wife at dinner. In the original this is done merely in his remark to her that Miss Gee is, he fears, a goner. In revision, Auden replaces this with four new stanzas in which the doctor, while rolling bread pellets, tells his wife what a funny thing cancer is, and how often childless women get it, and men too when they retire.

It's as if there had to be some outlet
For their foiled creative fire.

Thus he improves the story and at the same time points its moral. How well medical statistics bear out the theory I will leave to those who know.

"Miss Gee" is cited by Professor Spears as an illustration of Auden's use of the popular-song mask, where "the innocent form is made to convey an unexpected and ominously contrasting matter." This observation is well taken; but it is an open question whether, in this and other "light" poems of Auden, the artistic intention of combining the light and the ominously serious for a deliberate satirical end is *réussi* or *manqué*. We ought here to distinguish between the traditional popular ballad as represented in the famous Child and Kittredge collection, where, as we used to say, *das Volk dictet*, and the very different popular ballad of the scurrilous Elizabethan pamphleteer, or the risqué song of the English music hall, the French cabaret, and (sometimes) the American radio or television show. Mr. Auden is very well read in light verse, very clever at reproducing certain of the superficial features of the old popular ballad and the hillbilly song, but equally clever at sounding the note of the modern sophisticated ballad song. And the latter seldom has the "innocence" of the old folk form. There is about the music-hall and cabaret song, as part of its sophistication, something of the leering diabolism of the actual masks attached to their faces by professional celebrants in European festival saturnalia.

And that is sometimes the case with Auden's ballads. There is a gloating tone in detailing the spinster's ugliness and stuffiness that goes ill with the innocence of the old popular song. The old popular song would hardly begin with the archness of Auden's "Let me tell you a little story." It would not destroy the tragic effect of the central story by going out of its way to take a rap at the Oxford Groupers, confusing the issue by turning from the climactic event (here the sarcoma operation) to an incident (the dissection of the patient's knee) which leaves the reader asking, what bearing does this have on the story?

This is very far from the grave consistency with which a Voltaire, a Swift, or a Pope sticks to his ironic line. Even conceding the soundness of Auden's medical theory and the seriousness of his moral, he signally failed to achieve the artistic effect intended. He was betrayed by his fondness for exploding miscellaneous fireworks, scoring points; and he was thus betrayed, presumably, by the overdevelopment of his theoretical and rhetorical faculties, and the youthful underdevelopment of his sympathetic emotions.

The second one of the ballads retained by Auden, "Victor," confronts us with the most abysmally difficult problem that we have to meet in this study, with the single exception of the Vicar's Sermon in *The Dog beneath the Skin*. Our problem is to figure out the frame of mind in which the poem was written, at least as early as 1937, and still more the frame of mind in which it was found acceptable for publication in 1945 in the canonical work of a man who had definitely accepted the sentiments, the moral teaching, and the faith of orthodox Christianity. It is just possible that in 1940, or whenever the manuscript was prepared for publication in *Another Time*, he was still on the fence in the matter of religious belief and could excuse the doctrinal looseness of this poem in view of its high merits as a literary performance. But in 1945, how is that conceivable?

The plot of the ballad is briefly this. The hero, Victor, is from early childhood notable for goodness and piety, following his father in the stress he lays on not telling lies and on being "pure in heart" as the Bible prescribes. He is also neat and cleanly in his habits, does not even smoke, is diligent in his calling as a bank clerk, and is regarded by the manager as a decent fellow but "too mousey to go far." He has never been with a woman, and politely declines the invitation of his fellow clerks to go downtown with them on Saturday night. But for all that, he falls for the charms of a woman of loose character, who marries him because it is time for her to settle down. He soon discovers that she has bestowed her favors on all his acquaintances. He seeks counsel from his Father in Heaven and from all the forces of nature, and comes to the conclusion that Anna must die. He bids her "prepare to meet her God," and chases her round the house with a carving knife in his hand. He stabs her to death, and while her blood runs down the stairs, he declares himself to be "the Resurrection and the Life." After he is taken to the asylum he continues to claim divinity: "I am the Alpha and Omega, I shall come / To judge the earth one day."

It is said by several writers in a position to know that Auden was for years thoroughly "sold" on the theory that all physical diseases have mental causes; in some cases they are derangements of what we may call the Eros principle. "Miss Gee" is a serious case history in support of that medical truth. "Victor" is a case history illustrative of the truth that derangements of the Eros principle, or repressed sex energy, may produce insanity, and evidently of the corollary truth that religious mania may be the effect of — what shall we say? — puritan repressions bred by an over-strict conformity to bourgeois standards of morality. Naturally, too, religious mania is most likely to ensue in cases where the goody-goody character has been fostered by strict religious training in the home. Now, that, one would think, might sound like questionable or even subversive doctrine to thoroughly and consistently religious-minded people.

The problem is not resolved by a study of the revisions made by Auden in 1940 and continued in 1945. Most of these revisions are relatively unimportant. The most extensive is the excision of a stanza present in the original. Victor is chasing his wife round the house while she dodges behind the sofa and tears down the curtain rod, and then wrenches the door open and runs up the stairs. In the original Auden sustains the suspense by having her blunder into chairs and tables like a frightened June bug. But the poet wisely decided that this was a little too much of the movie business. In another stanza he steps up the irony in his characterization of the vamp.

> Her skin was like cream from the dairy,
> Her scent was like new-mown hay.

Here he makes a decided improvement with a touch that better suits the character of his hero.

107

> She looked as pure as a schoolgirl
> On her First Communion day.

The other alterations are hardly worth detailing. All but one; and that is of the highest significance. In the original poem as we have it in *New Writing* in 1937, there is a refrain which appears at the end of each stanza. In every case it is the same liturgical supplication, "Have mercy, Lord, save our souls from Hell," varied only in the pronoun according to context — our souls, your soul, their souls, my soul, and most often his soul and her soul. Thus to every stanza of this dubiously Christian poem is attached a formidably Christian refrain, with an effect that, to any simple, but not too simple, Christian reader must sound like blasphemy. And there is posed in its nakedness the crucial problem for interpretation and exegesis. The attachment of this Christian prayer to this type of poem is unquestionably effective in its histrionic way; it adds its element of shock to a piece charged with the sensational. It means the putting together of elements that don't belong together except as ingredients in an explosive that will make a big noise when it is detonated. The author at the time he penned it (some time, say, between 1934 and 1937), was almost certainly not interested in promoting the Christian gospel or saving souls from Hell. He was interested in promoting a half-baked medico-psychological theory containing, possibly, one part of truth to five parts of fancy; and through this, hastening the emancipation of his contemporaries from stuffy ideas on the subject of sex and society. He was mainly in reaction against what are called Victorian ideas. Every item in this poem declares his dislike for everything associated with Church and Sunday School. Tacking his prayer onto each stanza of the poem was a means of continually pointing up the ironic intention of the whole story. And when he made it fit for publication in 1940, at about the time of his conversion, the first thing he had to do was to cut out this refrain, which even he must then have realized was likely to give offense to God's unsophisticated children and to lovers of virtue as currently understood.

The poem, even so, could not be made acceptable to really close readers who took it as seriously intended and at the same time took seriously what they had been taught in Church and Sunday School. But then, it was such a brilliant performance, so riotously funny, it would be a pity to put it out of circulation! And it was so emancipated, so modern! We don't want religion to be sicklied o'er with the pale cast of puritanism. Surely there would be even church wardens capable of relishing a real piece of literary art in one of its ancient traditional modes.

But there will still be an insistent voice sounding in the ears of many readers, declaring that neither "Miss Gee" nor "Victor" is really so very funny, and that they are both shot through with a strain of frivolous and gratuitous cruelty. The violation of artistic standards is not so much in the seriousness with which the poet takes his quack medical theories, nor in the frivolity with which he treats the ethical problems connected with sex, as in the in- humanity (the insensitiveness) with which he exploits his ideas for the purposes of comedy.

But there was one of the "Three Ballads" that Auden did not elect to preserve, and this negative choice is perhaps as puzzling to a critical reader as his affirmative choice in the other cases. "James Honeyman" is the story of a very silent and studious child whose later life was dedicated single-mindedly to scientific re- search and invention. He did in due course marry and beget a son; but all his hours were spent in a little hut at the bottom of the garden (a complete reversal of the situation in Noel Coward's song, "The bushes at the bottom of the garden"). Here, like the poet Shelley, James Honeyman disturbed and frightened his neigh- bors by dabbling in explosive chemicals. The culminating triumph of his career was the invention of a new deadly gas known as Honeyman's N.P.C. His reputation spread wide in the scientific world, and he was visited by a foreign gentleman, who was, as it turned out, the agent of a hostile power. The final result was that, when the bombers came over his garden, he was choked to death by his own gas, along with his wife and child. James Honeyman was as reluctant to give up his life as his wife and child were to give up theirs. He wished he was a salmon in the sea or a dove cooing in the top of a tree. His wife assured him, with very natural irony, that he was far from being either dove or fish.

> But you invented the vapor
> That is killing those you love.

The moral of this piece is as plain as the nose on your face. Science is totally lacking in humanity, and scientists have no care for the destructiveness of the inventions they bring forth with great labor for the sole purpose of maximating their egos. (O Einstein! O Oppenheimer!) This is a very popular view among contemporary devotees of the Muse, and Auden need have no qualms about having given it poetic embodiment. But somehow he realized in this case that he had gone rather far with his comedy; and this poem he did discard in both collections that establish the canon. But "Victor" and "Miss Gee" are still there for our delectation.

We are more and more impressed as we go on with the amazing versatility of this writer, with the "infinite variety" of the parts into which he can throw himself, and the skill, the authority, with which he puts them over. But we do begin to wonder how it is possible for one serious poet to be so many men, and with some concern seek out the essential man behind the actor.

ℭ 9

Uncollected Poems of Serious
Ideological Import

THUS far we have considered revisions and eliminations in the case of poems which have been published by Auden
in book form. But we should also take into account the more than
a dozen of Auden's poems published in magazines and anthologies between 1930 and 1941 and never (so far as I have found) included in any collection made by the author. For many of these
have great interest both for his thought and his artistry as a poet.

The year 1933 was a red-letter year for Auden in more ways
than one. He was now confirmed (for some time to come) in a
philosophical position giving him an outlook on man, the world,
and history in their scientific, ethical, social, and political aspects.
And he had reached an early climax in public recognition as leader
in a new and promising literary movement. This year witnessed
not merely the publication of the second, revised edition of his
1930 *Poems*, but the appearance of nearly a score of poems in
half a dozen leftist magazines and anthologies. No less than seven
appeared in this first year of *New Verse*. The *Criterion* published
the now famous "Paysage Moralisé," beginning "Hearing of harvests rotting in the valleys," and the poem variously entitled
"What Do You Think?" and "The Hard Question." The *New
Oxford Outlook* published "The Malverns," discussed above in
Chapter 6, and the poem later called "The Climbers." As we have
seen in Chapter 6, the anthology *New Country* published the original versions of Nos. XIV and XV in *On This Island*. In the same

number it published, under the title "Prologue," the piece which appears in *On This Island* as No. I, with the same title; the poem later known as "Not All the Candidates Pass," discussed in Chapter 5; and — what is more important for our theme in this chapter — the first part of "A Happy New Year," still to be discussed. And then, finally, as if his following of Oxford intellectuals were not enough, Auden appeared in Volume 1, Number 1, of the Cambridge radical magazine, *Cambridge Left*.

Let us begin with a poem of Auden's that appeared in the very first number of *New Verse*. This was probably the most influential British organ of the literary and political avant-garde. In the first number, along with poems and essays in a similar vein by Louis MacNeice, Cecil Day Lewis, Herbert Read, I. A. Richards, and other advanced spirits, appeared a "Song" by W. H. Auden, which might be regarded as the call to arms, or the marching orders, for a group of guerilla fighters of whom he was already the acknowledged leader. Indeed, he and Rex Warner were here addressed by their first names in poems from "The Magnetic Mountain" by Day Lewis.

> Wystan, Rex, all of you who have not fled,
> This is our world.

"Submit to your star," he bids them, "and take / Command, O start the attacking movement!" Herbert Read, in an essay on "Poetry and Belief in Gerard Manley Hopkins," discusses the problem of belief in the poet. "True originality," he finds, "is due to a conflict between sensibility and belief: both exist in the personality, but in counteraction." This principle is exemplified by the mystical Hopkins, and we are prepared for finding it in the poets of the moment. And I. A. Richards similarly prepares us in an essay on "Lawrence as a Poet," which opens with the statement that "A fundamental fact about Lawrence's poetry is that its reader cannot escape from the problem of belief."

This certainly applies all along to Auden, and is strikingly exemplified by this opening "Song." It is really a ballad, taking the from of a dialogue between a rich young man who wonders why he feels such a fool, "As if I owned a world that had had its day," and a critical friend who is quite prepared to enlighten him on this subject. The young nob desperately proposes various ways of extricating himself from his humiliating situation; and each time his critic exposes the futility of this line of action. The rich man will throw his money in the gutter for workmen to pick up. His friend assures him the workmen will not get it; it will be used by the armament firms for shooting them down. He will get a factory job and fraternize with the boys. His friend assures him the boys will have nothing to do with him.

> For they know you for what you are
> That you live in a world that has had its day.

It will do him no good to go to an island and have the natives "set him free." The natives have "sampled your sort before," and are in no mood to welcome those "who come from a world that has had its day." It will be equally useless for him to set up author in an attic and write a book on such an uninteresting subject as "a world," etc.; or consult a parson or priest in hopes of going to heaven at least, for he doesn't believe them any more and they won't give him ease; or try the brothel and the syringe in his arm. The critic then has the floor through three stanzas, bidding the poor rich man remember that he's not the kind to fight at the barricade, and that while his son may be a hero and carry a gun in the next war, he is no hero himself, but is destined to "go down with your world that has had its day."

This, like the three ballads of *Another Time*, is a "lighter poem" in style, but intended to carry a deadly serious message. Well, perhaps not deadly serious, for it has all the zest of college men working off steam in a run-in with the police. It is a good translation of Marxian ideology into the terms of an effervescent imagination. It is indeed an admirable marching song for adventurous young men enlisted in an ideological Foreign Legion. This is the way it must have seemed to Auden and his friends in 1933. In 1945, it must have seemed to be not merely the carrier of false doctrine but a rather ludicrous expression of the spirit of callow youth. And one can quite understand why he did not wish to have it exposed to the critical examination of posterity.

Indeed, Mr. Auden seems to have disinherited this brain-child from the very start. He did not include it in the second edition of his poems published in September or November 1933, nor the other collection of *Poems* in 1934, nor in *On This Island* (1936), nor in *Selected Poems* (1938) or *Some Poems* (1940); and it does not have a place in the canonical collections of 1945 and 1950.

The sentiments here expressed are not peculiar to this poem, but were reflected in a number of those published in 1933 and 1936, and even in some that were retained in 1945. And there is a close thematic relation between it and No. III of *Poems* 1930 and 1933, "Since you are going to begin to-day." This is addressed to a conservative of the old culture who would like to begin the new life or to "abdicate" before it is too late, but who is assured that it is already too late. All such belated efforts at reform or escape are doomed to failure, with those who are "holders of one position, wrong for years." *

This piece from *Poems* was reproduced in 1945 under the fancy title "Venus Will Now Say a Few Words." This title does correspond to a special complicating theme in the poem. It involves indeed the double theme of (first) the Eros principle and (second) the elimination of types which in the evolutionary process have become obsolete. But this is simply, in slightly altered form, the Marxian theory of the inevitable elimination of the capitalist class. The poem is still mainly concerned with the obsolescence of a "world that has had its day." And in spite of a minor appropriateness of the new title, it serves mainly in 1945 to disguise or soften down the implications of the poem as it first appeared.

The *New Verse* "Song" does not have the subtleties of this and other poems on the same theme. It is a lively and amusing composition. But even before the end of 1933 it must have seemed to

* This phrase is salvaged by Auden from a piece which appeared in Spender's hand-printed volume of his friend's *Poems* not reproduced in the 1930 volume, but given entire by Isherwood in his *New Verse* notes on Auden's early poetry. In this poem Auden was speaking of the pedantry of scientific students of any subject presuming to explain things in terms of "because."

> Unanswerable like any other pedant,
> Like Solomon and Sheba, wrong for years.

Auden too blatant a piece of propaganda to deserve inclusion in his *Poems*. It was the opening gun of a campaign which in 1945 had become ancient history — a chapter from the time when he was sowing his wild oats. In theme it was almost identical with No. III of the *Poems*. But in this latter poem symbolic indirection takes the place of bald statement; the vein is not "light"; and there is nothing on the surface of it to make its author squirm. So that, while it is a less effective composition than the "Song," it did not come under the axe. In 1945 the "Song" was perhaps quite forgotten and the question of reproducing it did not even come up.

Another magazine poem from 1933 never reprinted by Auden appeared in the summer number of *Cambridge Left*. In this same number there is a serious political article by J. D. Bernal on "The End of a Political Delusion," and in the following number, for winter 1933–34, an article entitled "Left?" by J. Cornford. These essays are of great interest for the light they have to throw on the ideological position occupied by Auden at this time, and upon the presumable import of many of his poems during the following five or six years. The political delusion to which Bernal refers is what is sometimes called gradualism. The author looks back to the nineteenth century and traces the growing disillusionment of writers and artists faced with "the grim realities of capitalism." He notes the futility of their hopes of meeting the situation with mere radical theorizing. Impressed by the truculent imperialism of the wealthy, the intellectuals "realized that something must be done about it, and unwilling to accept the cruel analysis of Marx, decided that capitalism must be morally regenerated and turned to beneficent ends by the genteel admonitions of radicalism and Fabianism." But "the war smashed forever the idea of peaceful and continual progress," and "the collapse of 1929 brought down at one stroke the myths of capitalist prosperity and social democracy." Intellectuals went in for various forms of escapism, turning to their private dream worlds of art and science. "To this we owe the efflorescence of the last decade, of Joyce and Picasso and T. S. Eliot, of Freud and Einstein and Dirac." But the depression finally made such evasion impossible, and "Fascism marks the culminating disillusion of the bourgeois intellectual." He is faced with the choice between fascism and war on the one hand and on the other a genuinely revolutionary movement, which is "largely and indeed essentially a working-class movement." The objective of the intellectual must be "the establishment of a classless socialist world state, the only state to which an intellectual can give unqualified allegiance." Bernal, like Malcolm Cowley two years later in the United States, is advising the writers of his time to find their salvation in solidarity with the working class.

In his article in the following number, Cornford indicates the Marxian inspiration for this same program by a quotation from the Communist Manifesto of 1948.

Finally, as the class struggle nears its decisive stage, disintegration of the ruling class and the old order of society becomes so active, so acute, that a small part of the ruling class breaks away to make common cause with the revolutionary class, the class which holds the future in its hands. Just as in former days, part of the nobility went over to the bourgeoisie, so now part of the bourgeoisie goes over to the proletariat.

Of the younger poets who have best exhibited "the revolutionary fermentation," Cornford names Auden first, along with Charles Madge, Stephen Spender, C. Day Lewis, and two others now less well known. And the party of reaction in literature is represented by Eliot, Joyce, and Pound with their evasive "subjectivity." He discusses some of the difficulties attending on the experimental character of the new movement, "the obscurity and crudity which are the growing pains of every vital movement," but quotes two stanzas from Auden's *New Country* poem, "A Communist to Others," as an example of virile, unambiguous verse.

This may seem an unnecessarily long prologue to my brief comment on Auden's "Interview" in the first number of the Cambridge magazine. This poem, never reprinted by Auden, is a rather flimsy exercise in irony, in which he is still having fun with his old boyhood game of spies and counterspies. The speaker is some person in authority in a secret organization, and the person addressed is seemingly a spy reporting to him for instructions. This secret agent is taking considerable satisfaction in the role he is playing. He has escaped from somewhere in a submarine, "with a false beard, *hoping the ports were watched.*" But he needn't be vain about it, for it isn't snowing and no one will take him for a spy. He is evidently a person of some consequence in polite society. Due credit is given him for his "annual camp for the Tutbury glass workers" (in Auden, a favorite device of the ruling class for corrupting those who might otherwise be revolutionaries), and for his "bird-photography phase," and the winter he spent in Prague, though not everything about that episode is to be mentioned publicly. He is finally dismissed with somewhat cryptical instructions and a strategic map of the country.

Such is my understanding of the poem, and my presumption is that these conspiratorial characters belong to the party in power, the "ruling class," and it is on them that the satire falls. But other interpretations are possible. The secret agent who wants to be taken for a spy is greeted by the man in authority with these words: "Having abdicated with comparative ease / And dismissed the greater part of your friends." This might suggest that the person thus greeted is one of the old order, as in the *New Verse* "Song," and *Poems* No. II ("Venus Will Now Say a Few Words"), who would like to "abdicate" or get to the frontier before he is caught, but is assured that it is already too late for that since he belongs to "a world that has had its day." In that case, the man to whom he reports and who gives him so many cryptical warnings may belong to either party. It is pretty hard, at this distance, from Great Britain and from 1933, to distinguish between friend and foe in these somewhat faded romantic play-worlds.

Where ideology is involved, it may be with performances as inconsiderable as this that a poet becomes the recognized leader in a literary movement. But if Auden had not something more substantial than this to depend on, he would never have achieved the reputation or reached the stature that he has.

In the lengthy Part I of his *New Country* poem "A Happy New Year," Auden was again indulging in a perfect carnival of boyish fun at the expense of a whole host of reactionary stuffed shirts. He was playing the exhilarating role of rebel sniper from an attic window upon a streetful of tanks sent by an oppressive foreign power to put down native freedom.

But this is only the surface manifestation of a moral philosophy striking deeper roots. That in his socialist ideology Auden was supported by a more comprehensive vision of man and the world is suggested by his dedication of the *New Country* poem to Gerald Heard. This speculative humanist philosopher had already in 1933 published at least three of his long series of books dealing with human evolution and history; and Auden's dedication makes it probable that he had read and been influenced by one or more of the earlier volumes: *The Ascent of Humanity*, 1929; *The Emergence of Man*, 1931; *This Surprising World*, 1932. For the gist of these books, so far as it suggests the probable philosophical attitude of Auden at this period, one cannot do better than quote from the summary of the argument given by G. Lowes Dickinson, in his Introduction to *The Ascent of Humanity*:

The human consciousness is engaged in a secular process, spiral in character. The most primitive societies . . . are undifferentiated herds in which individuals have not yet developed. . . . Later by degrees . . . individuals begin to emerge. They become priests, kings, monks, philosophers, men of science; and the more they develop the more they slough off the social and corporate sense, until . . . at the period we call the Renaissance . . . they stand alone, intellectually sublime and morally monsters. But this development is involved in an inherent contradiction. The more the individual seeks and acquires the less he is satisfied, and Hamlet succeeds Caesar Borgia.

Then, when the movement has run into this impasse, if it has not destroyed civilization, there begins to emerge a new form of consciousness. It is above the individual as the earlier form was below him. Henceforth it begins to be the business of man not to acquire but to understand, and to understand by a cooperative effort. The age of science has dawned and at its dawn we stand. The problem before us is whether the higher consciousness thus emerging will be able to control the lower, that is bursting out all about us, with the cry of individuals newly released for the fruits that have turned so sour in the mouths of their predecessors.

From Lowes Dickinson's summary I quote at such length because it seems to me to throw much light on many poems of Auden all the way down to 1940, on the sonnets and Commentary of "In Time of War," and even on the sonnets of "The Quest," though in these latter Auden was sloughing off the secular point of view for the strictly religious. Lowes Dickinson remarks, of the view he outlines from Heard's book, that it "lays stress not on physical but on psychical factors." It is this, in Auden, that differentiates him from the strict materialism of Marx. The "higher consciousness" that is emerging is "above the individual as the earlier form was below him." This may be the key to passages in the earlier poems which some recent critics would interpret in terms of Christian theology. And a reading of Heard, to whom Auden addressed his "Happy New Year," may help to keep these early poems where they belong, within the framework of a secular humanism later repudiated. Auden is a poet, and Heard's "higher consciousness" often takes with him the image of Love. Even in his "A Communist to Others" (discussed in Chapter 6), he refers his "comrades" to the "love outside our own election" that everywhere "holds us in unseen connection."

As for Heard's enthusiastic preoccupation with "the age of science," that would not have been unwelcome to the Auden of 1929 and 1933. It was somewhat later that the poet's disparaging references to science began to appear, and they were most frequent after his conversion, when science was more regularly identified with deterministic materialism, as well as with the mechanization of modern life and our vulgar passion for gadgets. As twentieth-century science more and more abandons the dogmatic materialism of the nineteenth, our poets grow more and more alarmed about it. While our scientists ever more urgently object to the development of destructive weapons, our poets go on blaming them instead of the politicians and the voters who inspire the politicians. And science is even held to blame for the gadgets with which housewives reduce their domestic labors and their laundry bills, and for whatever there is of ugliness in our urban landscapes.

But the poem addressed to Gerald Heard does not move on this high level of constructive philosophical thinking. It follows rather the strategy of the rebel sniper — satirical and destructive of anything in the oppressive reigning order that can be brought within gunsight.

It is, it seems, a frosty still December morning, when the poet has a day off from teaching in his Scottish boys' school. He climbs up for a view of the Clyde and finally sees Loch Lomond below him. Through three long stanzas he pays his respects to the lovable Scotch country, and then, on the moor, he becomes aware, as in a vision, of a great gathering of Englishmen representing "the dingy difficult life of our generation." They include a motorcyclist proud of the speed with which he has covered a mile, and a band of boys and girls in bathing suits (strangely enough for the season), a pretty sight if they hadn't had to keep stopping "because their drawers were constantly slipping" (British prudery?). Then came a band of horns and miscellaneous musical instruments, and a choir singing a hymn by John Bacchus Dykes, and then the saxophone boys in fantastic costumes. Next came the "main bodies," notable for their shamefast glances and awkward stares, lanky or lame legs, their "stammering over easy words," spasmodic laughter, and drawling speech to conceal their fears. Indeed a dreary picture of English manners in an age of bourgeois decadence!

And last came the stuffed shirts — the figureheads of the British social order. The statesmen are well represented by eminent leaders of all political parties — Ramsay MacDonald (very much pleased that "at last he'd been invited to Leicestershire Meet"), Baldwin, Churchill, Snowden (who had been Chairman of the Independent Labor Party), Austen Chamberlain (author of *Peace in Our Time*). The armed forces were represented by several distinguished officers who had served in India and Africa, and by Lawrence of Arabia flying over in a Bristol Bomber. Finance and industry were represented by Sir Thomas Horder (created Baron in 1913), by Sir Alfred Mond, Lord Beaverbrook, and Sir Montague Norman (Governor of the Bank of England); the Boy Scouts and Girl Guides (symbol of near-fascist regimentation) by

Lord Baden-Powell (Baron since 1929); economics and government service by Maynard Keynes (prominent at the Peace Conference in 1919, author of *The Economic Consequences of the
Peace*, created Baron in 1942). Outright fascism was represented
by Sir Oswald Mosley. Psychology and medical science were represented by Ernest Jones (who introduced psychoanalysis to England and America, but evidently not the correct Groddeck and
Homer Lane brand). Entertainment was represented by Maisie
Gay and Sir Harry Lauder; religion by Father D'Arcy; and literature by Wyndham Lewis and the escapist poets, Eliot, Pound,
and the Sitwells, who "were giving a private dance." It is remarkable how many of these notabilities, when you look them up,
prove to have been Cambridge men, thus enabling the Oxford poet
incidentally to thumb his nose at the rival university. Maynard
Keynes he notes sulking in a ditch and blubbering, "In Cambridge
they think I have brains."

The young schoolmaster was truly giving himself a holiday,
and the young poet having the time of his life, as if he were a
yokel in a booth shying balls at every head that came into view.
And before he has done he works himself up to even higher
flights of daring and fantasy. The lower ranks of these people are
dreary enough, but some of them become unruly under so much
organized authority; they cry out for freedom, and are promptly
rounded up by the secret police and carted off to the Government
San. Then the general gives orders for military action to begin;
the Eagles are ordered to attack on the North and the Tigers to
occupy the South, and the several hordes march off toward their
objectives.

One cannot begrudge the young poet the pleasure he took in
thus contributing his mite to the Revolution. But one can readily
see why he left this piece out of *On This Island* and all subsequent
collections of his poetic work.

In order to reconstruct the atmosphere in which this work took
shape, it is worth while to consider the volume in which it was
printed together with four other poems of Auden's. This volume
is packed full of what we used to call "proletarian" writing —

revolutionary prose articles by Michael Roberts, Day Lewis, Spender, and others in the movement, and poems by Lewis, John Lehmann, Charles Madge, Michael Roberts, Spender, Rex Warner, and others of like mind. And curiously enough, it was published at the respectable Hogarth Press for those reputable citizens and eminent members of the Bloomsbury Group, Leonard and Virginia Woolf. A thousand pertinent reflections come to mind. Two will suffice, and out of the mouths of Eminent Victorians. "But where," asks the author of "The Blessed Damozel," translating Villon, "where are the snows of yesteryear?" And then the author of "Locksley Hall": "The old order changeth, yielding place to new."

ℭ10

More Uncollected Poems

O NE cannot hope to hunt out every poem of Auden's, orphans of his prodigal genius, published in magazines and anthologies of the thirties and left to gather dust on library shelves. But I will mention here or in the Supplementary Notes such others as I have run down, treating here those that have the greater interest for our study and relegating to the notes those which mainly serve to make the record more complete. In this chapter, we will begin with more of the light verse, take note of certain more serious pieces, and have something to say of poems which served as rough drafts for later more important compositions.

Among lighter poems that provoke serious thoughts about the Protean temperament of their maker is "Foxtrot from a Play," which appeared in *New Verse* for April–May 1936, but which, so far as I can discover, was never reprinted by Auden. This poem has no ideological implications. It is an excellent piece for rendering in music hall or cabaret. It is sung alternately by a man and a woman, who join at the end in singing the final stanza. The whimsical theme is the variety of objects for which the sentiment of love is entertained; these include rifles (for the soldier), books (for the scholar), the stage figures Mae West and Fred Astaire, as well as Airedales and Pekinese. Each stanza ends with the gracious though somewhat tepid assurance to the singer's special darling, "but you're my cup of tea." In the final duet are recited the loves of birds and beasts. The song concludes:

The trout enjoys the river
The whale enjoys the sea
And dogs love most an old lamp-post
But you're my cup of tea.

Isherwood has a portrait of his friend "Weston" in his auto-biographical novel, *Lions and Shadows*. If we can take this for a faithful rendering of the impression made on him as a young man by Auden, it has its light to throw on the poetical theories, and perhaps on the personal temperament, which lie behind the composition of this piece, light as it is. "To be 'clinically minded' was, Weston said, the first duty of a poet." This will account for Auden's heavy emphasis all through on his notion that physical disease is the symptom of a moral malady. It will also account for something in his attitude toward love. For the poet, Auden argued in the twenties, "Love wasn't exciting or romantic or even disgusting; it was funny," and it must be handled "with a wry, bitter smile and a pair of rubber surgical gloves." It was not implied that this was the way the poet felt *personally* about love. That it was for him an exciting theme is evidenced by a large part of all that he wrote; that it was not funny is the impression given whenever he is not writing in the lighter vein. It was, it may be inferred, his painful duty to treat it as funny, since it is the primary duty of a poet to reveal to men the diseased condition of their souls.

Well, that love is funny is the primary assumption of anyone who tells funny stories on that theme; and many of those most given to such funny storytelling are persons for whom love does not appear to be particularly romantic or exciting. I would not suggest that we should regard love as a subject immune from the glance of the comic muse. But I fancy there are plenty of quite ordinary people who, when they read Auden on this subject, have an uneasy feeling that he is not talking of quite the same thing as they have in mind.

Perhaps the poet decided that the rather vulgarly racy association of images with which his "Foxtrot" comes to its conclusion, while it would suit the mood of a *boite de nuit* in the small hours, might seem off key when spread in sober print on the pages of a poetry book. This opinion, however, was not shared by Oscar Williams; and in 1946 he made this poem available to Auden fans in its integrity in his *Little Treasury of Modern Poetry*.

Another piece of light verse dropped by the way is "Blues," which appeared in *New Verse* in May 1937. It is one of the cabaret songs written for Hedli Anderson, but not included with the others in *Another Time*. It begins with the lines "Ladies and gentlemen sitting here, / Eating and drinking and warming a chair." It is a merry reminder to these pleasure-seekers that Death is everywhere ready to take over. He may be the one sitting next to them in the cabaret. He may be a "high-stepping blondie," for whom you will become "a sugar daddie and do as you're told." He may be a G-man, a doctor listening to your chest, a real estate agent, a teacher whose one theme is the Tomb. Large use is made of current slang, some of it perhaps imported from America — "hot-seat," "slow worker," "the dotted line," "broke." It is written in jolting anapests in the manner of the popular song adapted to modern use. Mr. Auden may have concluded that it was too popular in tone for long-time wear, and its anapests too lumpy-footed. Or he may have felt that he had treated his solemn theme with excessive flippancy. The cabaret celebrants might be able to take it in their stride if they had enough champagne under their belts; but the sober reader might think that the macabre was carried too far.

By the year 1939, when Auden came to the United States to live, he was the most famous of all British poets of his generation, and his contributions in prose and verse were eagerly welcomed by our most influential literary magazines. In 1940 the *New Republic*, which had already featured five "Sonnets from China," published in a single number the entire set of twenty sonnets comprising "The Quest," one of which had earlier appeared in *Poetry*. In 1941 the *Atlantic Monthly*, in two successive issues, ran the whole of Auden's extremely "highbrow" poem of more than 1700 lines later called "New Year Letter." And still other American periodicals published poetry by Auden, including the *Nation*, the *Partisan Review*, and the *Southern Review*. Even the *New Yorker* discovered in Auden's "lighter poems" a talent that would appeal to readers of Phyllis McGinley and Ogden Nash; and in their number for August 24, 1940, appeared a lively music-hall piece entitled "The Glamour Boys and Girls Have Grievances Too."

This is represented as being sung by choruses made up of Movie Starlets and Juveniles, Female and Male Powers Models, and Athletes Male and Female. The burden of their singing is the boresomeness of the roles they have to play before the American public.

> You've no idea how dull it is
> Just being perfect nullities,
> The idols of a democratic nation.

Mr. Auden had been impressed, as all of us are, by the flat and flashy character of much of our popular entertainment, and the low animal level of vitality and "pulchritude" from which so many of our heroes and heroines are drawn. And in this spirited poem he gave us just what we should expect from a good-natured critic representing a more ancient and demure culture, the parent of ours. No one could take umbrage at this sort of thing. But the author himself was the first to see that this is not the stuff of high art, and not his forte, and he seems never to have reprinted this in any of his books.

In any critical reflections that occur to us on the poems here described, we ought no doubt to keep in mind that Auden was a professional writer, who was presumably making a living by his pen in a world not inclined to offer much of a living to poets. He would naturally try his hand at a variety of things that were likely to bring in the means of subsistence. And it is clearly to his credit that, so often, he declined to admit to his collected poems work that, on consideration, seemed to him ephemeral.

But Auden's rejections were not confined to poems in the lighter vein. Some note should be taken here of a poem of deeply serious intention which he did not admit to the canon. This appeared in the anthology *New Writing*, in the same 1937 issue with the ballads of "Miss Gee" and "Victor" discussed in Chapter 8. Like so many of Auden's poetical compositions, it bears simply the title "Poem," and must be identified by its opening lines, "Under the fronds of life, beside / The flowers' soundless hunger." It was not in any of Auden's early collections, in *Another Time*, or in either the 1945 or the 1950 collection. And yet it has exceptional interest in relation both to Auden's philosophy and to his evolving poetical technique.

The theme of this poem is Man shown in his contrasted setting of lifeless stone, dumb vegetation, and the relatively inarticulate and helpless lower animals. Among all these he is known for his intelligence and cunning, the means he has invented for destroying all rivals for power, his ruthlessness, his grandiose loves and visions, including his vision of universal peace, with "hunter and victim reconciled," and the lion (or tigress) lying down with the lamb. The poem ends on the gloomiest note to be found anywhere in Auden's writing, with Man betrayed by his ever fresh loves and ever fresh defeats, and left with the griefs that follow upon his continuing defeats and disillusionments.

The writing is close-knit and often cryptical, but not characterized by the code-symbolism prevailing in his poetry in the 1930 and 1936 volumes. The thought is not so much dramatized, or rendered in terms of its "objective correlative," but is more directly expressed in the discursive manner so much in use in the poetry of *Journey to a War, Another Time, The Double Man*, and in the volumes published in the fifties. This is not to say that there is here no obscurity, no tangled thickets for the reader to penetrate. The most difficult stanza is that dealing with Man's relation to his mother, his nurse, and his father—always, in modern psychology, a crucial feature in determining how a man comes to his emotional and mental set. Here there is, of necessity, symbolism of the kind so diligently studied by Freud and Jung. But it is what we might call line-by-line symbolism rather than that symbolism which, in so much of Auden's poetry, is the groundwork of the entire poem and provides its action and scenery.

Much more readily intelligible to one at all well acquainted with anthropology and comparative religion, is the literal, non-symbolized account of the ways in which Man has come by his cosmic and religious philosophy — by the tabus prescribed by the ghosts of his ancestors ("ruled by dead men never met") or the revealed cosmogonies of religious dreamers ("by pious guess deluded"). As for the ideal of universal peace among earth's denizens, that "dream of vaguer ages," we recognize this as the "golden age" of Hesiod, Plato, and Don Quixote.

This is not, certainly, as an imaginative whole, one of Auden's finest creations, certainly not to be compared with his "Spain 1937." But it is perhaps the most comprehensive view of Man's "condition" to be found anywhere in Auden in so small compass. It is also the most despondent view, in a mood perhaps induced by events in Spain in this year 1937, where the poet spent some time as ambulance driver or stretcher bearer with the Loyalist Republicans. It was obviously written at a moment when his heart was not supported by any hope or faith from outside itself. The hopes of socialism were greatly dimmed. He had not yet gone to China to meditate, on the battlefronts, upon the growing menace of fascism, and to summon lovers of freedom, humanist-wise, to exert their will power in the struggle "to construct at last a human justice, / The contribution of our star." And it was several years before he gave up the humanist faith for what he calls here the "pious guess" of supernatural religion.

But a poem is not made or unmade by the degree of hopefulness expressed; it is made (always assuming the gifts of art) by the sincerity and depth of the author's thinking and feeling. I will not say there was any insincerity in the Auden inspired by Marxism, or by liberal Humanism, or by Christianity; and surely, given sincerity, the inspiration of his faith is an added merit in a poet. But where the poet feels the call to prophecy and propaganda, there is always the danger that his *esthetic sincerity* may be put under a strain. This is what we have to say sometimes of the poet Auden. And it is an actual relief to come upon a poem, like this one, in which, as in "Journey to Iceland," his actual disillusionment and grief, even perhaps his cynicism, is expressed without any undue consideration of his role as prophet and propagandist.

Still, it is easy to understand why Auden, in 1940 or in 1945, should have hesitated to include a poem so devoid of "faith" and edification as this one. And since as poetry it is not quite in a class with, say, "Journey to Iceland," he might have considered that he was justified in rejecting it on purely artistic grounds.

A number of Auden's poems published in periodicals were manifestly experiments or rough first drafts for later more finished work that better satisfied him. Such is a long "Speech from a Play," published in *New Verse* in February 1935. It is done in a sort of joggly blank verse, and is a discursive account of an endemic malady of the spirit which, from the time of Columbus and Magellan on, has caused us men to be "harried and haunted by the hounds of fear." We are driven on to perpetual hard labor in the amassing of capital, by means of which we can exploit our less industrious and saving fellows. We are none of us happy, since we suffer from a fatal division between heart and head, separating "that which we feel from that which we perceive / Desire from data." The tender among us will have to pierce the hard skin of the tough, or we shall all "in a scandalous explosion of the stolid perish."

This is, as the author must have soon realized, a lumpy and shapeless piece of writing, not worth reprinting. But it would serve, like other discarded magazine pieces, as a quarry from which he could carve out materials for work more happily conceived. There is one passage here in which he brings in the industrial revolution. This, he suggests, was one effect of "the gospel of work" which Wesley "spent all his life in the saddle preaching." And here we have half a dozen lines that were later used, with minor variations, in Auden's Commentary on "In Time of War." These may be found in the revised version on page 341 of the *Collected Poetry*. Here we have, to use the phrasing of the original, "machines created by clergymen and boys" attracting men "like magnets from the marl and clay / Into towns on the coal measures." There is the same reference to the economic process by which those who save exploit those who do not, driving a bitter bargain with "the careless" ones. In both cases we have hatred "germinating in tenement and gas-lit cellar," and in both we have the rich sitting, heedless or apprehensive, while the coming war casts its ominous shadows before it. Anyone acquainted with the literature of economics will know where to find all this in Marx or in Engels if not in Adam Smith.

I will leave for a note an account of two poems published in the *New Republic* in 1938, which were not reprinted, but which served as preliminary essays toward certain sonnets of "In Time of War," and will here turn directly to a number of sonnets that found early publication in periodicals but were not republished in book form (see p. 269). The first of these, in *New Verse* for July 1933, entitled "Poem," begins with the line "The fruit in which your parents hid you, boy." This is an extremely puzzling and difficult poem to wrest a meaning out of, with images crowding so close they smother one another. But it is unusually challenging to the imagination and the thought, with highly original turns of expression suggesting deeps to be plumbed. What I make of it I offer with great diffidence; but it is important to make something out of it, if only that this will bring us clues to the understanding of a much greater and more moving poem, Auden's "Journey to Iceland." For in the concluding stanzas of that poem there are several phrases lifted bodily out of this early sonnet and all important for rendering the peculiar emotion that the Iceland poem carries.

In the early sonnet the dominant image is that of a child taking his nourishment from the parents whose death he is, and going calmly and indifferently forward on his own career, his own discovery of the meaning of life, the realization of his own aspirations and disillusionments. But if I rightly understand the poem, this child is symbolic of the life force itself, which moves all our lives, and having its own inscrutable teleology, is blandly indifferent to us individuals and the hurt that comes to us in the process. Auden may have been thinking of George Groddeck's con-

130

ception in *The Book of the It*, which he lists among his "modern sources" in the notes to "New Year Letter." But in "Journey to Iceland" Auden is writing more than commonly out of his feelings rather than his dogmatic faiths; and that is one reason why the poem has so moving a pathos. For even Iceland is not far enough removed from the contagion of the world's slow stain to give him a clear and certain vision of that ideal Place to the discovery of which his heart is committed. Iceland swarms with "the jealousies of a province." "The indigenous figure on horseback" is asking all the old desperate questions about justice and human isolateness. "The fabulous country" recedes as fast as one moves toward it. And the poet here gives voice to a sorrowfulness that he very seldom allows himself to express, considering that this would be a fatal weakness and a prelude to defeat.

Among the expressions which Auden takes over from the earlier poem is the characterization of the child, the young, as that "for whom all wish to care," presumably because the young child is the promise of better things in the future. But promises are not to be believed. And in "Journey to Iceland" we read that there are in our time no "favourite suburbs," native home

> of the young for whom all wish to care;
> The promise is only a promise, the fabulous
> Country impartially far.

The early sonnet ends with an account of how "you" (the life force) moving all our lives

> Send back the writer howling to his art,
> And the mad driver pulling on his gloves
> Start in a snowstorm on his deadly journey.

These are the most extraordinary images in the poem. The syntax is irritatingly hazy. But the images were not lost, and are reproduced almost without alteration in the concluding stanza of "Journey to Iceland."

> Tears fall in all the rivers. Again the driver
> Pulls on his gloves and in a blinding snowstorm starts
> Upon his deadly journey, and again the writer
> Runs howling to his art.

I will not venture to say just what was meant by the mad driver. It may have been poor Man setting forth with desperate bravery into the blinding snowstorm of life. It may have been Groddeck's It. It may have been the life force itself setting out on his inscrutable errands. Or it may have been whatever more esoteric power is thought to activate the life force (the Greeks were not certain whether to call it Fate or God). Perhaps the author himself did not know which of these abstractions is symbolized in this formidable figure. Perhaps if he had known clearly which it was, ideological scruples would have entered in to ruin the poem.

In any case, we now understand why the poet was willing to cancel his early poem that provided so many brilliant touches for the magnificent piece that followed. The loss of an early sonnet, however rare, is a small price to pay for the strong and beautiful conclusion to "Journey to Iceland."

In *New Verse* for October 1933 there appeared "Five Poems" (all sonnets in sequence), of which Auden retained the fifth, later No. XXIX of *On This Island* and entitled "Meiosis" in the collections of 1945 and 1950. The other four he discarded. All five are closely bound together in thought, and through the final one connected, I believe, with the earlier sonnet last discussed and so with "Journey to Iceland." In the first four of them the "I" character is addressing another, who is first shown sleeping beside him and presenting a temptation which the sleeper resists. The other is then shown as having gone north and left the "I" alone on their holiday island. The one who is gone is beautiful and likely to prove false. The one who remains is struggling to free himself from a love which has "one wish and that is, not to be."

The final poem, which Auden retained, is more difficult and "metaphysical," and is sharply distinguished from the others by the introduction of a third-person character known only by the pronoun "him." I certainly have not the hardihood to undertake an authoritative explication of this poem in detail; but there are clues which one cannot resist following. The first clue is a reference back to the earlier sonnet. We have in the later poem three personages: Love, and he and you. And you is spoken of as "the seed to which he was a mother." In the same sense, in the earlier poem, "you" is represented as "growing" at the "core" of "the fruit in which your parents hid you, boy." And he is accordingly, as I have suggested, the bearer of the life force that moves forward indifferently through the hurts and deaths of individual mortals. And he (the you) is accordingly now represented as being made free by love

> To take the all-night journey under sea,
> Work west and northward, set up building.

He (you) is also represented as not yet grown to his full height, but — if the pronouns have not confused me — destined to become "the flood on which all move and wish to move" — which I take to be a more hopeful version of the "deadly journey" into the snowstorm undertaken by the mad driver pulling on his gloves. It is, we might say, Auden's rendering of Tennyson's notion of that "one far-off divine event to which the whole creation moves." And the main point of the poem would seem to be that this benign cosmic movement will not be stemmed by any "hopeful falsehood" of private self-centered loves ("the romantic lie in the brain / Of the sensual man in the street").

In the five sonnets in sequence, the first four would seem to be the simple record of an actual love affair between two definite persons. In the fifth there is a sudden passage without warning to a higher, abstract, and general plane of reference. There are references back to the circumstances of the particular love affair, but there is a sudden arbitrary shift of pronouns; the one who has gone to sleep alone in his northern house is suddenly raised in rank to be a symbol of the cosmic force of love, while the one who remains on the island (now "he") has become the generalized human being through whom the life force moves to realize its inscrutable aims, but who is still subject to those "hopeful falsehoods" that get in the way of the larger realization. In IV "you" now sleep alone in your northern house. In V love generalized has taken the all-night journey under sea, is working west and northward, and has set up building (figures that suggest the "working" of the Unconscious in sleep, and the constructive force of the superego or super-Eros as a cosmic life force?).

In the original sequence, certainly, the reader was left floundering, or (like "him") "fighting for breath," as the author without warning passed from persons of flesh and blood in their material setting to his mythological abstractions. It is as if the poet had suddenly realized that he was being too personal and that he ought to draw some larger lesson from the particular case and, as it were, give it the sanction of a Platonic Idea. The subject of love is forever leading poets into cloudy sophistications. They seem to feel that they must either reduce it to something degrading or elevate it into something ineffable according as their mood is satirical and disillusioned or prophetic and metaphysical.

The reader might have been able to pass from the lower to the higher plane if the transition had not been so sudden, and if he had been able to recognize the first-person protagonist of the earlier sonnet in the remote and impersonal "he" of the final one. But here he must infallibly have felt that he was lost in the woods. This is a familiar impish trick in Auden — what we might call his referential hide-and-seek or trick of referential obfuscation. In this case, along with the other obscurities in the symbolism, it served to set this poem off sharply from those which preceded it in the sequence. In dropping the first four sonnets, Auden must have been moved by a sense of this disparity of tone and substance and of the jolt he gave his readers in making the transition. Or again, he may not have cared for the personal tone of the poems he dropped. He may have shrunk from the suggestion of the intimately autobiographical.

In any case, he was able to salvage from the second sonnet the makings of a lyric to be used as the speech of a Mad Lady in *The Dog beneath the Skin* and published later without any such dramatic intention in the 1945 and 1950 collections, No. XXIX of the Songs and Other Musical Pieces. The holiday island, "the verandah and the fruit," "the tiny steamer" in the bay, with its uncanny hooting, and the lovers' "ugly comic servant" are all taken bodily from the discarded sonnet, in which also "you" have "been away." We cannot tell what it was about this particular stage set that made it persist so tenaciously in the poet's imagination. But it offers another instance of his faculty for putting old poetic material to new uses.

ℭ11

Letters from Iceland

THERE is another group of poems not included in the collections of 1945 and 1950, and the most extensive of all such exclusions except for the lyrics not kept from the plays. This comprises all but three of Auden's poems which appeared in his and MacNeice's *Letters from Iceland* (1937). The only ones to be collected were "Journey to Iceland," which appeared separately in the *Listener* for October 7, 1936, and in *Poetry*, January 1937, and Nos. XXVI and XXVII of the Songs and Other Musical Pieces, both of which were also published in magazines in January 1937.

But these other poems from Iceland are a case by themselves, and in his not including them in his *Collected Poetry*, one would not for a moment suppose that Auden meant to exclude them from the canon of his poetical writings. No one could possibly doubt that, for a long time to come, the volume in which these poems appear, along with several by MacNeice, will somehow be made available to readers of English, if only for its great auto-biographical interest. Of the two longest poems, one is the joint composition of the two men, their so-called "Last Will and Testament." There would be obvious reasons for neither poet's including this in a collection of his own verse, altogether apart from its subject matter and artistic quality. And it is certainly too long to be included in Auden's collection of his "shorter poems."

The "Last Will and Testament" is a spirited piece of half-fooling in which the authors pay their compliments, sincere or ironical, to numerous friends, adversaries, and contemporaries generally, under the comic pretense of bequeathing to them possessions, qualities, or tastes and opinions which in many instances they already have, or which they would particularly abhor, and which the poets clearly do not have it in their power to bestow. To Hilaire Belloc they bequeath "all the roadhouses in Herts . . . that he may drink and live"; to Father D'Arcy, the famous Thomist, they leave "St. Thomas Aquinas and his paeans"; to Gerald Heard "the new Peace he has won"; to Geoffrey Grigson of *New Verse* "a strop for his sharp tongue before he talks." But, more ambiguously, to Leonard and Virginia Woolf they would leave "the twin towers of the Crystal Palace." On people they scorn or hate they are pretty rough. Thus with the leader of the English fascists:

> And to Sir Oswald (please forgive the stench
> Which taints our parchment from that purulent name)
> We leave a rather unpleasant word in French.

They are not too respectful toward great figures in government. To the prime minister Stanley Baldwin they leave "the false front of Lincoln Cathedral, and a school of empire poets." To Vickers, the munition makers, they leave

> The Balkan Conscience and the sleepless night we think
> The inevitable dangers of their dangerous trade.

Considerable mild fun is made of dignitaries of the Anglican Church. With the Nonconformists, the fun is not quite so mild, and with Rome not mild at all, since to Rome they leave "all the lives by Franco gently stopped" — with more in the same vein. They pay affectionate tributes to their parents and families, and lavish all kinds of good wishes on their personal friends and confederates.

This poem is a rich mine of biographical information about two distinguished poets, and whatever they might wish to do about it themselves, literary scholars and publishers would never allow it to go out of circulation. But once again, there is rather too much of Puck in it for them to wish to see it yet in their collected verse, though unquestionably this neglect will be remedied by the time their literary executors begin to assemble their complete works.

Auden's "Letter to Lord Byron," in five parts, is, in the strict sense of the word, one of the most entertaining of all his writings. It is, to begin with, a brilliant tour de force in poetic technique, being done, not to be sure in Byron's Spenserian stanza or ottava rima — Auden begs off from the latter as beyond his powers — but in skillfully wrought rhyme royal — and with a wit and gusto that need not greatly fear comparison with Byron's. Especially delightful are the inspirations that come to Auden in the manipulation of feminine rhymes. The poem is, however, an example of what is called "light verse"; and "light verse, poor girl, is under a sad weather," and nowadays "treated as démodé altogether." It is considered that this style ought to be confined, except in special cases, to "the more bourgeois periodicals." And then, this is one of the longest poems he has written, and if included in the same volume with "New Year Letter," "For the Time Being," etc., it might upset the balance of light and serious, and give to Auden the witty entertainer and *improvisatore* an emphasis that at that time he did not desire.

There is, however, nothing in the "Letter to Lord Byron" that the later Auden might blush to see exhibited over his name. The author of *Don Juan* in his time knew all that was to be known about the corruptness, hypocrisy, and hollowness of British and European society; though a rebel, he was more a satirist than reformer; and Auden does not undertake to convert him to the twentieth-century brand of revolution. The Industrial Revolution is brought in only to show the effect it had on the status of poets without patrons. The author does mention, on his return to England, rumors of war coming in over the BBC and the widening "crack between employees and employers"; and he does somewhat irreverently suggest in passing that the pious folk who believe in heaven are "happy, lovely, but not overbright." But these are merely news items from the twentieth century for the information of Lord Byron in the nineteenth, and will pass as witty sallies from one young man of the world to another.

Auden's communications to the elder poet are mainly on the subject of his (rather conservative) tastes in literature and art, and include his fastidious old world reaction against modern inventions. He gives him a sketchy outline of his own career down to 1945 — his ancestry, parents, and home, his youthful determination to be a mining engineer, his experience of public schools as pupil and teacher, his momentous going to Berlin (his "To Carthage then I came"), and the men who influenced his thinking. Apropos of Jane Austen, he ventures the opinion that "novel writing is a higher art / Than poetry altogether." He is pleased to note that Byron agrees with him "in finding Wordsworth a most bleak old bore." He confesses that in art he prefers figure painting to landscape and still life:

> All Cézanne's apples I would give away
> For one small Goya or a Daumier.

He mentions with approval the most promising of contemporary poets, Spender and Yeats, MacNeice and Eliot. And through it all he maintains the airy tone of one man of wit and breeding addressing another. No least hint of the grubby proletariat, though still less of the stodgy bourgeoisie! One can be pretty certain that Auden never had any intention of letting this poem sink into oblivion.

The three more of Auden's poems in *Letters from Iceland* not included in the collections, and the two more that were included, are all enclosures to friends or take the place of letters in prose. They are in the form of verse because the writer is a poet and likes to keep in practice in that medium. "Letter to R. H. S. Crossman, Esq." develops the notion that we are too prone to interpret individuals in terms of abstract categories in the vain hope of making them "real." We ought to take them as they come for their uniqueness; that is what makes them real, and it is the artist's business. So he decides to "let the camera's eye record" some of the individual details of landscape and people seen; he has evidently been reading Dos Passos. At first we say of this, it is the shrewd reflections of an artist, and good letter-writing. But before he is through, the poet takes over, and he records with vividness what seems to have been the prevailing mood with him in his Icelandic days. He has a vision even in Iceland of "a tradition sick at heart," of "Time the destroyer / Everywhere washing our will," and ends up with "the anarchist's loony refusing cry":

> No choices are good.
> And the word of fate can never be altered
> Though it be spoken to our own destruction.

In Iceland, the prophet in Auden was on a holiday, and he was at liberty to express his most despondent moods without censorship.

In a letter to E. M. Auden the writer encloses a poem meant to show "why people read detective stories." It carries the title "Detective Story," and it has to do with the purely accidental circumstances under which "the truth about our happiness comes out," and the "lingering doubt" on the last page of the story as to whether the verdict of the court was just.

> But time is always killed. Someone must pay for
> Our loss of happiness, our happiness itself.

This little poem has overtones or undertones of greater emotional power than it promises at the start.

The "Letter to William Coldstream, Esq." is longer and less well organized (as poetic art) than that to Crossman. It is mostly an account of what the tourist had observed in a fortnight of Icelandic excursions. The two friends were meeting the challenge of a publisher who had handed them a theme on a plate.

> You went to such and such places with so-and-so
> And such and such things occurred.
> Now do what you can.

Nothing much *had* occurred in the way of adventures; so Auden proceeds to describe what small matters he had taken in with his eyes. His poem is, as he tells his correspondent, "a little donnish experiment in objective narrative." But when he is through with that he gives him, along with a poem of MacNeice on "Iceland," the piece in verse that will best express his own deepest feelings during this fortnight of sight-seeing and listening to alarming news from Europe in the pleasant voice of the wireless announcer,

"like a consultant surgeon," telling the world, "Our case is hopeless. I give you six months." It is a ballad-like dialogue between
various excited lovers of life — farmer-and-fisherman, traveler, im-
passioned lover, dreamer-and-drunkard — on the one hand, and on
the other Death, with his "soft answer," assuring all these enthu-
siasts that "not to be born is the best for man." All they can do
is go on with the formal-patterned dance in which as living beings
they are willy-nilly engaged. This lyrical ballad is reproduced in
the 1945 and 1950 collections as Song XXVI, "O who can ever
gaze his fill."

In another letter to E. M. Auden, the poet encloses a poem
suggested by "a picture of the seven ages of man" that he had
seen "in some book or other." This is Song No. XXVII in the
collections, beginning "O who can ever praise enough." This song
is not so cheerful as its opening suggests. It is indeed a variation
on the same theme as the other song. Precious is "the painted
tree / And grass of fantasy" — the visions of childhood, of the
traveler, the lover, the poet, and the old man trustfully nearing
the tomb. But experience separates man from his father's love and
his mother's womb, and after a week of nights sleeping with a
wanton, he becomes "bride and victim to a ghost,"

> And in the pit of terror thrown
> Shall bear the wrath alone.

The three poems selected by Auden for inclusion in his *Collected
Poems* are no doubt the best of those which accompanied the
Letters from Iceland, though something could be said for the
"Letter to R. S. Crossman, Esq.," and even for "Detective Story."
All of the poetry written in Iceland is transitional in style. It does
not have the clipped phrasing, the high condensation, and evocative symbolism that give their cryptical effect and pungency to
the work in the earlier volumes. Nor does it have the learned allu-
siveness, the intellectual density and Jamesian elaboration of
phrasing that characterizes his work in the forties. It is less modernistic and avant-garde than either the earlier or the later work.
It is simpler and more traditional in manner. It may be true that
"Journey to Iceland" is the only poem in this volume that ranks

with the best things in *Paid on Both Sides* and *Another Time*. But there is nothing here that a modern poet need be reluctant to sign, neither the lightly cynical and worldy "Letter to Lord Byron" nor the lyrics interspersed in the prose correspondence.

These latter have one merit that should not go unnoticed. They represent a temporary truce to prophecy, reformism, and system-making. Their gloom was natural enough considering the date and what was going on in central Europe and Spain. Here, on vacation, the poet's mood of pessimism goes uncensored. And uncensored moods, where they are genuine, have this great advantage for art that they need not be warped to meet the requirements of any gospel. This is not to question the importance of gospels and faiths as a part of an artist's equipment; but simply a reminder that an artist must be free from ideological compulsions if he is never to falsify the faith that is in him.

That Auden failed to include in the *Collected Poetry* certain pieces of verse from the *Letters from Iceland* does not mean, I think, that he has repudiated them, or that they will not continue to be made available to his readers in some form or other.

ℭ 12

Paid on Both Sides and *The Dance of Death*

BETWEEN 1930 and 1938 were published five dramatic compositions, two of them written by Auden, and three by him in collaboration with Christopher Isherwood. All of them contain many passages in verse interspersed among the prose: choruses rhymed and unrhymed, songs in ballad-like rhyming stanzas, dialogue exchanges in blank verse or in rhyming verse. Many of these passages fall naturally into poetic units susceptible of being taken separately. From three of these plays, Auden reproduced a considerable number of such poetic passages in the *Collected Poetry*: from *Paid on Both Sides*, *The Ascent of F6*, and *The Dog beneath the Skin*. From two of them — *The Dance of Death* and *On the Frontier* — he included none. If we regard his inclusions and exclusions from the plays as forming a chapter in the establishment of the Auden canon, we should make at least a brief survey of the situation in each of the five dramatic pieces.

We will first consider the eloquently contrasting cases of *Paid on Both Sides* and *The Dance of Death*. The first of these was a "charade" published in both the 1930 and the 1933 editions of the early *Poems*, which also appeared in the *Criterion* for January 1930 in most distinguished company — among others Ezra Pound, with an essay on Horace, T. S. Eliot as translator of "A Humanist Theory of Value" by Ramon Fernandez, and J. M. Robertson with an essay on "Shakespearean Idolatry." While it bears the modest label of "charade," this is a tragic story of a border feud between rival houses whose males, inspired by their vengeful mothers, kill each other off from generation to generation. Except for the north of England setting it might be a Kentucky feud from days that old men can still remember. At a climactic point it is reminiscent of *Romeo and Juliet*, when, at the wedding feast of a son and daughter of the rival houses, it is declared, "now this shall end with marriage as it ought." But the tragic conclusion has a different turn from Shakespeare's. For the groom's mother bids him kill the man who had killed his brother. So his brother's killer is trapped and shot and the feud goes on. The farm will now be sold and be abandoned to erosion and the moles. For even the strong man is defeated and "his mother and her mother won."

This piece is a charade in the sense that the pictures, tableaux, and dramatic actions represent something beyond themselves. This is, of course, transparently a manifesto against national wars, and an illustration of the way that many of men's finest qualities — their manliness and their family feeling — may conduce to the perpetuation of a senseless way of life. For they are "sick of this feud," and ask, "What do we want to go on killing each other for?" The term charade is also suggested by many features of the drama which are purely symbolic and make it as different as possible from the ordinary realistic play. Such are the introduction of Father Christmas as a character, and the representation of the wounded prisoner's groans by jazz instruments at the back of the stage. Such is the comic doctor, who has discovered the origin of life and received the morning star as decoration, and who, for his operation, takes from his bag "circular saws, bicycle pumps, etc." There is also the anachronistic combination of features natural to an old border feud with others characteristic of contemporary England, such as the fighters' taking a "side-car" when they have "time for a quick one."

Most expressionistic and unrealistic of all is the very general use in the verse passages of a style taken directly from Anglo-Saxon poetry, with its energetic alliterative lines, its kennings, its lack of articles, its descriptive phrases following their nouns, its staccato succession of parallel statements, and even such pecul-

144

iar rhetorical features as the statement of a positive fact in negative terms.

> Fighters lay Groaning on ground
> Gave up life Edward fell
> Shot through the chest First of our lot
> By no means refused fight

The use of the Anglo-Saxon style also brings in much imagery
from an earlier culture that serves as evocative symbolism for
things in contemporary experience.

The chorus from which the above passage was taken, "Day was
gone Night covered sky," was not included by Auden in his
1945 collection, perhaps because it was almost *too* faithful an imi-
tation of the Anglo-Saxon epic, perhaps because it is exclusively
a picture of action and virtually devoid of thematic symbolism.
But he did include all but one of the most evocative and incantatory pieces: the magnificent choruses, "Can speak of trouble,
pressure on men" ("Always in Trouble"), "The Spring unsettles
sleeping partnerships" (in 1945, "It's Too Much"), "To throw
away the key and walk away" ("The Walking Tour"), "Though
he believe it, no man is strong" ("Year after Year"). He included
the fine speech of John, "Not from this life, not from this life is
any / To keep" ("All Over Again"), the responsive song of Anne
and John, "The summer quicken all" (same title in 1945), and
Anne's speech in remembrance of the dead, "To-night the many
come to mind" ("Remember").

One famous passage he fails to reproduce. It consists of a verse
speech by John beginning "Always the following wind of history." This rejected passage, together with the following chorus,
"The Spring unsettles sleeping partnerships," was made familiar
to every (American) schoolboy by Louis Untermeyer in his
Modern British Poetry (1942 and 1950 eds.). In the discarded passage John speaks of the loud voices of his generation,

> Abrupt, untrained, competing with no lie
> Our fathers shouted once.

Their fathers taught them war, love-making, athletic sports, but
did not prepare them for the time

> When to gaze longer and delighted on
> A face or idea be impossible.

And in their acute disillusionment with the world, these young men have a longing to be reduced to the mineral level, where one might see this green world "sterile as moon." In the chorus that follows, the actual approach to sterility is pictured, with references to the industrial decay that followed on the postwar boom, and to the mere "euphoric dreams" which keep men from looking up and saying "I am good." And the chorus ends with a vision of dead armies and a repetition of the death wish:

> Better where no one feels,
> The out-of sight, buried too deep for shafts.

Thus the chorus is organically linked to the preceding speech and does but complete the line of thought started there.

Why the poet turned his face against this first half of what is essentially a single piece, must remain a matter for speculation. Perhaps in 1945, in his growing fondness for tradition, he did not like to reproduce this slur upon the fathers, this suggestion that the present generation had been taught evil doctrine. It was included, among a selection of lyrics from the play in *Some Poems* in 1940, and had appeared, along with the entire text, in *Poems* 1934 and *Selected Poems* 1938. And so it was naturally included, with the entire text, in the *Collected Shorter Poems* in 1950. Its omission would have involved a violation of the integrity of the work. And it seems not unlikely that, in the interval between the two later collections, Auden had come to feel so secure in his new position that he could risk the exposure of his youthful indiscretions, or had even grown tolerant of the abrupt, untrained voices of a generation in reaction, as is normal, against the teachings of their elders.

Apart from the pieces mentioned, there is very little else that could be detached from the text of the play and serve as an independent poem. There are odds and ends of versified dialogue that could not well stand alone. The one exception is a speech of some twenty-eight lines in rhyming couplets assigned to a mysterious character called Man-Woman that has no obvious connection with the action. This Man-Woman is clearly a symbolic personage intended to represent something in the personal life of any man related to his social behavior in the larger context. The terms of the social or moral problem as here given are those of the intimate love life. Perhaps the hyphenated Man-Woman character is meant to make it apply equally to persons of either sex in the heterosexual relation according to the other person involved. Some obstruction or perversion of the relation of the ego to the other seems to be in question in the symbolism itself; and it seems to center in the notion of "self-abuse."

One is aware of psychological subtlety and ingenuity in the management of the erotic symbolism. But one is also aware of considerable confusion in regard to its application to the social theme of the play, and does not know whether this confusion is in the writing or in one's own understanding. Perhaps Auden, reviewing this piece in his maturity, realized the presence of this confusion in the writing or the probability that it would be present for most readers. In any case, one can understand why Auden did not reproduce it in his 1945 collection. It was, however, included in the charade whenever this was given entire, and does accordingly appear in the 1950 collection.

In 1945, as we have seen, *Paid on Both Sides* was represented by a very high percentage of all the detachable pieces of poetry, but was not reprinted in its entirety as a dramatic composition. In 1950 it was restored in its entirety, in spite of its length of more than twenty pages. It thus became for British readers an integral part of the Auden canon. It has little clear ideological significance except as it deprecates mere wars of revenge, which could not be offensive to Auden in any period of his writing.* And it contains

* There are indeed obscure intimations of what later takes more definite shape as a quasi-Marxian position. There are expressions of revolt against the tradition of the fathers and mothers; references to industrial ruin and decadence in the individual and in social relations, and to the heroic quests of men who cross the border and go into "exile." And there are two places in which "the left" suggests a socialist orientation. Most of these appear in passages not reproduced in the 1945 collection: "Always the following wind of history," the Man-Woman speech, and Aaron's speech, "There is no time for peace." We shall see later that Auden was much less on his guard in 1950 against vestigial traces of the old ideology than he was in 1945.

much more excellent poetry than any of the plays that Auden wrote alone or in collaboration with Isherwood.

In 1933 was published *The Dance of Death*. It was reprinted in its entirety in *Poems* 1934. It was not included in *Some Poems* 1940 (fourth impression 1944) nor in either the 1945 or 1950 collections. What is still more striking is that no extract or verse unit was included in either of these canonical collections. And this in spite of the fact that it is about the same length as *Paid on Both Sides* and contains a much higher proportion of verse to prose.

The reasons for this very significant difference in the author's treatment of the two dramatic compositions are obvious. They are both ideological and esthetic, and so intimately bound together that it is hardly possible to consider them separately.

As theater *The Dance of Death* is a sort of modernistic musical show, all song and dance and pantomime with occasional bits of comic dialogue. It is symbolical and didactic. Like the later Auden-Isherwood plays, it is strongly influenced by German experimental drama of the twenties and thirties, and especially by the plays and operas of Bertold Brecht. There is perhaps some suggestion of Brechtian expressionism, but the play conforms more nearly to the types which Brecht labeled epic drama and epic opera. Eric Bentley has referred to the "rather sketchy extravagandas" of Auden and Isherwood as the "best imitations of Brecht," though it is his opinion that Auden, "despite his comedic and poetic brilliance, his borrowings from Eliot and Brecht, and his collaboration with Christopher Isherwood, has not made a dramatist of himself." *

* Mr. Bentley, who, as director, has "created" some of Brecht's dramas in Europe and the United States, has given illuminating accounts of Brecht's theory and stage craft in *The Playwright as Thinker* (Reynal and Hitchcock, 1946) and *In Search of Theater* (Vintage Books, 1954). In *The Playwright as Thinker*, Bentley has reproduced from the notice appended to Brecht's opera *Mahagonny* (1928) the list of contrasting features which differentiate the "epic drama" from the traditional form. More recently Geneviève Serreau, the French translator of Brecht, has traced the stages of Brecht's work and furnished considerable information on its staging in Germany, France, Switzerland, the United States, and England. She has also

Paid on Both Sides AND *The Dance of Death*

The term "epic" serves to signalize the *narrative* character of the new type as opposed to the strict confinement of the well-made play within the limits of the chosen dramatic situation. This goes with the relatively non-naturalistic stagecraft and the want of realism as that term applies to the typical late-nineteenth-century drama. In all stages of Brecht's work, while there is plenty of realism, the drama is not confined to the strict rendering of the present scene; there is always a wider historical reference, and a frequent succession of scenes bound together more by the comprehensive theme than by the particular dramatic situation. Thus we have the technique of interruptions as opposed to the old technique of dramatic concentration and liaison. This lends itself to the effect of *Verfremdung* or "alienation" — the emotional distance set between the author and his subject matter, between the spectator and the story, and even (if possible) between the actor and the character he impersonates. The intention is to keep the spectator from using up all his emotional force through his participation in the drama, and to bring him rather, as a thinking and acting being, to intellectual conclusions that may form a basis for action. Another feature that tends to promote this alienation, at the same time that it entertains the spectator, is the large use of music and incidental songs even in pieces that are not properly operatic. Another contributing factor is the strain of irony in the author's style, signalizing his objectivity and detachment from the characters, which frequently led to the charge of "cynicism" against Brecht, especially in the twenties.

It may be partly this intention of *Verfremdung* that results in the effect of ambiguity which I note in *The Dance of Death* as well as sometimes in the Auden-Isherwood plays. And I should say that in general the Auden-Isherwood cynicism (or irony) is more superficial and smartly "sophisticated" than Brecht's, and that there is in the English plays more of the tone of the saucy cabaret song, and more of casual slapstick and satirical burlesque.

In *The Dance of Death*, the audience make their comments in

given Brecht's second list of contrasting features that differentiate the "epic opera" from the Wagnerian. (*Bertold Brecht Dramaturge*, Paris 1955.)

149

cockney and sometimes join the actors on the stage. The undifferentiated behavior of men in the mass (*Massemensch*) is symbolized in pantomimic action. At one point the cue seems to be taken from Vachel Lindsay's poem-game, "King Solomon and the Queen of Sheba." There the Negro "congregation" enact in pantomime the various parts in support of their leaders representing Solomon and the Queen. "We were the oxen . . . We were the sweethearts . . . We were the swans . . . We were the sailors," etc. In *The Dance of Death*, the cockney audience represent the features of a storm at sea: "We are the lightning. Crash, Fizz. / We are the thunder. Boom . . . We are the rocks," with appropriate noises. The funniest thing in the play, for anyone who has tried to say things right in the German language, is the exchange of elementary idiomatic talk in English phrases that are a literal translation from the German. How goes it then? It goes me well. Comest thou with? Self-understandingly I come (*selbstverständlich*). Thou seest dreadful out (*Du siehst schrecklich aus*).

It was not for nothing that Auden followed up his Oxford training with a stay in Berlin. He learned to lisp in German, and he and Isherwood seem to have made themselves acquainted with the contemporary German stage. It was Isherwood who translated the incidental songs for Brecht's novelistic version of *The Threepenny Opera*, his musical play based on *The Beggar's Opera*.* Auden and Isherwood were doubtless early acquainted with the socialist-pacifist plays of Ernst Toller, author of *Massemensch*, whose lyrics in *No More Peace!* were translated and adapted by Auden in 1937. And it may well have been the example of Brecht that suggested to Auden his activity since 1939 in writing opera librettos, referred to in Chapter 16. Perhaps Auden had also seen performances of the Russian and Swedish ballet.

The central figure in *The Dance of Death* is the solo Dancer, who leads the chorus of bathers in their singing and their athletic

* *Der Dreigroschenroman*, München, n.d.; *A Penny for the Poor*, London, first published 1937. Geneviève Serreau states, rightly or wrongly, that Isherwood made the English translation of Brecht's play, the *Dreigroschenoper* (French, *L'Opéra de quat' sous*), staged in New York by Mendelsohn and Neher in 1937.

exercises with dumbbells and medicine ball. He symbolizes the death wish that Auden considers the dominant motive of European society in the capitalistic age. The Announcer explains at the start the theme of the piece. "We present to you this evening a picture of the decline of a class, of how its members dream of a new life, but secretly desire the old, for there is death in them. We show you that death as a dancer." In the opening chorus the bathers invite their European friends to join in the rites of sunbathing and health-building which are so important for the bourgeoisie in distracting their attention from the more urgent social problems of the time. Then the Dancer does a solo dance "as Sun God, creator and destroyer," while the Announcer warns the audience against this divinity. He may be good for flowers and doves, and tempting to young people in "their green desire," but in succumbing to his wiles, "Perhaps they'll find they've been very mistaken indeed." While the chorus were bathing, the Dancer made away with their clothing, and substituted uniforms from an old musical revue, where the chorus were "Soldiers of the King of Kings." Uniforms suggest another war, and the proletarian audience sing a song, urging people to "seize the factories and run them yourself." They are going to overthrow "the capitalist state." The Manager urges the Dancer to do something to "get us out of this trouble." The Dancer now represents the demagogue, while the Announcer explains that of course "we must have a revolution," but that conditions are not the same here as in Russia, and what we want is "a revolution of Englishmen for Englishmen." "After all, are we not all of one blood, the blood of King Arthur, and Wayland the Smith?" He is down on "the dictatorship of international capital," but very strong for Anglo-Saxon racism. The fickle audience are easily taken in. They begin their revolution by beating up the Jewish manager, and then they assume "ship formation" and sing an extraordinary lyric about how "the ship of England crosses the ocean" and how they are all of one blood, with a chorus beginning "Then hurrah for me and hurrah for you."

They are now all happily on their way to the Promised Land.

Unfortunately a rough storm blows up, everybody is in a panic, and the Dancer himself falls in an epileptic fit. A Doctor forbids him going on with the show; but an influential Sir Edward, with a still more influential friend behind the scenes, persuades the Doctor to let him go on. But he makes it a condition that they shall keep away from all exciting subjects — "No politics, for instance." The actors organize a colony of seekers "true to the inner self." There is a little quarrel over whether the girls shall be admitted to leadership. The men agree that "Man must be the leader whom women must obey. He must go forward into the unknown at dawn, while she waits at home trusting and believing in him," etc. This dispute is accommodated by making the girls into "scenery." And now they sing of the healing joys of simple country life for people out of touch "with flowers and such."

The revolutionary spirit takes a new direction; for now what is needed is "a revolution within." And here we reach the climactic point of the irony. One of the characters declares that he will no longer dance, along with other beautiful youths; for the Eternal Word has no habitation in any such natural things, and whoever would enjoy the Primal love, "must leave behind / All love of his kind / And fly alone to the Alone." In time the chorus are brought around to this mystical substitute for revolution; and what they need now is a Leader or Pilot. The Dancer goes into action as the Pilot, but this time he falls and is paralyzed from the feet up. While he is dying the chorus sing the terms of his testament. He is obviously a symbol of the dying capitalist order, and much orthodox socialist doctrine is worked into their singing. The part of Luther and Calvin in promoting laissez faire in the Protestant world, the enclosing of the commons by "the bourgeois," their bringing the peasants into squalid towns, putting them in factories and doing them down — themes we have encountered before in serious poems of Auden. It all culminates in the couplet:

Then they ruined each other for they didn't know how
They were making the conditions that are killing them now.

However, these people don't yet know they are ruined, and we have a lively song in honor of Alma Mater, or Good Old England, to the tune of "Casey Jones." The Jewish manager has returned and set up "a cosy little night-club just like home," which he calls Alma Mater. Thus we have, in obvious symbolism, the way in which nationalism is supported by self-indulgence, commercialism (the Jewish proprietor), and the old school tie (Alma Mater). Everybody is happy, the girls and boys with their anti-foreign prejudice, the Blackmailers and Coiners and Old Hacks and Trots who know how to make their profit out of the status quo. At the end of the singing, the Dancer is dead. And to bring the curtain down, we have Mr. Karl Marx, welcomed by the Mendelssohn Wedding March, pronouncing the moral: "The instruments of production have been too much for him. He is liquidated," and then leaving the stage to the strains of a Dead March.

Much of this satirical allegory it is impossible to take seriously as representing the author's position, it is spelled out in such copy-book capitals. But there is no other way of taking it unless we are to suppose that the author is on all sides at once. The socialist manifesto of the cockney audience is in terms of a child's game:

> One, two, three, four,
> The last war was a bosses' war.
> Five, six, seven, eight,
> Rise and make a workers' state.

Mr. Karl Marx for the curtain, to the accompaniment of German marching tunes, declaring that the Pilot was liquidated by the instruments of production, is a perfect figure of fun. The recommendation of a mystic among the characters to leave behind all love of one's kind "And fly alone / To the Alone," is not this a point-by-point parody of the position which Auden's detractors accuse him of taking himself in his religious poems from "New Year Letter" on? As regards the gullibility of the populace, the sophistry of demagogues, the childishness of jingoism, the lure of the Führer principle, there is no difficulty. We all agree that those are fair targets for satire. But when it comes to the sharp opposition between capitalism and socialism, between the religious and the secular grounds of action, the satirical intention constantly misfires. The progress of the thought is perfectly clear and unmistakable. We know which side we are supposed to take. But the style of presentation is such that we cannot resist laughing at every position as it is stated.

The causes for this confusion seem simple enough. Auden was trying to get down to the popular level, to make use of the current "myths" that are the common heritage of everybody; to take advantage of the kind of song and dance that draws multitudes to the music hall. But that requires such a simplification of the terms of discourse that it makes a mockery of all serious thinking on matters social, political, or religious.

The other cause for confusion, not unrelated to this, is Auden's inveterate disposition to give unrestrained play to his wit, his sense for the absurd. This made him an unreliable propagandist for socialism, a follower whose support was welcomed, but who could not be altogether trusted by those who were seriously committed to the cause. One wonders whether his continuing penchant for parody and burlesque in his religious poetry may not, in the minds of those seriously committed to Christian faith, make him an equally unreliable partisan there.

In any case, this bald Marxian doctrine, the materialist interpretation of history, and this satirical treatment of mystical faith were sufficient to make *The Dance of Death* unsuitable for inclusion in either the 1945 or the 1950 collection, entirely apart from considerations of style and artistry. There were half a dozen catchy songs that might have been taken by themselves, but none which had any of the imaginative quality of his serious work in this period. There is nothing here of the basic humanity, none of the mysteriously haunting symbolism of the lyrics in *Paid on Both Sides*, no single piece that would be a loss to the body of English poetry. One finds oneself in entire agreement with Auden in the verdict passed by him on this play. Whatever one may think of the ideology that informs the piece, the poet as artist had made *fausse route*; he had taken the wrong turning. And his artistry was not sure enough in this medium to obviate the element of confusion inherent in the ideology itself. It was clearly impossible to assimilate this matter to the tone and substance of his later work.

154

ℂ 13

The Dog beneath the Skin

*T*HE DOG BENEATH THE SKIN (1935) was
the first of three plays written in collaboration with Christopher
Isherwood. I suppose we may assume that it was Auden's assignment to write the verse for these plays. Any poetry written in
whole or in part by Isherwood would naturally be unavailable to
Auden for reprinting in the *Collected Poetry.** *The Dog beneath
the Skin* contains more than two dozen detachable pieces in verse
— songs, choruses, etc. And Auden was able to salvage from this
play five poems for the 1945 collection, as well as a prose sermon.
In the case of this play, the poems (as well as the prose) admitted
to the later collections are even more significant than those rejected. They are particularly interesting as examples of Auden's
ingenuity in fitting old material into the fabric of new thought,
and (to change the figure) particularly challenging to a reader
wishing to compare the flavor of the old wine in the old bottles
with that of the same vintage in its new containers.

The verse pieces in this play are much more diversified in quality and intention than those in *The Dance of Death.* Many passages are in the manner of Gilbert and Sullivan, such as the one
in which the comic notabilities of Pressan Ambo are introduced
by themselves. There is the Vicar:

> Here come I, the Vicar good
> Of Pressan Ambo, it's understood.

* One cannot be certain, of course, that none of the lyrics not reproduced in Auden's collections were in part or in whole the work of Isherwood; but the evidence of style makes this doubtful.

His business is to expound the truth, train the Youth, "and guard the moral order." There is the General who won his fame at Tatra Lakes and who now rules his house like a brigade "with discipline of iron." And there is the General's wife who declares that "Woman, though weak, must do her part," and explains how she has done her utmost to advance throughout the world "the just and English glory." This sort of thing Auden will not perpetuate by inclusion in his *Collected Poetry*.

There is very lively singing by two journalists and the choruses, suggesting how much goes on behind the scenes in political life, in the newspaper world, and in the minutest incidents of ordinary life. In every case they find, of the persons referred to, that "they're in the racket too." There is a financier who sings dolefully of the efforts he makes to be liked, the hospitals he has founded, etc., all in vain, for nowhere can he get anything but nasty looks. Paradise Park is a fool's paradise, the place where you make your imaginary escape from the ills of life — into love, into the poet's solipsism, into the hypochondriac's love of his illness; and it has its own little ditty. The nationalistic advertising slogan "Buy British" is taken off in a cabaret song, "Love British!" In the course of his travels abroad and in England, the hero sees his full share of night life, and the seamy side of things is made comic in songs by the proprietors of cafés in Red Lamp Street. The ambiguity of the word "love" is made comical by waiters in the Nineveh Hotel who provide you with a female companion to your taste, and ask whether you will have her roast or on Japanese toast, "with Sauce Allemagne, sir, / Or stewed in white wine, sir?"

The general corruptness, boredom, and spiritual illness of bourgeois society is thus exhibited with considerable gusto in a succession of tuneful episodes very tenuously held together by a plot that has no greater complication than that of a search for the lost squire of Pressan Ambo, who turns out to be the man who was accompanying the searcher all the while disguised as a dog. Auden is a Greek scholar and trusts us to remember that *cynical* is derived from the Greek word for dog.

At times there turns up some piece in verse that is less in the vein of music-hall lyrics. In one such, two chorus leaders sing of the shadow of night creeping over the face of the earth, favoring sleep for vagrants and losing gamblers and wakefulness for lovers. There is some trace of cynicism here too, but it is somewhat veiled by a note of imaginative pathos. This chorus, "Now through night's caressing grip," was reprinted in *Selected Poems* 1938 and *Some Poems* 1940, and appears, virtually without change, in 1945 as No. XIX of the Songs and Other Musical Pieces. Another not too obviously, if at all, cynical piece has had a more curious history. It is Song No. XXIX, referred to in Chapter 10 as being made up of materials salvaged from an early sonnet in *New Verse*. Within two years of the magazine appearance of this sonnet, the song derived from it was used in *The Dog beneath the Skin*. And there it did take on a satirical or clinical interest not present in either the discarded sonnet or the 1945 song. It is sung by the inmate of a lunatic asylum, by the First Mad Lady! There is, to be sure, nothing specifically crazy about this song. This poor woman is recalling circumstances from her life before "you" had "gone away." Perhaps in the madhouse setting, one might find something suspicious in the "tiny steamer in the bay / Startling summer with its hoot," or still more in "our ugly comic servant / *Who is observant*" (this last phrase was not present in the sonnet). The author was evidently casting about for words to put in the mouth of his Ophelia and these lines came in handy. When, later, they were tucked in among the songs in 1945, they could be used without change, except that we have now an ugly comic servant "who *was* observant"; the experience is relegated to the past, where it serves merely to call up the details of a scene which must have greater evocative power for the author than it can have for the reader.

A poem of much deeper significance is that which bears the title "Legend" in 1950 and "I Shall Be Enchanted" in 1945. This is taken from the first scene of the play, when the chorus is speeding the young hero on his travels. I have referred in Chapter 3 to the slight but meaningful verbal alterations made in 1945 in order to assimilate the thought to the Eros-Agape formula. The chorus

are addressing love, who is to accompany the hero on his pilgrimage, urging this volatile spirit to adjust itself to the various con-
ceptions of love that prevail in different localities. It may be
thought to furnish the key to the whole dramatic composition.
The hero, one gathers, must pass through many phases of love
before he finds in it what he has always wanted, his faithful,
though disenchanted, his *simplest* (in 1945, his *finite*) love. However, I will not undertake to show how this program is carried
out, if it is carried out, in the following musical revue.

But altogether the most loaded with meaning and most imaginatively haunting of the pieces taken over from the play is "The
Witnesses," which in both of the later collections occupies a
strategic position as the final poem in Part I. This is a portion
of the introductory chorus, and is made up of speeches by the
leaders of the two semi-choruses, and a singing duet of the
leaders in unison. This concluding duet is taken from a poem
of Auden's called "The Witnesses," first published in the *Listener* for July 12, 1933, and reprinted in two anthologies: Alida
Monro's *Recent Poetry*, 1933, and Janet Adam Smith's *Poems of
Tomorrow*, 1935. The original poem consists of three parts, all
in the same lively ballad meter. In the play, as in the later collections, Auden retains only the third part. The two first parts are
sheer doggerel; but they have great interest as an early treatment
of themes (the Hero, the Pilgrim, the Exile) to which Auden was
to return many times in his later work. They tell the story of a
very gifted young man who one day said good-by to his mother
and set out on very extensive travels and adventures. He rescued
maidens, overthrew giants, and slew great dragons. But in the end
he came to a desert, and in discouragement sat down between two
black rocks. He there decided that he was not after all "the truly
strong man," and asked to die. His request was granted. All that
remained was to give the moral of the story as a warning to any
others who fancy themselves in the heroic role and do not wish
to die. This was done in the third part, where the Two, guardians
of the gate in the rock, explain that the hero has "disobeyed their
word." Here the image of the two black rocks is abandoned for

that of the "reef" and the "whirlpool" (Scylla and Charybdis?). But as the black rocks were to the left and right of the hero in the desert, so these two guardian spirits are watching you "on your left and on your right."

One is reminded of the famous chorus from *Paid on Both Sides*, "To throw away the key and walk away" ("The Walking Tour"), where we have a similar adventurous going into exile, "following a line with left and right / An altered gradient at another rate." And again there are the Lords of Limit invoked in the poem from 1933 republished in 1945 under the title "Not All the Candidates Pass." These "witnesses," as we have seen in Chapter 5, are they who set "a tabu 'twixt left and right."

In 1945, we may assume, these words "left" and "right" are without political significance, or at any rate do not imply a recommendation of the leftist way. In *The Dog beneath the Skin*, as I shall suggest a little later, they are probably double- or multiple-faceted in their connotations. It was certainly a time — '30, '33, '35 — in which these were for Auden ideologically "hot" words. If we take them in that sense, we must understand them as a warning to steer a course between the reef and the whirlpool, but certainly also with an inclination more to the left than the right. But their reference here is not exclusively or narrowly political. It would seem obvious that in this poem, whether in '33 or '35 or '45, Auden has in mind the great basic problem for any earnest man of discovering the truth that will "save his soul" in some fundamental sense of that phrase. In the parts of the chorus that were added in *The Dog beneath the Skin* we are reminded that these young men tossing on their beds are waiting for "the lot that decides their fate," and that the casting of the lot is in their own hands.

> Look in your heart and see:
> There lies the answer.

This lot and this choice have, it is to be presumed, both a political and a moral character, and the two are not to be separated. If in the young man's heart he "chooses to depart" on this perilous quest, he must walk "the empty selfish journey"

> Between the needless risk
> And the endless safety.

Calling this an "empty selfish journey" is certainly confusing, and can with difficulty be understood, unless we assume that it is a warning of the emptiness and futility of the quest when not undertaken in a selfless spirit. One of the pilgrim's chiefest perils is that of deceptive "expansive dreams," when sailors tell their fish stories,

> The expansive moments of constricted lives,
> In the lighted inn.

The lighted inn is the equivalent of the bar with its mirrors in "September 1, 1939." The "expansive moments of constricted lives" anticipate the "euphoric dream" of those who haunt the bars — "the romantic lie in the brain / Of the sensual man-in-the-street."

This figure of the lighted inn, the fish stories, and the expansive dream is in the duet taken from the doggerel ballad; and it is one of many images that lift this third part of the ballad definitely out of the class of doggerel. The main image of the mysterious Two perpetually watching, from left and right and over the garden wall, is the begetter of a number of related images that build up the shivery atmosphere of mysterious threatening powers, as when behind him the adventurer becomes aware that (as at Dunsinane)

> The woods have come up and are standing round
> In deadly crescent.

Woods have a large place in Auden's imaginative realm of childish fears. Not so poetically pure is the assemblage of hobgoblins:

> the woman in dark glasses, and the hump-backed surgeons,
> And the Scissor Man.

The Scissor Man is perhaps a bit too much out of the nursery. In 1945 Auden gave a mythically more elevated tone by substituting "the hooded women" for "the woman in dark glasses"; but it is doubtful whether the original was not more effective, with its touch of realistic modernism. One of the most effective touches of all is in the dry sinister understatement in the following:

Something is going to fall like rain,
And it won't be flowers.*

It is a curious accident that this poem from the early thirties, by
virtue of its opening line, "Young men late in the night," should
find itself in such a strategic position at the very end of his most
serious group of shorter poems. For it is probably here, so far as
it is possible in any one poem, that we have the very center of
this man's moral endeavor for himself and the message which he
feels bound to deliver to others longing to give spiritual value to
their living. It is only one side of his many-sided nature, and does
not adequately represent the numerous facets of his restless and
unpredictable genius. But it does point to what is probably his
most serious, as it is the most constantly recurring, concern.

If, however, Auden was able in 1945 to incorporate this poem
in the body of his approved work, this was, one suspects, in spite of
connotations which it carried for him in its context in *The Dog
beneath the Skin*. These connotations can fully be apprehended
only when we take into consideration another poetic unit from
the same play which he did not choose to reproduce — that constituted by the semi-choruses of the Epilogue. And the crowding
ambiguities that beset so much of Auden's work might pass unnoticed if we left out of account the earlier poem from which
Auden drew the major part of this Epilogue, and the apparent
modifications of meaning which the earlier verse took on when
it was thus fitted into the text of the play. The earlier piece, called
simply "Poem," appeared in the anthology, the *New Oxford Outlook*, just a year before the publication of *The Dog beneath the
Skin*. The opening lines were identical with those of the Epilogue,
"Love, loath to enter / The suffering winter."

The theme of this poem is Love unwilling to face the winter
weather of disillusionment, betrayal, and all the ugly forms that
this passion may take when fallen upon frustration and perversity.
Love had wished to linger in the halcyon weather of "precocious
charm" and allow itself to be taken in without question by "sum-

* A popular American song in the early twenties had the refrain "It's not
raining rain to me, / It's raining violets."

mer's perfect fraud." But the poet summons the benign principle
to grapple with suffering and degradation, and "among the sterile
prove" its "vigour." So far the play follows the poem, except for
the omission of some forty lines in which the poet develops in
considerable detail the squalid and beastly, the perverse, helpless,
and fear-ridden situation of the lovers who have been caught in
"the stricken grove." This powerful image is taken from Canto
XIII of the Inferno, where those are punished who have died by
their own hands and have "turned themselves to trees," forever
stunted, befouled, and mutilated by the raids of harpies. And then,
in some twenty-five lines not reproduced in the play, he develops
the theme of how Love, turning to "the night-side," being kind to
death, discovers in "each frozen ghost" the possibilities of regeneration, so as to re-educate them, as we might say, and lead them
back from their hell into heaven itself, watching in their faces the
process by which their wintry love grows "into an honest summer." None of this is kept in the play except the reference, there
not explained, to these "ghosts who chose their pain," and the final
lines in which they

> Walk in the great and general light
> In their delight a part of heaven
> Its furniture and choir.

What takes the place of all the omitted lines is the second semi-
chorus, and the final one-line chorus, with its adaptation of the
famous Marxian formula: "To each his need: from each his power."
This final line, of the Epilogue and the play, gives us our clue to
the interpretation of the poem in its revised form, and is our reminder that in the play its original meaning has been substantially
modified — both amplified and delimited. In the second semi-chorus
(all new) the poet is addressing not Love the healer but those
who have witnessed the play. They are adjured to mourn not for
these "ghosts who chose their pain," but for themselves, men who
"cannot make up their minds." They must rouse themselves to the
act of choice if they are to recover from their self-hatred, and find
their place

> Determining not this that we have lately witnessed:
>   but another country.

What they have witnessed is the decadent life of Europe as it exists. "Another country" is that of the sound life, of "disciplined love," which will come into being with the socialist revolution. The word "country" is the same figure as appears in *New Country*, the title of the anthology in which several of Auden's poems were published, a volume of avant-garde and mainly socialist writing.

But in the earlier poem there is, so far as I can see, no reference to the social condition of Europe. At any rate, the poem stands without need of such reference, as a picture of love in its personal aspect, immature, and in some way perverse. Whether it is in the strict sense sexual perversion which the poet has in mind it is difficult to say, for the ambiguity we have noticed in other poems attaches to such dark touches as the "self-regarding hand" and the "honest summer." We are reminded again of the "dishonest path" of the "bachelor mind" and "the isolated dishonest (or personal) life" discussed in Chapter 5. We are reminded of the Freudian view of sexual deviations as characteristic of youth on its way to maturity. "The charm mature" of lovers in the "general light" of heaven is contrasted with the "precocious charm" in which the wintry lovers rejoiced "with unbroken voice." And in the whole context, by association of ideas, the "sterile" lovers suggest forms of love that are not productive of new life. The faithless "summer vows" of the unregenerate lovers, featured in the original poem, might also, in the whole connection, be taken as referring to the unstable relationships reputedly associated at least as much with homosexual as with heterosexual love. At any rate, it is a self-centered "undisciplined" love that leads these miserable lovers into the stricken grove.

Here of course we have the common term between a purely ethical doctrine of love and a doctrine of love as conceived in early Marxian theory. The Humanist, the Socialist, and the Christian can all agree that love should be "disciplined" and regardful of others. And it is doubtless true that Auden when he wrote the original poem was an adherent of Marxist doctrine. There was certainly nothing in that poem inconsistent with Marxist doctrine. But it does not appear to have that particular slant. In the play, by adjustment and manipulation, it was given that slant; and this intention was clinched by the adaptation of the famous slogan in the concluding line. And in the new context, the immature love, the precocious charm, might be taken as "correlatives" of intellectual rather than erotic backwardness. The dream from which the lovers were afraid to wake might represent some old-world pre-Marxian social ideal, and summer's perfect fraud might be the falsity of capitalist theory.

When it came to making up the canon, the original might well have suited the poet's book, unless he had reservations on other grounds than those of political theory. But the poem had already been used in the play, and its form in the play would not be acceptable because of ideological implications. Perhaps Auden had simply forgotten the existence of the earlier version.

And this brings us back to the poems already discussed, which Auden did choose to reproduce in the later collections. The first, from the opening scene, is that in which Love is reminded of the need to steer the young men, and especially the young hero, through the many phases of love characteristic of youth and prevailing in different localities, and so bring him in the end to his faithful and "simplest" love. This we now realize is essentially the same theme as that of the Epilogue in its original and even in its later form. The second of the poems is the set of choruses later called "The Witnesses," with its reference to those critical spirits that are watching the hero from left and right. And so we are confirmed in our assumption that in the play these directional references do indeed have their political intention, and that here the theme of adolescent and mature love is closely associated with the political theme in the earlier chorus from Scene I, "Enter with him / These legends, Love," as well as in the Epilogue, "Love, loath to enter / The suffering winter." If we went so far as to put two and two together, we might arrive at this bald definition of the theme:

The miseries and immaturities of adolescent love may be cured by the more favorable conditions brought about under socialism. Well, it is not quite so simple as that, or rather it is simpler still. It all depends on the individual choices of the young man himself. In the Prologue, he is bidden, "Look in your heart and see: / There lies the answer." In the Epilogue, he is bidden: "Choose therefore that you may recover: both your charity and your / place." Here his place is clearly to be found in the reformed society. And the connection shows that what is intended is not simply a private moral resolution to follow the right ideal of love, but also, and indistinguishable from that, the resolution, the deliberate decision, to espouse the cause of the collectivist state. That would seem to be the affirmative doctrine enunciated in a play mainly devoted to negatives — that is, the satirical representation of bourgeois decadence. And this interpretation is supported by the opening chorus of what I have called the Prologue, "The Summer holds: upon its glittering lake." This introductory part of the Prologue, to which I shall refer later, gives a bird's-eye view of European corruption and decadence. Here the poet tells us that "Man is changed; but not fast enough." As in the Epilogue, immature man is "blithe in the dream / Afraid to wake," we read in the opening chorus:

> In the hour of the Blue Bird and the Bristol Bomber, his
> thoughts are appropriate to the years of the Penny
> Farthing:
>
> He tosses at night who at noonday found no truth.

And immediately after, we read, in a passage later adapted in "The Witnesses":

> The young men in Pressan to-night
> Toss on their beds.

Sex-tortured young men toss on their beds as well as those vainly seeking truth. Everyone knows how closely the personal problem, with its accompanying anxieties, may be bound up with the anxious philosophical problem. It is a theme familiar among psychologists and father confessors, but seldom plainly stated in poetry. What is needed for the resolution of adolescent problems is some kind of conversion. In *The Dog beneath the Skin*, this takes the form of conversion to the socialist faith.

There is one more point that might be made, though here we are certainly groping in the dark. If we are right in thinking we make out, among the shadows of "the stricken grove" and among "the diverse forms" assumed by love in the first-scene chorus, a reference to the deviationist forms of love to which young men are liable, and which sometimes linger on into manhood, we might extend our tentative definition of the theme of the play so as to include this corollary: Even the deviationist forms of love are susceptible of conversion to the standard or "normal" forms under the benign influence of the socialist faith. The poem taken from Scene I is in 1945 given the title "I Shall Be Enchanted," and in the poem, when the hero's "desire of legends tire(s)," he will find love "disenchanted," that is, freed from its evil spell. Here of course the "desire of legends" is, on the ideological level, in its implications, like the lover's cherished dream, the Blue Bird, and "summer's perfect fraud." But there is also the level of the personal and erotic, and the two separate motives are ingeniously (even if somewhat ambiguously) woven together in the composite theme of Love's Coming of Age.

Another possible source of ambiguity is the final image of the redeemed lovers walking "in their delight a part of heaven." This is almost certainly a figure of speech corresponding to the earlier figure of "the stricken grove" in Dante's hell. It does not imply the author's belief in the hell and heaven of Christian faith. But it might be taken for that by an unwary reader not familiar with the ways of the poetic imagination, or one anxious to find in the early poem something to suit his own ideas and aware of the fact that since the poem and the play were written, this poet had become a true believer. And for such a reader color might be given to the more religious interpretation if he had come upon the following interesting statement in John Lehmann's *The Whispering Gallery*, referring to the collaboration of Auden and Isherwood in the writing of their plays: "Christopher told us that he had to keep a sharp eye on Auden to prevent the characters flopping down on their knees on the slightest pretext." Isherwood was evidently more interested in the satirical and comic modes in propagandist drama, whereas Auden wished to emphasize the moral and affirmative elements in their social faith. I don't suppose Isherwood in his figure of speech meant to imply that Auden was turning religious on his hands. If he was, we are caught in a web of contradictions from which we can never hope to extricate ourselves. The ambiguities are thick enough without that. And while some readers may think I have conjured these ambiguities out of thin air, through literal-mindedness and misprision, I can only bid them try to make their own way among these luxuriant growths of doctrine and fancy.

The pieces thus far discussed are not, from the point of view of pure esthetic effectiveness, among Auden's finest poems. They are not so impressive, to my taste, as any one of half a dozen poems in *The Dog beneath the Skin* that the poet has chosen, for inscrutable reasons, to let drop and not include in either of his collections of 1945 and 1950. These are all choruses of somewhat special character — in which he makes a panoramic survey of the actual human scene as it may be observed in large perspective by a traveler in postwar England and Europe. These choruses serve to introduce scenes in the show proper, but they do not form a part of it and do not share in its music-hall liveliness, tunefulness, and slick cynical irony. Neither do they have the marks of the typical Auden poem of the period as we have it in the 1930 and 1936 collections: the staccato movement, the clipped syntax suggestive of Anglo-Saxon verse, the esoteric symbolism, and the riddling enigmatic suggestion of hidden depths of meaning. They are written in free-verse lines of irregular length, unrhymed, sometimes almost prose paragraphs, lending themselves to the listing of parallel illustrative items, as well as to interpretative comment. They have their individual qualities of rhythm and imagery, but fall most nearly under the general type of verse of which Whitman is the most famous exponent, and of which Robinson Jeffers has in this century made the most impressive use. These poems are open and direct in their comment on modern industrial civilization; they have their moments of sneering irony, but this is almost lost in the over-all pathos of the poet's sense of the misery and degradation of life among poor and rich alike.

There is the opening chorus: "The Summer holds: upon its glittering lake / Lie Europe and the islands." Here he shows you first the English village of your predilection – of your fond childish memories – and then goes on from this to the actuality of "barns fallen, fences broken," the farmers' children who have "entered the service of the suburban areas"; then the fancy country villas, and the homes of the rentiers –

> nervous people who never marry
> Live upon dividends in the old-world cottages
> With an animal for friend or a volume of memoirs.

From this he is raised to his general vision of man whose evolution can never keep up with the pace of the changing world, and who cannot find the truth he seeks – "He tosses at night who at noonday found no truth." And so on to the particular village of his dreams and here too

> corruption spreads its peculiar and emphatic odours
> And Life lurks, evil, out of its epoch.

This chorus, together with the following semi-choruses of "The Witnesses," serves as introduction to the opening scene of Act I; and the whole of this was reproduced in his *Selected Poems* of 1938 and in *Some Poems*, 1940. But in 1945 and 1950, he dropped the opening chorus and retained only "The Witnesses." We can certainly say of the opening chorus that it is manly and forceful, and above all deeply feeling. But it does not have in manner quite the "marks" of either the early or the later Auden.

Another chorus reprinted in the *Selected Poems* but not retained in the later collections is that beginning with the long prose paragraph, "You with shooting sticks and cases for field glasses, your limousines parked in a circle," etc. These are the easy middle-class lovers of sport and art. But he takes them on a tram ride through the region of factories and alleys, past the great Power House, with its splendid dynamos and turbines and diesel engines, and then at once into the filthy crowded slums, "wretched and dirty as a run for chickens," with their blighted children and torpid, rotting adults. He is seized with "human pity"

> that life on its narrow littoral so lucky
> Can match against eternity a time so cruel!

From the prevailing despair of slum life he then turns to "the street of some of your dreams" — the impeccable, luxurious interiors "full of Ming vases," and the poor shamefaced, self-deceiving, envy-ridden people there, with their pitiful efforts to find themselves in love ("their magical acts of identification") —

> You may kiss what you like; it has often been kissed before.
> Use what words you wish; they will often be heard again.

Here we have, as never in the music-hall lyrics, and seldom in the real poems, the moral revulsion felt by this young man at the degradation and meaninglessness of what is currently called love; and, rightly or wrongly, this is treated by him as a type-symbol of the degradation and meaninglessness of our industrial age.

One of the longest choruses is that beginning "So, under the local images your blood has conjured, / We show you man caught in the trap of his terror, destroying himself." This is too abstractly expository and analytical to qualify as poetry in the common sense. It has the prophetic eloquence of the man with a gospel, but little of the imaginative appeal of a poet taking his departure from nature or from people. But it is a perfect textbook in the psychological analysis of the motivation that drives people into their several avenues of escape — sickness and crime, good works, asceticism, religion, art, vegetarianism, money making, and the cult of power in its various forms. It is a "must" document for anyone wishing to interpret many obscure passages exhibiting Auden's typical oversimplification of the psychosomatic theory of disease. On the side of poetic art, it bears somewhat the same relation to Auden's better work as Eliot's choruses from "The Rock" bear to "Prufrock," *The Waste Land*, and *Ash-Wednesday*. It concludes with a curious Marxian parody of the passage in *The Waste Land* in which is rendered the threefold gospel of the thunder. In Eliot we are bidden to give, to sympathize, and to control, with appropriate imagery for each. In Auden, we are reminded of our excellent hospitals and schools and bidden Repent; of our precision instruments and bidden Unite; of our great knowledge and power and bidden Act.

The failure of Auden to reprint this piece is not a great loss to poetry; but it does deprive us of what might be of considerable help to the general reader in the understanding of much genuine poetry that he has made available to all.

Three of the choruses begin with a poignant contrast between the happy state of the lower animals and man with his intelligence which has plunged him into a morass of moral bewilderment and desperation. One of these, beginning "Seeding and harvest, the mating of lions," etc., turns out to be an account of our magnificent hospitals and our pitiful way of resorting to disease as escape from our passions: "see passion transformed into rheumatism; rebellion into paralysis; power into a tumour."

The best of these three choruses is the one that the author has wisely chosen to reproduce, beginning "Happy the hare at morning, for she cannot read / The Hunter's waking thoughts." This appears in 1945 as "The Cultural Proposition," in 1950 as "Culture." The poem starts out with an interesting picture of animal and vegetable organisms painlessly going through their life cycle; and then turns to man and the ways he has found "to defend himself from his knowledge." (This helpful explanatory phrase was added by Auden in revision.) There follows an account of man's "places of refuge and the tabernacles of his peace" — of his books and sports and thickets for love-making, his arts and music — "The galleries are full of music, the pianist is storming the keys, the great cellist is crucified over his instrument." And all this so that we may not hear the warnings of the sentinels, the sighs of the poor, and "the thud of their falling bodies / Who with their lives have banished hence the serpent and the faceless insect."

Here, unquestionably, Auden has chosen the best piece, from this miscellaneous and mottled collection, to represent his modern-day version of the prophetic gospel of Ecclesiastes and Jeremiah combined.

"Prothalamion" and the Vicar's Sermon

BUT there were two more pieces from *The Dog beneath the Skin* which Auden chose to reprint in his canonical collections, one in 1950 and one in 1945. And here an old-fashioned reader must confess his inability to comprehend the reasons for the poet's making the decisions he did. The first is a cabaret song from a farcical scene set in a corridor of the Nineveh Hotel. It is in celebration of the wedding of the hero to a shop-window dummy. Auden did not admit this to the 1945 collection; but in 1950 it is not merely admitted under the title "Prothalamion," but, because its opening line begins with a Y, it turns up in a position of special prominence, being placed next to the last in the main body of poems in Part I. It presents us with one of the most puzzling problems we have encountered. For the tonalities of the piece are so mixed, and one might say ambiguous, in effect that we just don't know what to make of it. It is as far as possible from the staid and almost conventionally philosophical style of the two other marriage hymns published by Auden. It is, on its own showing, a hymn celebrating "the union of two loving hearts," and the wedding guests are repeatedly urged to honor this occasion with glasses of champagne. On the overt level it is decidedly "light verse," but underneath one cannot fail to assume a satirical intention. The celebrants are gathered to "honour the god to name whom is to lie." And the erotic phenomena that are passed in review might suggest that most of what goes under the name of love is blasphemy against that godlike spirit.

The poem is in effect a riotous enumeration of all manifestations of the reproductive impulse known to nature — in the mating of birds, the pollination of flowers, the miauling of cats "on the tool-shed roof," and the "dutch-kissing" of boots and slavey on the back stairs. Even the perverse forms taken by the mating instinct when frustrated are brought under the general rubric. There is the vicar leading "the choirboy into a dark corner," and "the son who comes home to-night to his anxious mother." And not merely are the various ways of love given the singer's praise, but a general amnesty is declared on the happy occasion and indulgence asked for the boy caught smoking and the burglar caught breaking into the house; and in this hour of expansive feeling it is hoped that the uncle will "settle his nephew's bill" and that "the nervous lady's table gaucheness" may be "forgiven." By now we know enough about Auden's psychological theories to understand that the nervous lady's gaucheness is a sure sign of repressed sexuality. Considerable attention is given throughout to those repressed and frustrated, those returning alone to their narrow beds, the pale lovers that "have never been touched," and fourteen-year-old boys who are "beginning to realize just what we mean." There is even the cold heart's forlorn wish, "the desire for a desire." In this jolly saturnalia, everyone is encouraged to hope for release and satisfaction. As Auden likes to quote from Blake, "Everything that lives is Holy."

This is where the reader is left who comes upon this poem near the end of Part I in the *Collected Shorter Poems*, and does not know of its context in *The Dog beneath the Skin* and what function it is there supposed to serve. And he must conclude that somehow it was written sincerely in the interests of piety, and its intention was satire of the most obvious sort. In that case it would be a simple *reductio ad absurdum* of all pretensions to goodness, or even decency, in any movement of the animal or vegetable nature. It might have been written by St. Paul in one of his most worried tirades against lechery in all its forms, if it is possible to conceive of St. Paul as descending to irony. But in a writer of Auden's sophistication, the satire is bound to strike in so many directions that it cannot be effective in any one. The loving hearts whose union is here celebrated can hardly have relished the company they are called to keep, or have taken great comfort from the thought that it is better to marry than "burn." They would not enjoy seeing their passion reduced to a mere sexual appetite, on a level with the weeds in the field and the cats on the roof, and even with the perverted forms taken by repressed sexual cravings among vicars and teen-agers.

And so we are brought back to the chorus in *The Dog beneath the Skin* and the scene in the corridors of the Nineveh Hotel where the management of the hotel is feting the marriage of the hero to the store-window dummy. In such a farcical situation we are relieved of our sympathetic disgust in behalf of the married couple, or at least in behalf of the bride. We may even suppose that marriage to a department store dummy may be symbolic of mercenary unions, or unnatural unions, and consequently becomes an item in the satire along with all the other phenomena of sex reviewed in this chorus. The entire episode is one of many in which the authors show up the general rottenness or decadence that underlies the surface blandness of modern European society in a capitalist economy.

But in the 1950 collection Auden tells us nowhere that this poem is to be read in the spirit of an Aristophanic comedy. What he must rely on is the reader's understanding of the poetical technique described by Mr. Spears, in which the author's apparently jolly tone is an ironic mask assumed in order to give greater saliency to the serious satirical intention. The question for a critic is whether in this case the reader can be relied upon to appreciate this technique. The mask of jollity is so convincing that it may easily be mistaken for an at least partial rendering of something in the poet's personal feeling, and in that case it may tend to defeat its own satirical purpose. The implied disapproval of the fertility processes in nature is so sweeping that it includes the mating of birds and flowers, and when it comes to human beings it is difficult to reconcile it with the poet's philosophical position in any stage of his writing. We do not see how as a Christian he can disapprove of holy matrimony; as a favorer of the life force, how he can doubt the benignness of the Freudian Eros. And the mask of joviality in the chorus is so genial that the singers' benevolent wishes include an uncle's settling of his nephew's bill and the land-locked state getting its seaport. A simple-minded reader may think there is no alternative left him but a choice between universal license and ascetic misanthropy.

This is not to deny that the poem is highly interesting and very effective in its special way, representing a complication of feeling that any lively philosophic mind may occasionally be subject to. A broad-minded philosopher may well have moods in which every manisfestation of the life force may be taken simply as something falling within the order of nature and to be indulgently regarded accordingly. And even if a poet, underneath his satirical censure, may be a little in sympathy with the spirit of this "generous hour," even if, in spite of himself, and under the heady influence of the bridal champagne, he has entered a little into the mood he (ironically) invokes, this would simply show that a poet cannot manage all the time to be the mere agent of his didactic mission.

But however much we may wish to excuse the poet for this momentary, unconscious, and involuntary betrayal of his common humanity, we note that he would not admit this poem to his canonical works in 1945. Perhaps in 1950 he was more at ease in Zion, and need not so jealously watch over his tongue. We shall be interested to know what he will do about this poem in 1960.

The other piece chosen for republication (this one in 1945) is in prose. It is a sermon on sin and Satan delivered by the Gilbert and Sullivan Vicar of Pressan Ambo. Pressan Ambo is throughout represented as a stodgy country town, reeking with snobbery, pomposity, hypocrisy, and corruption. It stands for everything which the young squire is in revolt against. The scene in which this sermon is delivered is full of the most obvious satire against the jingoism, militarism, and racism represented by all the respectable people of the town. Plentiful cues are given in advance on how we are to take the Vicar's sermon and on the ends which the newly organized boys' brigade (uniforms designed by the

Vicar) are meant to serve. The curate is briefing the journalists on the program of this ceremonial occasion, including the Vicar's sermon "on Bolshevism and the Devil." The humble curate is clearly out of sympathy with the movement inaugurated by the Vicar and the other notables. Everything manly in him revolts against it, but he does not have the stamina to make his protest heard. The journalists are completely cynical about the whole thing, but prepared to give whatever picture of the proceedings will fall in with mass opinion. One of them is able in advance to strike the very key of the Vicar's harangue. "Standing outside all political parties and factions, for Church, King and State, against communism, terrorism, pacifism and other forms of international anarchy, to protect Religion and succour England in times of national crisis." The curate is amazed at the accuracy of this. "Those are almost exactly the Vicar's own words. However did you know?" And the journalist points out that there is nothing new in this ideological stereotype. "It's the usual, er . . . programme."

The dénouement of the drama comes after the Vicar's sermon, when the long lost squire of Pressan comes out of his dog's skin to denounce his fellow townsmen as "obscene, cruel, hypocritical, mean, vulgar creatures," and to invite those among them who have any decency left to join with him "the army of the other side" — the army, that is, of peace, humane collectivism, and international good will. The satirical intention is heavily underscored in the concluding tableau with stage effects that might have been taken from a morality play. There the respectable people of the community appear in appropriate masks, the General as a bull, the ladies as cats and turkeys, the Vicar as a goat. (The munitions makers remain discreetly in the background.) The General is making a speech, but is drowned out by the animal bellowing of his hearers. "Gestures and cries become more incoherent, bestial and fantastic, until at last all are drowned in deafening military chords."

This is the setting in which the Vicar's sermon on sin is delivered. And apart from the indications of context and dramatic pertinence, we are specifically reminded, in the stage directions, how

175

far the sincerity and sobriety of his intentions are betrayed by the rank emotionality and staginess of his manner. His manner, we are told, grows more and more "histrionic" as he proceeds, and by the time he reaches his climax, "tears pour down his cheeks, saliva runs from his mouth: He has worked himself up into an hysterical frenzy." At the conclusion of his sermon, there is a flourish of bugles, and the lads of Pressan parade in military formation, and listen to a rousing talk from a local lady, whose sons were "murdered" in an earlier war, and who lets them know, among other things, that "You'll learn to kill whoever they tell you to," and "What does it matter to me if you're all murdered?" — that is, so long as her sons are avenged. Then the General makes a speech announcing the marriage of their Patroness to "that well-known munitions manufacturer . . ." Etc.

As for the Vicar's message, it is deliberately rendered in a flashy, meretricious style suitable to the satirical intention — a parody of ecclesiastical baroque in the fabrication of which the author evidently took the keenest relish. One is reminded again of the schoolmaster's tone in the earlier "Address for a Prize-Day," and of the patriotic announcer in "The Dance of Death." "Remember," shouts the Vicar, "God is behind you: Nelson, Henry the Fifth, Shackleton, Julius Caesar. As for the enemy, those rats! they shall skedaddle like a brook; Nature herself is on our side." The first of these two sentences of jingo oratory was indeed too thick even for Auden when it came to republication; and these twelve words were stricken out. But that is all that a close reading will note as missing in the later version. And what is left is all in much the same vein of jeering burlesque. The Vicar is shown as a preacher of superior parts. He is allowed a considerable measure of Auden's own ingenuity in epigram and topical allusion to give intellectual point to his melodrama. Thus in his account of the great historical catastrophe of Satan's rebellion, which was accomplished in all apparent quiet. "No door banged, no dog barked. . . . No judge's sentence had been passed. Basedow's disease had not occurred. Love. Joy. Peace. God. No words but these. No population but angels. And after . . . *the whole lexicon of sin: the sullen proletariat of hell!*" Or again, in the modernistic rendering of Dante's doctrine of the universal movement of love towards God: "All actions and diversions of the people, their greyhound races, their football competitions, their clumsy acts of love, what are they but the pitiful maimed expression of that entire passion, *the positive tropism of the soul to God?*"

The sullen proletariat of hell; the positive tropism of the soul to God: these are indeed formulations worthy of being preserved in any florilegium of pithy sayings, along with the most striking of La Fontaine, of Pascal, Bernard Shaw, or La Rochefoucauld. These are flashes of wit that, in another mood, as in "New Year Letter," might serve to enliven Auden's own serious thought. But in the present connection they inevitably take on the burlesque hue of their surroundings and betray the misguided factitious cleverness of the Vicar.

The sermon begins with an arresting stroke of theatricalism: "What was the weather on Eternity's worst day? And where was that Son of God during the fatal second: pausing before a mirror in an anteroom?" Etc. It ends with a larmoyant evocation of a tired child's dream of heaven. There . . . "Thy saints move happily about their neat, clean houses under the blue sky! . . . Mother is waving from the tiny door! The quilt is turned down in my beautiful blue and gold room! Father, I thank Thee in advance! Everything has been grand! I am coming home!" Here each banal adjective and exclamation point is a touch gleefully added to a Marxist intellectual's parody of a bourgeois Sunday School paradise for Little Lord Fauntleroys.

But the reader may go through this amazing piece, sentence by sentence and sentiment by sentiment, and determine for himself the spirit in which it was composed and designed to be the *pièce de résistance* of this lively musical show. It is a manifest satire on the clergy enlisted in rabble rousing in the interests of nationalism, militarism, and capitalism (represented by the munitions makers — compare the slur on the Vickers firm two years later in "Last Will and Testament").

And yet this very sermon, without the slightest toning down, without the least change of wording or punctuation, except for the omission of one twelve-word sentence, was reproduced as Part IV of the *Collected Poetry* under the title "Depravity: a Sermon," where it was intended to be taken in all seriousness as a work of edification. That it was so intended is shown not merely by the general context in which it stands, along with "New Year Letter," "The Sea and the Mirror," and "For the Time Being." Lest there be any mistake, the author supplies a Note in which he admits that "those who are not professing Christians" may find this sermon meaningless, but proceeds to point out the positive spiritual lessons it conveys. Did he actually turn out for the Vicar so convincing a piece of ecclesiastical spellbinding that, in spite of himself, he was later taken in by it like one of the boys' brigade? It would be as if Defoe had been himself taken in by the planned ironies of *The Shortest Way with the Dissenters*. Or is it just possible that in the case of this sermon the literary artist got the better of the religious teacher: Auden was so pleased with the brilliancy of his performance that he felt he must include this show piece in spite of every risk of misunderstanding? And then at the last moment perhaps, when it was all set up in proof, being struck with belated misgivings, he added the prefatory note in a desperate effort to make it more conformable to good morals and sound doctrine?

What an ordinary reader cannot understand, whether or not he be a professing Christian, is how the same elaborate prose discourse of some 1500 words can be, in 1935, a hilarious burlesque of ecclesiastical rhetoric, hypocrisy, and time-serving, and in 1945 a sober exposition of spiritual truth. It is a question not merely of a shift of opinion by which a man comes to take seriously doctrines, attitudes, and mythological machinery which previously had been for him the object of ridicule. It is a question of radical change of taste, the complete relinquishment of certain esthetic standards in matters of style — as if, in the interval, the author had turned color blind and could no longer distinguish between the modes of burlesque and sincere exalted feeling. It is as if, in accepting the truths of religion, he had felt obliged to embrace along with them whatever he had previously found most unpalatable in certain exemplars of the clerical style.

The only clue to the considerations that might have blinded Auden to the absurdity of this Houdini trick is the following: In the Vicar's sermon the youths of Pressan Ambo are being alerted to the menace of communist diabolism; but every charge brought against communism in 1935 would hold equally well against fascism in 1936. For within a year of the production of this play, fascism had become for Auden the palpable enemy whether to socialism or to any sort of liberal humanism; while in 1945 both fascism and communism were still more unmistakable enemies of the Christian faith which had then taken the place of his earlier socialist-humanist ideology. And so what Auden had written in irony in 1935 might pass for sober gospel truth in 1945, providing only one could overlook the extravagances of the parody style, and ignore the undercutting effect of the original irony.

In Chapter 16 we shall see how in 1936 Auden was lampooning fascist dictatorship in his "Danse Macabre." And there too the Devil came in for much abuse, not because he was setting himself up against Deity (who had not yet seriously entered into Auden's philosophy), but because he was a dangerous rival to fascism. It is personified fascism who in "Danse Macabre" denounces the Devil; for the latter is champion of those democratic freedoms that are so abhorrent to dictators. And the irony of this opposition of powers is such as to make the Devil appear in a sympathetic light quite inappropriate to Christian thinking. For his adversary is a far more odious figure than the Devil, being nothing less than an image of Death himself.

"Danse Macabre" is more than anything else a pacifist manifesto. And the blackest feature of the fascist death-figure is his war-mongering and rabble-rousing nationalism. Thus he is ranged on the same side in the ideological lineup with the Vicar, the Church, the munitions makers, and all the most respectable people of Pressan Ambo. And the parallelism is carried even to the point of making him, like the Vicar, a horrified opponent of sin and "irreverent thinking" in the person of the Devil and his "sullen

179

proletariat." This hearty disapproval of sin fits in well with the poet's later Christian philosophy. But otherwise the terms in which the Vicar spoke in 1935 were better suited to the surely unchristian motives and passions which animated the fascist dictators in Auden's "Danse Macabre" and Toller's *No More Peace!* (see the following chapter), as well as the death-figure and his Mosleyite announcer in *The Dance of Death*. Whereas for the Christian poet of 1945 . . . Bless thee, Bottom! bless thee! thou art translated! It was too much to hope that this piece of ethical and rhetorical skulduggery could be turned to honesty and edification by a mere sprinkling of holy water in a pious moment.

One must suppose that Auden was simply unaware of what he was doing. And that he could be unaware of anything so obvious is our excuse for dwelling on this flagrant case. It is surely symptomatic of some radical and besetting confusion of thought to which he was occasionally subject. Or perhaps one should not speak of confusion of thought but of dramatic versatility. Auden has so mercurial and Protean a nature; he is so brilliant a player of parts: he knows how to change his stage character with the slightest alteration in his costume or make-up. Isherwood has told us of the many hats he wore as a young man and the transformation each hat made in his *persona*. There was the workman's cap with a shiny black peak bought in Berlin, the very broad-brimmed black felt hat; and above all, there was the panama with a black ribbon, "representing, I think, Weston's conception of himself as a lunatic clergyman."

This would not matter if Auden were simply an actor; or rather, it would then be all to the good. But Auden is also, I believe, a serious seeker after truth, sincerely concerned with character and conduct. The difficulty lies in combining the actor and the truth-seeker in the same performance. His trouble seems to be that he is not quite sure at a given moment whether he is preaching the gospel or playing the part of a lunatic clergyman. In this particular case, there seems to have been a total lapse of memory, and he simply placed the panama with a black ribbon on top of the workman's cap with a shiny black peak.

ℂ 15

The Ascent of F6 and *On the Frontier*

*T*HE ASCENT OF F6 (1936) is not, like *The
Dog beneath the Skin*, a set of loosely strung episodes made up
largely of music-hall songs. It has a fairly well defined plot in
which a serious psychological problem is developed in terms of
dramatic action. There is much of the fantastic and "expressionistic" (or non-naturalistic) about it, with metaphysical arguments
between a sort of Tibetan Abbot and a mountain climber, with
apparitions and voices across space, and Demons and mysterious
veiled Figures seen on the mountain top in the midst of hurricane
and thunderstorm, with voices commenting from the stage boxes
to right and left of the stage, and commentaries by singing choruses. Some of the characters also exchange sentiments in blank
verse. And there is even, at the monastery, a chant in a made-up
language supposed to be that of the Himalayan natives. But most
of the verse is decidedly pedestrian. And taken all together, there
is very little between the covers of this book that could be drawn
upon to swell the volume of a poet's work. Auden could find but
two pieces suitable for reprinting. And one of these had to be
eked out with new matter for the occasion.

Such, at any rate, was the situation in 1945. It is true that Auden
or his publishers had earlier tried three pieces of verse from the
play. In the *Selected Poems* (1938) were reprinted a song of Mrs.
Ransom's, "Michael, you shall be renowned," and a rhymed speech
by Mrs. A. In the first of these the mother of the hero is shown
by the theatrical spotlight seated on a darkened stage facing the

audience, carrying on a spectral exchange with her son, now far out at sea on the way to his mountain-climbing exploit. She is assuring him that he need not be afraid, for she is with him now and will be with him on the mountain. We then hear the distant frightened voice of young Ransom telling his mother of the Demon that threatens him. Then follows the song of the mother, in which she assures him that he will overcome the Demon and will be "mine, all mine." She will see that he is not misled. For

> A saint am I and a saint are you,
> It's perfectly, perfectly, perfectly true.

Ransom's exploit, we are to understand, is a kind of false heroism, engendered out of his extreme attachment to his mother, and this scene is highly important in developing the Silver Cord theme. Mrs. Ransom's song is pure doggerel, but dramatically right as a rendering of the perverse sentimentality of the mother. As a separate piece in a volume of poems, it will not stand up, and would simply be a cause of needless perplexity to the reader.

Later in the play comes the speech of Mrs. A on hearing over the radio of the death of one of the mountain climbers. Mr. and Mrs. A represent the ordinary, home-keeping people, suggesting the *petites gens* of Laforgue and of Eliot in *Murder in the Cathedral*, as described by Leonard Unger in *The Man in the Name*. They have no inclination for heroism and do not even care to hear too much about it in others. And yet Mrs. A, in the boredom and emptiness of her own life, feels that the "death of a hero" is "right and splendid." He will be spared the wasting away of his powers, the insulting onset of paralysis, ulcer, sciatica, or cancer, and the waning of passion as

> Beauty sliding from the bone
> Leaves the rigid skeleton.

Here again, this speech is dramatically right as it appears in the play. But it is not in the least Audenesque in style. It is bald and literal and doggerel-rhymed and joggly. In a volume of Auden's poems it would stick out like a sore thumb.

Rather better as poetic art is the interchange in Scene V of Act

II between Mrs. Ransom and the chorus, "Acts of injustice done." Mrs. Ransom's lines are all sentimental and childish, with their dark forests, reindeer, castle towers, and princess's cheek. The remarks of the chorus are concerned with more serious and realistic matters—justice violated, memory beset by fear, a "world turning in the dark," the greatness of Love in the end, and the eternal freedom of choice. This all serves to point up the contrast between the showy falsities of self-regarding sentiment and the stern inspiring realities of an ethic based on true and "disciplined" Love. This might pass in a volume of poems, but it does not bear the sterling mark of the true Auden.

There remain the two pieces that he approved for his *Collected Poetry*. The first of these is what appears in *Another Time* as "Funeral Blues" and as Song No. XXX in the two collections, beginning "Stop all the clocks, cut off the telephone." The first two stanzas are taken from the piece recited by Lord Stagmantle and Lady Isabel at the funeral of Sir James Ransom in the play. But the three last stanzas of that piece in the play were replaced in *Another Time* by two other stanzas that have no relation to the play. The scene in which this piece is found in the play is a strange mixture of allegory and burlesque, at the same time that the dialogue continues to pursue a serious and somewhat mystifying psychological theme. This Sir James Ransom is an extremely unsympathetic character, and we do not share the feelings of sorrow with which the speakers mourn his passing. After his sudden death while playing chess with his brother, the other characters "jostle each other, jump on each others' shoulders to get a better hearing and behave in general like the Marx brothers." It is in such an atmosphere that their speech in verse is recited or perhaps sung; and this accounts for the musical-comedy style of it all.

Auden was, as we have seen, a great one for saving odds and ends from earlier writing that might come in handy in later work. And evidently, some three years after the publication of this play, when casting about for something that might be worked up into a cabaret song for Hedli Anderson, he bethought him of this funeral song and decided that it would do well for a "Funeral

Blues." But the three last stanzas of the original referred too specifically to the circumstances and characters of the play. Besides,
they were inferior in quality and too monotonously lugubrious in
tone. And so he set to work and turned out two stanzas, to take
their place, that would round out the song with a proper sentimental effect. The dead politician now becomes simply some
woman's lover, whose relict, on the loss of her beloved, is sure
that "nothing now can come to any good." The two original
stanzas retained take their imagery from the world of telephones,
airplanes, and traffic cops; the new stanzas take theirs from things
familiar to the old ballads — the sea, the heavenly bodies, and the
points of the compass. They both have an underlying tone of
cosmic disillusion characteristic of the interbellum period. The
two fragments are pieced together without any striking evidence
of their separate origin. They make together a lively composition
in a vein appealing to world-weary modern readers as well as sophisticated nightclub audiences. It is worth preservation, and was
reproduced without alteration in both the later collections.

The other poem reprinted from this play is Song No. II in the
1945 and 1950 collections, "At last the secret is out, as it always
must come in the end." In the play it is sung by the chorus on the
hero's realization that his motives in climbing the mountain had
all along been more than dubious. He has, he says, been a coward
and a prig, and evidently has concluded that his main motive was
jealousy of his brother, Sir James, who was his mother's favorite.
It is not made too clear in the play whether, in the trial that followed his brother's death, a verdict was to be rendered upon him
or upon his mother. (His brother had certainly been guilty of
sending him on this dangerous climb, perhaps to his death, for
equally unsavory motives, including the passion for power.) In
any case, this deeply hidden family secret was now out, and the
chorus could gloat over it as people do gloat over the discovery
of others' secret shames. The chorus stands here, as in Greek
tragedy, for the mass commentary of the community upon the
action of the leading characters. But Auden lends to the fraternity
of gossips more than the Greek tragedians did of malice, *Schaden-*

freude, or relish for the humiliations of others, especially when they are objects of envy.

> The delicious story is ripe to tell to the intimate friend;
> Over the teacups and in the square the tongue has its desire.

This is, I think, the finest of all Auden's many poems in the lighter cynical vein. It reflects all the pleasure we take in the digging out of hidden things, and brings in several of our universally favorite sayings, "still waters run deep," "there's never smoke without fire," "there is always another story, there is more than meets the eye." We all have our guilty secrets, our secret shames; the Two are always watching us "over the garden wall." This complex goes back to our earliest childhood, and accompanies us through life. No one knows this better than Auden, and it is the secret of many of his most poignant effects. The tone is light here, and the instances such as might be found in any detective story. But it rises to moments of haunting beauty, when we have "the scent of the elder bushes" and "the clear voice suddenly singing, high up in the convent wall," and all perfectly worked in with the rest in the general solvent of Auden's sophistication.

On the Frontier (1938) is the least confused and the best constructed dramatically of all Auden's stage pieces whether written by him alone or in collaboration with Isherwood. And it contains decidedly more lyrical units detachable and available for reproduction in a volume of poems. It has very effective workers' songs, prisoners' songs, songs of male and female dancers and leftists, and three distinct songs by groups of soldiers. And there are also passages in verse between the hero and heroine, lovers who have been separated by war between their opposed countries, but who get together in some garden of the spirit and sing of the good life that is to come when better reasons prevail and the wars are over. And yet with all this available material, this is the one play of those written with Isherwood from which Auden has chosen to reproduce nothing whatever in his collected poems.

And the reasons are clear and simple. This is the most unambiguously anti-nationalistic and anti-militaristic of all Auden's writings; and his propaganda is entirely conducted on the level of the overt facts of human society without the remotest reference to the complications of psychology and the transcendentals of religion.

Among literary influences, one of the strongest was doubtless the plays of Ernst Toller, German socialist and revolutionary leader. In the preceding year, as we have seen, Auden had translated and "adapted" the lyrics in *No More Peace!*, the English (or American) version of Toller's *Nie Wieder Friede!* In this "thoughtful comedy," Toller had produced a double-barreled satire on the war-mongering of fascist nationalism under the shallow mask of peaceful intentions. The action is laid partly in heaven, where St. Francis, the paragon of pacifists, is tricked by the militarist Napoleon into provoking a war on earth, but mainly in the city-state of Dunkelstein, whose citizens all bear the names of Old Testament characters. A false rumor of war turns this little state instantaneously from the cult of peace to the more congenial pursuit of war, and from beneficent liberal government to dictatorship under the rule of the hairdresser Cain, set up as Leader by the banker Laban. The Peace Song of the children is readily turned into a War Song with very little change of words; we are reminded of the way the Boy Scouts in *The Dog beneath the Skin* were wrought up by the representatives of industry, army, and clergy, and turned into soldiers eager for war. There is also a lively song in which Laban and Noah summon young men to the "war that will end war," a cynical Financier's Song, an amusing Spy Song, and then — as the war fizzles out — a Song of Socrates, sadly disillusioned in his hopes that Reason would prevail among men, and a Song of Rachel, who acknowledges that the race of man is stupid, but insists that if he would only make the deliberate choice, man could possess the earth and all its fruits.

In the Dictator's Song, Cain makes his followers many attractive promises. He will save them from the dreariness of their little lives, cure their loneliness, give them the clue to history, teach them whom to hate and kill, restore their "unity of will," and above all relieve their headaches by preserving them from the necessity of thinking. Many features of this program are reproduced by Auden in the Commentary to "In Time of War," where the apostles of fascism promise to "halt the flood of thinking," to "confiscate for safety every private sorrow," and assure their followers that their "ignorance will keep off evil," and they shall be "consummated in the General Will."

At the time when he wrote *No More Peace!* Toller had pretty well given up the specific Marxian tenets in his humanistic socialism. The class struggle was played down, for Toller had long since been keenly aware of the evils incident to this doctrine. Under his surface cynicism and his dominant hatred of war, there is a serious vein of faith in the spiritual (though secular) resources of man's nature. The treatment of the whole subject is less baldly socialistic than that of the English authors of *On the Frontier*.

With them their play was mainly a pacifist document, but it was more realistic in its treatment of the economic causes of war and laid more emphasis on the class struggle. It was now 1938, the year when Auden and Isherwood went to China to report on the conflict in which the Chinese were defending themselves against the Japanese invaders. They were very well aware of the threat of fascism, which was for them represented by Japan as well as by Italy, Germany, and Spain. (Auden had been driving an ambulance for Spanish Loyalists the year before.) But for them the fascist cause (the cause of corporate statism as against freedom-founded democracy) was making strong inroads in all the free countries as well as in China — in the Commentary on "In Time of War," Auden specifically names England and "free America," Hungary and France as countries where "thousands believe" (in fascist doctrine), "and millions are half-way to a conviction." In every land the strongest supporters of fascist ideology are the vested interests — financiers, industrialists, the military, and the professional classes most nearly identified with these: the academic intellectuals and the clergy. These play upon the frustrations of the poor and the ignorant; they rouse in them the pride of race and nation, exploit the satisfactions taken in mob aggressiveness; and make their profit out of national rivalries and wars.

The one force that may be depended on to make headway against this fatal drive toward war is that of the workers united in the struggle to throw off the yoke of the exploiters, and to secure justice and peace for themselves and so for all. Their present weapon is the strike, but the time might come when it would be actual fighting. The class struggle is a brush fire lighted to stop the forest fire, the vast conflagration, of national wars.

This is the clear and unqualified teaching of *On the Frontier* from beginning to end. The opening chorus of men and women workers recites the killing labors of the assembly line, with a slave-driving major who wears pointed shoes and calls himself a gent, the baby dying, rent in arrears, pretty women prematurely aged. And it ends with invitations to a meeting tonight, and assurance that the workers will be notified when it's time to strike. The chorus of prisoners tells how industrialists and bankers in comfortable chairs are in control, with a Leader who "will have all our enemies shot." The judges and chaplains recommend obedience to constituted order. The Leader bids them put on his uniform and wave his great flag. The party of order think they are in for a thousand years, but "History, it happens, has other ideas." The party of justice may die by a firing-squad, but there will always be others to take their places. Then

> Truth shall flower and Error explode
> And the people be free then to choose their own road.

The male and female dancers and leftists urge their hearers not to be taken in by deceiving words, but to unite and act. You must learn "to know your friend from your foe." The Westland soldiers sing of the hardships of trench life for the subalterns and the self-indulgent luxury of the officers at G.H.Q. When a bullet struck the sergeant-major who had given the soldiers hell, "Where did it come from? Who can tell?" Later on the fraternizing soldiers of the two opposed camps recite all the humiliations and injustices of a soldier's life, and conclude:

> We're sick of the noise of shot and shell,
> And the whole bloody war can go to hell.

From this summary account of the tenor of these lyrics, a reader unacquainted with the play at first hand might conclude that they are simply a parody of the leftist line deliberately written to make fun of it by persons far to the right. But the play itself, when you read it, makes this supposition untenable. You see how war was brought about by the machinations of fascist-minded manufacturers in league with their puppet Leader, and made possible by the traditional patriotic sentiments of high-minded professional people living in "the Ostnia-Westland Room" on the frontiers between two countries, who by their passive acquiescence provoked the tragedy symbolized by the separation of their children, the hero and heroine of the story.

Auden and Isherwood were, of course, refined and sophisticated intellectuals. They knew that they were simplifying. They were writing a play for leftist audiences, and they were reducing the issues to their barest material elements. Only in the sentiments of the separated lovers do they sound the note of idealism that is so strongly sounded in the Commentary to "In Time of War." What they offer us in the lyrics of this play is the bare bones of the materialist interpretation of history.

This is ingenious propaganda, and perfectly sincere so far as I can see. But as poetry it was not directed at "those pure eyes / And perfet witness of all judging Jove." Auden was perfectly right, on esthetic grounds, in leaving it to the oblivion of a volume out of print. And even more on ideological grounds was he justified in forgetting it when he came to make up his canon in 1945. There was no conceivable way in which it could be assimilated to his later Weltanschauung as he did undertake to assimilate the vicar of Pressan's sermon.

ℭ16

Opera Librettos

AUDEN'S writing for the stage was not confined
to the plays mentioned in the preceding chapters. From as early
as 1937 to as recently as 1956, he has been much occupied from
time to time in writing lyrics for operas and other dramatic compositions involving songs. Such songs were a frequent feature of
the plays of Brecht and Toller, which may have turned Auden's
mind in this direction; and it is natural for one so much interested in the stage in general and opera in particular to associate
himself with eminent composers in the production of work in
which poetry and music go together as more or less equal part-
ners. The reader may be interested to know whether any of the
verse written under these circumstances was considered suitable
for inclusion in his collected poetry.

In 1937, as we have earlier noted, Auden translated and adapted
the lyrics for the American version of Toller's *No More Peace!*,
music by Herbert Muller. In 1939 was performed at Queen's Hall,
London, *Ballad of Heroes*, a sort of cantata by Benjamin Britten,
words by W. H. Auden and Randall Swingler. In 1941 is listed
Paul Bunyan, an opera by Britten, with libretto by Auden. In 1951
was published the libretto done by Auden and Chester Kallman
for *The Rake's Progress*, an opera by Igor Strawinsky. In 1953,
in the anthology *Botteghe Oscure*, appeared "Delia or a Masque
of Night: Libretto for a One Act Opera," by Auden and Kallman. In 1956 was published the libretto for Mozart's *The Magic
Flute* written in English by Auden and Kallman after the German
libretto of Schikaneder and Giesecke.

190

Of these six compositions it is only the first three, which appeared before the collection of 1945, that are strictly relevant to this study. Auden's versions of the songs in Toller's comedy are translations, or at most free adaptations, and naturally none of these was included in the *Collected Poetry*. Of the lyrics in *Paul Bunyan* only three were included in the collections, among the Songs and Other Musical Pieces. Nos. III and XXXII are light, engaging lyrics. No. VII, " 'Gold in the North,' came the blizzard to say," is a tuneful, but essentially tragic, "popular" ballad, recalling some of the sadder phases of American history and life — violence in the early days in San Francisco, the market crash in New York, and what love can do to you in glamorous Alabama. They are all reminders of the ways in which "America can break your heart." This is a fine poem in its kind. It is the sort of poem from his contemporaries with which Dylan Thomas used to open his poetic recitals before coming to his own work. But this opera, though performed at Columbia University in 1941 and copyrighted, was withdrawn before publication, both the poet and the composer considering it unworthy of their artistic ideals.

The *Ballad of Heroes* (score and libretto) is available in published form. The libretto consists of three pieces in verse: the first, for music in Funeral March tempo, written by Swingler, the third, Recitative and Choral, by Auden and Swingler together, and only the second, Scherzo, being the work of Auden alone. This consists of an abbreviated version of a poem first published in the *Listener* for February 17, 1937, then reprinted in *Another Time* in 1940, and finally, with two stanzas omitted, in the collections of 1945 and 1950, under the title "Danse Macabre."

This poem, in its several versions, presents us with an extremely teasing problem in interpretation. In the original and final forms it is a curious but not untypical example of Auden's way of distributing his ironies and telescoping his symbolisms. It is a galloping ballad-like piece in Auden's liveliest music-hall manner, such as those he wrote for *The Dance of Death* and the plays produced in collaboration with Isherwood. The person speaking in the poem is ostensibly one of those heroic deliverers that appear rather often in Auden's writing and are sometimes treated with a considerable tincture of irony. In this case, the deliverer is warning his contemporaries that the time is past for polite parlor discussion, diplomacy, storytelling, and piano playing. For the Devil has "broken parole" and is walking abroad in all sorts of innocent-looking disguises. His triumph would be fatal to the old pleasant way of life; and the speaker is summoning everyone to a crusade against the Devil under his leadership. He is himself the "Fortunate One," the "spoilt Third Son" of romance and fairy tale.

At the start, considering the date, this Devil naturally makes one think of Hitler, who in 1936 had re-established conscription in Germany, was building up a big air fleet, and was destined in 1938 to conclude the Munich pact with Britain and France. Or he might be the Italian or the Spanish dictator, or fascist dictatorship in general.

But, as it turns out, it is not the Devil himself, but his heroic adversary, who is the true representative of lethal war-mongering dictatorship. The Devil is no more for the pretended deliverer than a pretext, a cover for his own nefarious plots. The Devil is, to be sure, the wicked inciter to every private sin, and the world that has shaped under his suggestions is a horrible Sodom and Gomorrah, as well as a world of eating and drinking, buying and selling, of disobedience to authority and irreverent thinking. And it is the hypocritical, moralistic dictator who is destined to bring "liquid fire" and destroy "the cities of human desire." He himself, as befits his godlike station, is to feed on the rarest delicacies, live in a cathedral "with a vacuum cleaner in every room," ride in a platinum car, turn cartwheels in the street, and ring the bells all day.

The irony here is very broad, and rather passes the bounds of plausibility when the speaker informs his beloved victims that his ultimate aim is nothing less than to "rid the earth of the human race." No doubt the author has in mind the transparent inconsistencies and absurdities of the book in which Hitler managed to bamboozle a willing people though it was clear enough to all unprejudiced readers that he was simply a wolf in sheep's clothing.

192

Here at any rate it is clear that the heroic deliverer, while promising to put down sin in the world, is candidly admitting that, for those he is addressing fondly as "dear heart," the campaign to which he invites them means good-by to everything they cherish in life — means, in short, death.

It is here that we begin to realize how the symbolisms are doubling up. For there are many indications in the poem that this dictator-deliverer is another figure for Death, for the death wish operating in modern bourgeois society, as this was spelt out for us by Auden in *The Dance of Death.* He is a distinctively modern bourgeois figure, who proposes to compensate for the loss of the old devilish sins with the vulgar gadgets of modern industrialism, the vacuum cleaners and platinum cars ("conspicuous waste," as in the "theory of the leisure class"). As a rabble rouser, he is an ancient practitioner; we have met him in *Julius Caesar.* His parades and cartwheels and church bells are old stuff, but there are characteristic touches from modern bourgeois democracy.

And we must not overlook the special irony, the multiplied symbolisms (along with the Audenesque ambiguity) in having the warlike dictator so down on "mortal sin." He is down on sin, as he is down on "irreverent thinking," because he is above all concerned with order and unquestioning obedience. And as a representative of Death, he is down on sin because sin is associated with the gratification of natural impulse, and the repression of natural impulse is followed by disease and dissolution, and (again for the dictator) such repression tends to make people meek followers of constituted authority. As for "irreverent thinking," we have noted how, in the Dictator's Song in *No More Peace!* and the propaganda mouthed by fascists in the Commentary to "In Time of War," one of the chief promises of fascist leaders is to relieve their subjects from the headaches incident to the laborious process of thinking. The fascist wants to restore the people to the innocence of children or beasts.

And this is also, we should remember, the wish of those who support and profit by the capitalist system — the great manufacturer of *On the Frontier,* who has the leader on a string, the banker in *No More Peace!* who sets up the barber as ruler, the munitions makers in *The Dog beneath the Skin*, hand in glove with the gentry, the clergy, and the boy scout leaders. For the speaker in "Danse Macabre" may by implication, if not explicitly, have a further symbolic role. He is Death who dominates the modern bourgeoisie; he is fascist Dictatorship; and he is Capitalism itself, dominant in countries which pass for democracies. And if it seems peculiar for an unchristian German dictator to be so down on the Devil, that is not the case with either the Italian or the Spaniard, nor is it in this view the case with the leaders of thought in England and the United States. These are all down on sin and irreverent thinking.

If this seems farfetched, it is because our memories are short, and the allegories of 1937 are hard to decipher in 1957. It might refresh our memories to take a glance at an old periodical which has been called to my attention by a book-loving friend who is an admirer of Auden and collector of Auden items. This is the *Booksellers Quarterly* of May 1939, volume one, number three, edited by Terence Holliday, a man evidently greatly concerned with the freedom of the press, opposed to the forces that threaten this freedom, and hospitable to writers of like mind. Among those featured in this number are such notable names as Albert Maltz, Willem van Loon, Donald Ogden Stewart, Dorothy Parker, and W. H. Auden. These writers are united in their concern over the Nazi censorship of books, including, among others, the works of Alfred Adler, Karl Barth, Edward Beneš, Ernst Cassirer, Benedetto Croce, and Albert Einstein. They are united in their concern over the growth of anti-Semitism in the United States. They are interested in the movement to help get Spanish writers out of concentration camps.

It is evident that this periodical, official journal of the Booksellers Guild of America, was devoted to the cause of democratic freedoms and eager to rally liberal forces against the threat of fascism. Auden's appearance in this company only reminds us of what we know, that he was an earnest and active worker for liberal causes. But there were two items that have a more special relevance to his "Danse Macabre." One is a list, given on request, of seventeen books published between 1912 and 1934 by Bruce Barton, editor of several widely read magazines, congressman, and chairman of the board of Batten, Barton, Durstine, and Osborn, the famous firm of advertising counselors. The remarkable thing about this list is that fully half of these books are on religious subjects — Jesus, St. Paul, and the resurrection of the soul, while the other half is made up of books on financial subjects, life insurance, political subjects, and books whose general character is sufficiently suggested by the title of one of them published in 1920, *It's a Good Old World*. The compiler of this list is ironic in her reference to the "inspirational" character of Barton's writing, "the crass go-getterism" of some of these volumes, and the frequent "appearance of God and Mammon in double harness under the auspices of Mr. Barton's muse." My point in mentioning her note is to remind us of the tendency among liberal writers to associate the exploitation of piety with the exploitation of the proletariat by the leaders of our commercial order. Like the liberator in "Danse Macabre," capitalism in our democracy is down on sin and irreverent thinking.

Still more relevant to "Danse Macabre" is Auden's article on "effective democracy," which was an address delivered by him to the Foreign Correspondents Dinner-Forum in New York on March 16, 1939. Of this address, the editor says, not with too great accuracy, that it is "an eloquent indictment of the Rome-Berlin axis, and a moving appeal for a united front among the democracies." Auden's address is actually an appeal to the so-called democratic nations to bring about real democracy at home before it is too late. The Weimar and Spanish republics were an easy prey to the fascists because they were weak, and they were destroyed by fascism because they were democracies which threatened not only to find their people work, but to guarantee their liberty as well. But "Fascism is not afraid of a political democracy like England, which is not really a democracy at all." England and the United States "are rich, are powerful nations, and the United States, at least, cannot be crushed by foreign intervention, like

Spain. If we can make a decent society in our two countries, we have nothing to fear from the Fascists . . . and it is still just possible that we can. We still have a slight chance." If we are unable to take advantage of this chance ". . . it will not be Germany, it will not be Italy, but our own people who will . . . rise up and sweep us away, and by God, ladies and gentlemen, we shall deserve it."

This earnest appeal for social reorganization at home within the body of the great political democracies is, from a literary point of view, a quite different sort of thing from the high-spirited play of ironies about the multiple-symboled figures of devil and deliverer in the 1937 poem. But it does serve to throw light on the ideology reflected in that poem and enables us to appreciate more of its glancing ironies.

The poem is little subject to the charge of ambiguity by readers thoroughly versed in the ideology and capable of appreciating the ironic method. When I speak of the Audenesque ambiguity in the original "Danse Macabre," I have in mind for one thing the horror that this death image expresses for Sodom and Gomorrah, which are associated with the gratification not of natural but of "unnatural" impulses, and might be expected to come under his special favor. But these too are the work of the Devil, and the oratorical strategy of the righteous Führer is to make the Devil look as black as possible.

For us who read, of course, the net effect of this strategy is to range all our sympathies on the side of the Devil, who, if the speaker stands for Death, must himself stand for Life, and if the speaker stands for tyranny, must stand for freedom. Well, that would appear to be precisely the poet's intention, at least in 1937, in regard to these symbolic figures. Bernard Shaw before him, and some say Milton, had found much to like in Satan. The ambiguities spring, perhaps, from the inherent difficulties of the symbolistic, or allegorical, opposition. It was unfortunate, dramatically, that the Dictator had to be so candid in admitting that he was a Death figure. We do not fall in so readily as our medieval forebears with the dramatic conventions of the morality play.

It is also unfortunate that Sodom and Gomorrah are brought in as typifying that indulgence of natural impulse of which the Devil is sponsor, even though this is done by his odious puritanical defamer. It gives the genial rebel an air of being just a bit too broad-minded, and makes us wonder why on earth the poet allowed himself to drag in this confusing reference to the cities of the plain.

The greater difficulties show themselves, however, in 1939 in the cantata, and in 1945 when we find this poem incorporated in the approved works of Auden. In 1937 the poem was in main intention a pacifist manifesto, and it was the war-mongering, rampant in England as well as in the fascist states, against which the satire is mainly directed, as it was in Toller's *No More Peace!* and in Auden and Isherwood's plays. It is true that Auden had done civilian service with the Republican forces in Spain, and he sympathized with those who went to fight there for the Republic. But they were fighting for peace and liberty and *against* war and tyranny, fomenter of war.

But as the months went by, and in Poland, Austria, and Czecho-slovakia, the warlike threat of Hitler became more and more ominous, Auden must have become increasingly convinced that war was unavoidable and that the forces of freedom must be made ready for the fight with fascism. In '38 Auden and Isherwood had witnessed the agony of China fighting back against the Japanese invaders. The world had witnessed the German annexation of Austria and the Munich pact; and in March 1939 the dissolution of the Czechoslovak state and the occupation of Prague. Hitler was demanding the return of Danzig, Britain and France were pledging their support to Poland in case its independence was threatened.

All these events have had their effect on the poet's attitudes, and the old poem as it appears as part of *Ballad of Heroes* has a radically altered character and *Tendenz*. The old poem was a blast against war-mongering at home or abroad. *Ballad of Heroes* was in effect a call to arms against a foreign threat.

The most curious and puzzling circumstance here is the quite different tone of Auden's New York address, which was presumably written after the composition of the cantata, which was ready for performance on the fifth of April. Auden's New York address was delivered more than two weeks earlier, on March 16, but it required no long preparation, and might well have been affected by later world events than the cantata, events which must have been featured in newspaper headlines within twenty-four hours of their occurrence. It was on March 14 that, under Hitler's pressure, the Czechoslovak federal state was dissolved. On March 15 German troops marched into Bohemia and Moravia, and occupied the great capital city of Prague. And it was on the very day of Auden's address that Bohemia, Moravia, and Slovakia were officially added to the Reich as "protectorates." And yet there is in his address, at least as printed, no slightest reference to the fall of that great liberal democratic nation. It is as if the poet had not yet taken in the significance of these events — had not realized how much nearer they had brought the probability of world war. Perhaps he was deliberately refraining from any remarks that would be sensational or alarming. Or he was simply following the momentum of ideas long held. What still concerns him is the slight chance that the democracies may reform in time and the likelihood that, if they miss this chance, these powers will be overthrown not in international war but by domestic revolution. It is as if the cumulative effect of two years' events had not yet registered with Auden.

And yet already preparations must have been under way for the performance of a musical composition with words which could hardly fail to have the effect of foreshadowing world war and rousing Englishmen to appropriate action.

Ballad of Heroes is no longer pacifist or anti-nationalist — let alone anti-capitalistic — except in a purely nominal way. In the opening and concluding verses, the plain English public at their shop doors are called upon to recognize the greatness of those who go forth from among them "to fight for peace, for liberty, and for you." Up to April 1939 such fighters for peace and liberty had been chiefly volunteers for the Republican armies in Spain; but the Queen's Hall audience must have felt that this appeal was equally in behalf of those destined to fight against fascism in Germany. The *petites gens* who stay at home, with their "life's despair and its evil taste," will have their "power and pride" restored by those like them ridden with fear, hating death and loving life, who go forth to "destroy the destroyer." Beyond the sound of the guns across the hills is heard the murmur of pigeons bringing "secret messages of peace." For these men will be fighting to build love's city and bring to full flower "the dignity of man" (famous phrase from Malraux' *Condition humaine*). In 1937 Auden was translating Toller's scornful song in which the banker of Dunkelstein celebrates "the war that will end war." In 1939 Auden and Swingler are, without irony, singing of British soldiers who "die to make men just."

How then can Auden work into this wholehearted and patriotic *Ballad of Heroes* the sneering ironies of his "Danse Macabre"? He does it by dropping out more than half of that poem, leaving no hint of the central opposition between the relatively harmless Devil and the utterly devilish figure of Dictator-Death. He drops both the speaker's identification of himself as the legendary deliverer and his admission that his aim is to "rid the earth of the human race." He drops out his sermon against the petty life of buying and selling, disobedience to authority and irreverent thinking. He drops out his account of his private luxuries, vacuum cleaners and platinum cars, and his public parades and cartwheels and bell-ringing. Indeed this rabble-rousing Deliverer makes no appearance at all in the cantata unless possibly in the enigmatical reference to the horrors of Sodom and Gomorrah and the unidentified "I" who is to employ liquid fire to "storm the cities of human desire," which in this context really makes no sense. Of course the cantata audience would not make out a tenth part of the words sung, and would not worry much over the precise meaning or relevance of this passage. But for anyone reading the libretto in printed form, it will be quite impossible to determine from what is given here the identity of this "I."

Is it Jehovah, as in the Bible, or is it destiny, or war, or the

199

Devil, or Death, or fascist Dictatorship? And if fascism is meant, then what sense does it make for anyone not thoroughly grounded in the theory of repressions as the cause of disease, insanity, and death? What can even a trained psychologist make of the horror felt by either Death or the Devil or the fascist Dictator at the spectacle of Sodom and Gomorrah? That it is (mainly) fascism the author has in mind is shown by his retention of the lines in which the command to join their crusade comes from "order and trumpet and anger and drum / And power and glory." Actually the general effect of this piece in the cantata is to *identify* or telescope the two figures who were so sharply opposed in the original poem. That makes it simpler and more suitable to the conditions of musical rendering. It would make it go down more readily, too, with the polite audience at Queen's Hall, who might not be converts to the liberal new brand of morality. But the most probable guess of all is that Auden was here simply making thrifty use of as much of the old magazine poem as would meet the requirements of the joint enterprise of music and poetry. Sodom and Gomorrah are imaginatively effective images, and liquid fire and a holocaust of human desires are appropriate enough to a picture of the horrors of war. As for the "I" who utters these prophetic words, poets are always fond of personifying the forces of good and evil operative in history; it made good sense in the original poem; and the author simply did not stop to think of the abysmal confusion into which a critical reader might here be thrown. This is one of the most dismaying examples of the bewildering effect of fitting an old poem into a new and alien context.

As for the contrast between the effect and message of the March 16 address in New York and the April 5 cantata in London, it is natural enough, perhaps, that Auden's reactions to world events should have been of several kinds and that one or another aspect of his thought should have come to the fore according to the special circumstances under which it was made public. In addressing an American audience in March, it may have seemed wiser to stress the basic ideological theme — the urgent need for social reform within the nation in order to make democracy "effective" and forestall revolution. In joining with others in a musical composition to be performed in England in the same early spring, it may have seemed more important to prepare Englishmen for a threatening international struggle with fascism; this might there seem to be a necessary preliminary step toward social reform at home, the building of love's city and restoration of the dignity of man. At any rate, world struggle against fascism — the Devil-Dictator — in which Englishmen would go forth from their homes and die to make men just, was a theme more suitable for musical rendering than the complicated business of social reorganization in the forum of local politics; and the threat of class warfare and social revolution might better be ignored in a cantata to be performed in Queen's Hall, London, in the year 1939. Such are the conditions to which a poet must conform in adjusting old work to new circumstances.

In June 1940 the original poem was restored in its entirety in *Another Time*. That year and especially perhaps the early months of that year, would seem to be a period during which Auden was an indeterminate "double man" — a territory disputed between the evenly matched forces of the old and the new Adam. The poem was brilliant and lively and full of engaging subtleties, and it fell in with the poet's penchant for light ironic verse. It was printed entire. In 1945 it was reproduced without change except for the omission of two stanzas of no great significance one way or the other. They are simply an elaboration of the point that the Devil has many disguises: he may be "a baby that croons in its pram"; he may be a plumber or a doctor or an athlete "superb at ice-hockey." The dropping of these stanzas has obviously no philosophical bearing; the author may have felt that they watered down his theme with unnecessary detail. But otherwise the poem is retained intact, and once again we are faced with the problem of how the poet could reconcile himself to making public at this date a piece so out of key with his religious opinions.

It does involve, to be sure, a satire on fascism, and that is something that might be thought to save it for the purposes of edification. But the opposition between fascism (or Death) and the Devil is still there in all its starkness. And in the comparison the Devil is still a relatively humane and innocuous figure, and the representative of life forces as against the forces of death. He is no wheedling hypocrite or political sophist. He does not share the modern vulgarity of his adversary, or his "democratic" rabble-rousing appeal. If Bourgeois-Fascism-Death is bent on emptying the earth of mortal sin and stifling human desire, then we are sympathetically compelled to take sides with the Devil in favor of sin and desire. If Fascist Death wishes to suppress irreverent (that is, independent) thinking and disloyalty toward the totalitarian regime, then we find ourselves on the side of the Devil in favor of rebellion and liberty of thought.

The strategy of the thing is all wrong for a poet wishing to win us over to the Christian point of view. This is, you may say, a mere fault of miscalculation in the poetic conception, in the dramatic setup that requires us to make a choice between the Devil and the deep blue sea. But this ambiguity was hardly present in the poem as originally conceived and in the context of the earlier unregenerate thinking. The Devil there was really a good fellow and not far wrong in his ethical theory. The fault there, if it was a fault, was in the supersubtlety and overcomplication of the ironies and symbolisms; in supposing that English readers could make sense out of a work that proceeded from assumptions so foreign to their way of thinking. The fault appears when a work intended for the consumption of liberals in the know is made a part of the canon and given the *nihil obstat* of a Christian poet in 1945. And it is hard to conceive how so acute an intelligence could have been oblivious either of the confusions raised by this poem in the mind of the ordinary reader, or of the sufficiently clear but unacceptable interpretation likely to be put upon it by an informed reader who had followed the course of the author's thinking from the start.

The later librettos need not hold us long. They are all readily available in print. The story of *The Rake's Progress* is taken from

Hogarth's celebrated series of pictures, but with many ingenious embellishments — psychological, romantic, and supernatural. Rakewell's pursuit of the gratifications offered by Nature results in a disillusionment and emptiness of spirit worthy of a twentieth-century Don Juan. Instead of an ordinary ugly rich old woman, Rakewell is married, for obscure metaphysical or psychological reasons, to the famous Baba the Turk, who, when her veil is removed, reveals a full and flowing beard. His ruin is accomplished by a faithful Shadow, who gratifies all his desires and then proves to be the Devil in disguise. When the abandoned love of his boyhood comes to visit him in the madhouse at the end, he believes himself to be Adonis and takes her for his ideal Venus; he begs her forgiveness, and his love is purified and his soul redeemed upon his deathbed.

"Delia or a Masque of Night" is an elaborate allegory based on George Peele's *The Old Wives' Tale*, "a pleasant conceited Comedie, Played by the Queene's Majesties players," and printed in 1595. This rude old play is considerably developed and refined upon, with touches added from the Wife of Bath's Tale, from *Macbeth*, and from Renaissance allegorical poetry. It has to do with a brave young knight who comes to save the heroine from her abductor, the sorcerer Sacrapant. There is also an amateur sorcerer, transformed into a bear by the professional. There is an old Crone whom the knight must agree to marry, and so lose his beloved Delia if he is to save her, but who reveals herself in the nick of time as the beautiful Queen of Elfland, alias Nature, alias Diana. There is a magical light which guarantees the immortality of the sorcerer; for none can work to his distress save "a son born motherless." But the knight Orlando proves too much for him when he declares that "born of a mother dead was I." There are comic episodes, and an allegorical pageant in which the characters are Time, Mutability, Toil, Age, Pain, and Death. And the whole piece mirrors the age-long struggle between the powers of Night and Day.

The powers of Dark and Light are again in conflict in *The Magic Flute*; but here a diplomatic reconcilement is brought about between the strenuous idealism of the princely lovers and the less exacting and earthy bent of the comedy rustics, Papageno and Papagena. This was implicit in the original German libretto; and it may well have been this, along with his love for Mozart, and the theme of eternal conflict between Good and Evil, that attracted Auden to this undertaking. But the original libretto involved certain confusions which the English translators have wished to clear up by discreet rearrangements in the order of scenes.

It will be observed that in several of these operatic pieces Auden is dealing with themes which have often engaged him in his more sober poetic compositions — the Quest, the Hero as Deliverer, the Testing and Redemption of the Hero.

It would be going unduly out of our way to attempt a critical appraisal of these musical fantasies, which came too late to be considered for inclusion in Auden's collections in whole or in part. There are traces here and there of the spiritual philosophy and metaphysics of his later years; but these works do not deal directly with the sacred themes of Christianity. These themes, grounded in Biblical lore, are pretty well fixed in traditional authoritative form, and do not invite the free excursions of the modern poetic imagination, though Auden has tried some of them out in "For the Time Being." It is perhaps enough to say that these opera librettos are too inveterately, if somewhat loosely, allegorical, they deal too largely in magical spells and charms, and are too heavily literary in derivation, to be taken very seriously as poetry as it is conceived in our time. Coleridge and Wordsworth would have agreed that they are products of fancy rather than imagination. They do exhibit the virtuosity in handling diverse literary modes that has always characterized Auden. Their style is suited to their conception and to the traditional requirements of the operatic form. In a superficial way they are good imitations of Elizabethan poetry in its lighter vein. Archaisms abound, and word order and naturalness of language are constantly sacrificed to the exigencies of rhyme. They doubtless made good songs, but as poetry they are largely jingles.

They need not be treated with critical solemnity. They have been one means of eking out a poet's slender income. And they represent, let us say, the hobbies of a highly gifted poet — music, Mozart, magic, and all that range of objects and words emanating *numen*, which, as Auden has told us in his Oxford lecture, held fascination for him as a child, and are indeed, in one form or another, the proper subject matter of poetry. The enchantments of faërie and necromantic lore are not often regarded, in serious poetry today, as likely means of evoking religious awe. But they take us back to the imaginative world of childhood, and offer healthful relaxation for the burdened mind of the man of letters.

ℂ17

The Three Long Poems

THE *Collected Poetry* includes three long poems dating from the early forties, "New Year Letter," "The Sea and the Mirror," and "For the Time Being." My undertaking does not call for any lengthy discussion of these works for the simple reason that the author found no occasion for revising any of them or leaving out any portions of them in making up his collection. "New Year Letter" appeared first in the *Atlantic Monthly* in the January and February numbers of 1941, and was republished without any essential alterations, first in the British volume *New Year Letter* and the corresponding American volume *The Double Man* in 1941, and then in the 1945 collection. "The Sea and the Mirror" and "For the Time Being" were published together in the volume entitled *For the Time Being* in 1944, a small portion of "The Sea and the Mirror" having already appeared in the *Partisan Review* in the fall of 1943, and were republished without essential change in the *Collected Poetry*. There was evidently nothing in these poems that was objectionable to the author on philosophical grounds. And he seems to have been well enough satisfied with them as works of literary art to let them stand as they were.

And here I will allow myself to record very briefly my personal impressions of them as literature. "New Year Letter" is, in my opinion, much the best of the three. But it has no pretensions to being a work of imaginative creation, unless perhaps in the sense in which this is true of Pope's "Essay on Man." The poetic imagination is indeed called into play in the peroration or invocation of some thirty-five lines beginning "O Unicorn among the cedars," in which we are reminded somewhat of Eliot's symbolism in "Ash-Wednesday" but very little of Eliot's poetic method. Otherwise this poem of more than 1700 lines of rhyming tetrameters is an informal philosophic dissertation, in which the poet, meeting the challenge of a world caught in the toils of its wickedest war, exposes the errors of rationalism, naturalism, scientism, etc. It is brilliant and witty talk in verse, and gives the author occasion to review his reading in poetry, history, social science, philosophy, and theology, with provocative comments and allusions to everybody from Cotton Mather to Rainer Maria Rilke. It would, together with the notes, be an ideal starting point for a university course in the Humanities or the Philosophy of Religion. In its way it is very well done; it at least has the dash and vigor of poetry; and is very well worth including in his collected works if only for the light it has to throw on the mental process that led to the author's conversion.

The two later poems deal in considerable measure with themes and personages, from Shakespeare and the Bible, that give scope to the poetic imagination. But considered as literary art, they impress me as distinctly inferior to "New Year Letter," and as marking indeed a relatively uninspired interval between Auden's poetry of the thirties and that of the fifties. More than half of "The Sea and the Mirror" (Caliban to the Audience) is a long-winded disquisition in prose on (as I understand it) literary-art-in-an-age-of-naturalistic-unbelief. It is in effect a clever but tiresome parody of the style of Henry James in his famous Prefaces. Perhaps the best thing in it is a reminder of Kafka's *Castle*; here, at the end of a sentence of nearly 150 words, is characterized the dramatist's hope "that, exhausted, ravenous, delayed by fog, mobbed and mauled by a thousand irrelevancies, it has, nevertheless, not forgotten its promise but is still trying desperately to get a connection."

"For the Time Being" is perhaps the least successful of Auden's larger creative efforts. It is a "Christmas Oratorio," and it suffers from the glib falsetto into which Auden so readily falls when he undertakes these artificial operatic forms. It is a sort of first try at *The Age of Anxiety* theme in terms of the Nativity story. But Joseph and the Shepherds and Simeon do not serve him so well as Quant and Emble and Rosetta in their New York bar. His allegorical touches are thinner than the Seven Ages and the Seven Stages of the later more consistently developed fable. The lyrical verse is sing-song and flimsy as operatic libretto. The characters and situations lack imaginative substance. This you feel most strongly if you put them alongside of Eliot's "Journey of the Magi" and "A Song for Simeon," from which he may have taken suggestions. Auden's treatment is more pretentious, less simple, and his scenes less well realized in concrete detail. Everything in the fable is a vehicle for the strained paradoxes of theological metaphysics. "Space is the Whom our loves are needed by, / Time is the choice of How to love and Why." Eliot and the Existentialists are all about us in the wings. Auden's desert and garden are pale echoes of Eliot's famous symbolic creations. Eliot's moveless center (from Aristotle and Dante) is baldly invoked and given a smart new turn: "O where is that immortal and nameless Centre from which our points of / Definition and death are equi-distant?" Kierkegaard is here with his paradoxes: "The Real is what will strike you as really absurd"; "O where is the garden of Being that is only known in Existence / As the command to be never there . . ."

There is a good deal of Hamlet in modern dress. Thus we have Joseph: "My shoes were shined, my pants were cleaned and pressed"; "The bar was gay, the lighting well designed." Eliot does not have to resort to this kind of thing to make us realize that his Magi were men like us. This reaches its climax in the fugal-chorus in which Caesar is ironically magnified as the triumphant ruler of the Seven Kingdoms. Here is allegory in its baldest form, along with ironic sarcasm laid on with a trowel, with the kind of humor that consists in making the ancients employ the terms of modern Philistia, and even a seasoning of the Jabberwocky that was to be so generously used in *The Age of Anxiety*. There is the Kingdom of Abstract Ideas: "Instead of inflexions and accents / There are prepositions and word-order." There is the Kingdom of Natural Cause: "Instead of reciting prayers, we note pointer-readings." In the Kingdom of Credit Exchange, "Instead of My Neighbour, there is Our Customers; / Instead of Country Fair, there is World Market." In the Kingdom of Inorganic Giants (machinery?), "When we want to go anywhere, They carry us." In the Kingdom of the Organic Dwarfs (rationalization?), "Last night it was Ouch-Ouch, tonight it is Yum-Yum." And finally, in the democratic Kingdom of Popular Soul, "When he says, You are wretched, we cry. / When he says, It is true, every one believes it." Thus the poet brings his assorted artillery of wit to bear, and in one fell swoop disposes of all his pet peeves. Perhaps the best piece of writing by classical standards is the long prose meditation of Herod on the dangers threatening civilization from the reputed birth of a Son of God. He is the truly enlightened ruler, and much disturbed that such a responsibility should be laid on him. He ends up in bewildered complaint: "I've tried to be good. I brush my teeth every night. I haven't had sex for a month. I object. I'm a liberal. I want every one to be happy. I wish I'd never been born."

The song of the soldiers that follows is very much in the vein of similar songs in the socialist-pacifist plays, only more sophisticated, as befits the more transcendental character of his theme. And this brings us to the realization that his undertaking in this oratorio is very similar to that in the earlier plays, and his performance on the whole not very unlike in quality. In both cases he is making propaganda for a cause and suiting his style to that.

Auden was by nature drawn to the footlights, and he had considerable talents for what we might call the intellectual variety show. But he was also deeply serious in his pursuit and promulgation of truth. And it was when he took himself most seriously as a promoter of truth that he was the least serious in the service of the Muse. In 1945 he could look with critical objectivity on the profane propaganda of the thirties. But in his Christmas oratorio his propaganda was for a sacred cause and the cause that his heart was in at the time he made his collection. He could not apply the same critical standards to this work, and was accordingly content to reproduce it in its entirety.

ℂ 18

Collected Shorter Poems

THE Auden canon for poems published up to 1945 was pretty well established by the *Collected Poetry*. But something further must be said about the *Collected Shorter Poems*, which corresponds to the American collection so far as the shorter poems are concerned.

The British collection does not include anything from *The Double Man* (1941), or, in its British title, *New Year Letter*. "New Year Letter," the title poem of that volume, is too long to qualify. And the author fails to republish either the Prologue or the Epilogue, entitled, respectively, in 1945, "Spring 1940" and "Autumn 1940." Nor does he republish any of the twenty sonnets which in *The Double Man* comprise "The Quest," nor any of the nine pieces in verse which were interspersed among Auden's prose notes to "New Year Letter." *

Naturally, again, the 1950 collection does not include the other long poems in the 1945 collection, "The Sea and the Mirror," and "For the Time Being: A Christmas Oratorio," nor either of the longish *prose* pieces, "Letter to a Wound" (from *The Orators*) and "Depravity: A Sermon" (from *The Dog beneath the Skin*).

What 1950 does include is short poems from the following volumes: *The Orators* (1932), *Poems* (1930, 1933), *Look, Stranger!* (1936; same as the American volume *On this Island*, 1937), *Journey to a War* (1939), and *Another Time* (1940). It also includes

---

* Their titles in 1945 are as follows: "The Labyrinth," "We're Late," "True Enough," "The Diaspora," "For the Last Time," "Montaigne," "Blessed Event," "Aera sub Lege," "Luther."

the whole of the charade *Paid on Both Sides* (from *Poems* 1933, 1930), and a few odd pieces in verse from the Auden-Isherwood plays and from Auden's opera *Paul Bunyan* and the Auden-MacNeice *Letters from Iceland* (1937). It also includes the fourteen poems starred by the poet in 1945 to indicate that they were then published for the first time in book form. Curiously enough the stars are continued in 1950 with the same footnote, though obviously they had already been published in book form, in 1945.

Except then for the poems mentioned above as not included, *Collected Shorter Poems* makes up for the British reader the Auden canon as *Collected Poetry* does for the American reader. And it is a matter of interest how far the two collections are in agreement where we have found revisions made in 1945 from the text of earlier published versions of the poems, stanzas omitted, or entire poems eliminated. In a careful comparison of the two texts in all such cases, I have found that where 1945 differs from earlier versions, 1950 agrees with 1945 even down to the least important punctuation mark.* I have also compared the fourteen poems starred in 1945 and 1950, and in only one case do I find any variation, involving a printer's error in one or the other text.† Of the fourteen starred poems I have found the originals of only four in previous magazine or anthology versions. "To You Simply" appeared originally in the anthology *New Signatures* in 1932. In 1945 two lines were left out of the third stanza for some inscrut-

* I have noted three variations of 1950 from 1945, which represent obvious misprints in the later text. In Song XXXI, "That night when joy began," in the eighth line, "grows credulous of peace" (identical in *On This Island*) is in 1950 misread, "*crows* credulous of peace." In Sonnet XXII, "In Time of War," 1945, and *Journey to a War* both have the correct French in "il y a de la joie," where 1950 has the defective "Il y de la joie." Sonnet XIII, 1950, has "mourning" in the phrase "the morning's injured weeping."

† In "Christmas 1940" the sixth stanza ends in 1945 with a reference to how the real world "of self-enduring instants may endure / Its final metamorphosis and pass / Into invisibility at last." In the last line, 1950 has "visibility" in place of "invisibility." The passage occurs in the discussion of a very fine point in religious metaphysics; and I would not undertake to say which of these opposed readings better suits the position taken in the poem. I incline to think the change is a deliberate correction of a misprint.

able reason,* commas added here and there, and capitals dropped from the pronoun "you." In all these changes 1950 faithfully follows 1945 except for one comma. "Kairos and Logos" appeared in the *Southern Review* in the spring number 1941. The only variations in 1945 were in minute matters of spelling and still less significant matters of punctuation. In all these 1950 is in strict agreement. "Canzone" appeared in the *Partisan Review* in the September–October number. I find no variation whatever in either 1945 or 1950.

As for stanzas omitted in 1945 from poems retained, in every instance noted of such omissions, the same stanzas are still absent in 1950. "At the Grave of Henry James" appeared in the *Partisan Review* for July–August 1941. We have seen in Chapter 5 that three important six-line stanzas were omitted in 1945 from this original version of the poem. Also one word was altered, more than a dozen changes of punctuation and several alterations were made in regard to the capitalization of personified abstractions. In all of these changes 1950 follows 1945 with absolute faithfulness.

When it comes to entire poems in earlier volumes of Auden's poems rejected in 1945, 1950 generally follows the earlier collection. In the case of "Always the following wind of history," not reproduced in 1945, this is part of *Paid on Both Sides*; and evidently whatever reasons led Auden to leave it out of his first collection when it was a question of choice among separate individual pieces from that charade, they did not appear strong enough to justify him in interrupting the continuity of this dramatic composition when giving it as a whole in the later collection.

With more than a dozen of the poems in 1945, the titles are changed in 1950, but without alteration of their text or character. Sometimes the titles are simplified and shortened. "The Cultural Presupposition" becomes "Culture." "Please Make Yourself at Home" becomes "Like a Vocation." "As Well as Can Be Expected" becomes "Taller To-day." "We all Make Mistakes" becomes "A Free One." Where "September 1, 1939" is changed to

---

* Second line: "Nor the ghost houseless"; fourth line: "Nor the tongue listless."

"1st September, 1939," we simply have an adaptation to British usage. "Something Is Bound to Happen" becomes "The Wanderer." This is the famous poem beginning "Doom is dark and deeper than any sea-dingle," and the new title is perhaps intended to remind us of the likewise famous Anglo-Saxon poem of the same name which strongly influenced Auden.*

These changes of title shed no further light on the textual revisions and eliminations which are the subject of this monograph. But they do serve to add to the general confusion that besets a study of Auden's work. Already in 1945 it was hard enough to identify Auden's poems by title. Now an additional bar to understanding is set up between English and American readers when they wish to refer to one of Auden's poems. But there is one mitigating circumstance: 1950 has an index of first lines, and the American reader with 1945 before him can readily ascertain the first line of a poem and look up its title in 1950 — if he also has a copy of 1950!

The new British titles are most often a distinct improvement over the American ones of 1945. As a young man Auden was of the opinion that poems should have no titles. They were presumably works of art in a class with the abstractions of certain modern painters, or better, with musical compositions distinguished only by key and opus number (and we have in poetry no equivalent for the musical key). The danger in a title is that it too greatly limits, and may even misrepresent, the purport of the poem. This danger was certainly exemplified over and over again in the titles bestowed by Auden in 1945 on the nameless

---

* Auden did reading in Middle English as well as in Old English while at Oxford. The first line of this poem echoes a Middle English homily, in which God's judgments (domes) are spoken of as secret and deeper than any sea dingle (the derne beoth and deopre then ani sea dingle). See Morton W. Bloomfield, in *Modern Language Notes*, December 1948, pp. 548–52.

Other titles altered in 1950 are the following: "Are You There?" to "Alone"; "As We Like It" to "Our City"; "Do Be Careful" to "Between Adventure"; "In Father's Footsteps" to "Our Hunting Fathers"; "I Shall Be Enchanted" to "Legend"; "Make Up Your Mind" to "Easy Knowledge"; "But I Can't" to "If I Could Tell You"; "Pur" to "Like a Dream"; "Two's Company" to "Never Stronger"; "What Do You Think?" to "The Hard Question."

poems from earlier volumes. These titles were often arresting enough in themselves — proverbs and piquant colloquial phrases — but they all too often give a facetious or commonplace air to poems which did not originally have this and cannot be made to have it without serious violation of their poetical essence and value. When the clowning spirit in Auden takes over, the reader gets off to a wrong start and has great difficulty in reading the poem in the spirit in which it was written. The 1950 titles often restore the poem to something like its original tone. But the chances are that the 1945 titles will stick, at least for that large part of the reading public that gets its books from New York instead of London.

One more point of useful information in this connection. In 1945 pieces taken from *Paid on Both Sides* have their own titles, whereas anyone wishing to look them up in 1950 would not know where to look unless he already knew that they come from the charade, since they occur in the unbroken text of that drama, and are not listed in the index of first lines.

Another point more important for our study. In both collections poems of various dates taken from earlier volumes are thrown together without regard to temporal sequence, subject matter, style, theme, or progress of thought. But in both collections the order of the individual short poems is alphabetical, based on the first word of the first line. Accordingly, in Part I ("Poems") in 1950, allowing for the occasional intrusion of poems from earlier publications retained in 1950 but not in 1945, and for the absence here of poems taken from *Paid on Both Sides*, and others taken from the "New Year Letter" volume the poems are run in the same order in the two collections. Similarly in Part III (Songs and Other Musical Pieces), where the poems have no titles, they follow in the same order with the same numbering, except that No. XXXIII, being taken from *Paid on Both Sides*, is not included in this part in 1950, and the succeeding five poems have a correspondingly lower number. The sonnets and commentary of "In Time of War," as in 1945, occupy a part to themselves, VII in 1945, IV in 1950.

From all this the inference is clear enough: In publishing the *Collected Shorter Poems*, Auden or his publisher used the texts of the several poems as they appeared in the *Collected Poetry*, either because they were more conveniently available, or because Auden wished them to be regarded as canonical. However, presumably for reasons having to do with publishers' rights or policy, he included nothing whatever from *The Double Man*; and he did include the full text of *Paid on Both Sides*. As for the other poems excluded in their entirety, he followed in 1950 the line taken in 1945.

But here he made four notable exceptions. In the case of three considerable poems from *On This Island* rejected by him in '45, his decision was to reprint them and thus, so to speak, restore them to the canon. And he added one more considerable poem not approved in '45, made up from a chorus in *The Dog beneath the Skin*. This "Prothalamion" we have discussed at some length in Chapter 14. It would appear that he had rediscovered it in the interval since 1945, or had found merits in it not before discerned. Indeed, it might seem that in '45 he had himself sensed that ambiguity in the final import of the poem which the ordinary reader may continue to feel. He might have been in doubt whether to class it among his sacred or profane work. But with the lapse of time and the further settlement of the poet in the secure convictions of his maturity, his awareness of any dubious implications of the poem may have grown dim. He may have come to see how, in proper company, it might be so taken as to serve for edification. For the satirical representation of the immoral and the unsound is the left wing of a poet's forces marshaled in behalf of the right and noble.

Of the poems from *On This Island* rejected in 1945, one is that addressed to Christopher Isherwood, No. XXX, which he now reprinted under the title of "Birthday Poem." I have noted earlier, along with possible reasons for discarding this piece, other considerations that favored its retention. And it is easy to imagine how the mellowing influence of time may have made the author more ready to admit the autobiographical references and bring back in circulation this tribute to an old friend and literary collaborator.

Another of the restored poems from *On This Island* is No. XV, now reprinted under the title "Two Worlds." This poem we have discussed in Chapter 6. Here again we may postulate the mellowing influence of time. Auden had long since cleared himself of any involvement in "the contest of the Whites with our Reds," or of conspiratorial activities in the socialist underground. He might well consider that his youthful errors of the mid-thirties had come under the statute of limitations. Besides, as he may have considered, the final emphasis of the poem is less on the partisan passions that divide men than on the deep-rooted "wish to be one" that promises to unite them whether in time or eternity.

No. XV was reproduced in "Two Worlds" without variation except for two minor changes which must almost certainly be ascribed to printer's errors. In the seventh stanza reference is made to those

> Who within earshot of the ungovernable sea
> Grow set in their ways.

The 1950 volume has "Who within *the* earshot of the ungovernable sea." That is a violation of settled English idiom that Auden would never be guilty of, with his propensity to leave out articles even when they are conventionally called for. In the ninth stanza there is reference to those who

> May, by circumstance linked
> More clearly act our thought.

The 1950 volume has here an intrusive "s" that sounds more like the printer than the poet. My assumption is that Auden made absolutely no alterations in the text of this poem as it stands in the 1936 version.

Then finally there is No. XVII, eliminated in 1945 and restored in 1950 under the title "The Malverns," beginning "Here on the cropped grass of the narrow ridge I stand." I have noted in this poem what might have been for the mature Auden mitigating features. Perhaps it was his definite identification of the enemy as a foreign statism rather than a native bourgeoisie that reconciled him to this poem and led him to restore it in the later collection. Only, in doing so, he made a compromise with his earlier policy of complete elimination, not reproducing the poem entire, but cutting out seven stanzas in a row, or one full page out of five in the original text.

And here he lands the curious student in considerable perplexity, for what he cut out would seem to be more conformable to his approved views than much of what he retained. He retained the slighting references to Church and its worship — the luxury liners laden with souls, the high thin continuous worship of the self-absorbed, and the medieval monks who fell prey to "angel assassins." He left out his recommendation of a "disciplined love" as alone capable of rightly employing the engines of modern industry and warfare, his warning against materialism, the denial of liberty, and the psychological malady of the death wish —

> the will of the insane to suffer
> By which since we could not live we gladly died.

I cannot find anything in the rejected stanzas that might have seemed to the mature Auden a cause of offense, unless, just possibly, the flat statement made by the bones of war that

> the major cause of our collapse
> Was a distortion in the human plastic by luxury produced.

This might have seemed to the later Auden too baldly materialistic or deterministic in its account of how human character is "conditioned." Or perhaps again, the mere appeal to a humanistic "disciplined love" for salvation did not seem to him to suit his later pattern of contrast between the secular Eros and the divine Agape. And since the passage of seven stanzas in which these items are embedded constituted a single continuous dramatic utterance (by the "bones of war"), he may have thought it most convenient to drop the whole thing.

Still another hypothesis may be entertained as to the poet's reasons for cutting out these stanzas. The passage just quoted assigning "a distortion in the human plastic by luxury produced" as "the major cause of our collapse" might be objected to on artistic as well as on philosophical grounds. And it so happens that it *was* objected to on artisitc grounds by Randall Jarrell in the *Southern Review* essay already referred to. "Auden's effective rhetorical use of abstract diction," wrote Mr. Jarrell, "sometimes degenerates, in the later poems, into the flatness and vagueness, the essayistic deadness, of bad prose." And he instanced this very passage as "bad enough," though not quite so bad as things in the later poems. I have given reasons for assuming that Mr. Auden would have read this article when it appeared in 1941. And it seems not unlikely that Mr. Jarrell's criticism may in this case have struck home, and that Auden sacrificed these seven stanzas in order to get rid of the rhetorical abstraction that gave offense.

But there is still another possible artistic consideration that might have led to the omission of these seven stanzas. They are cast in a different verse-and-stanza form from the rest of the poem. The poem as a whole is in elaborate eleven-line stanzas with lines of varying lengths, such as were affected by seventeenth-century writers of odes. The rejected page is in three-line stanzas of five-accent lines ending with one of four lines, similar to the Italian terza rima but without rhymes. It may have been a sheer craftsman's scruple that led the author to dispense with this portion of the poem.

The *Collected Poetry* of 1945, then, may be considered the comprehensive authorized version of Auden's poems down to 1950, with this exception: in the *Collected Shorter Poems* of 1950, the four poems last discussed were restored to the approved canon of his poetical works.

ℂ19

A Summary of Findings and Conclusions

M Y AIM has been, first, to present the facts in regard to the revisions made by Auden in his poems when preparing the text of his *Collected Poetry* of 1945 — verbal alterations, the cutting out of passages of some length in many of them, and the entire elimination of others; and then, secondly, to determine, so far as possible, the considerations that probably moved him to make those revisions and eliminations. I have also wished to determine how far in the *Collected Shorter Poems* of 1950 Auden followed the text of the 1945 collection, and what probable considerations moved him to make the very few variations that he did from the earlier text.

It appears that, in all three categories, his probable reasons for these changes and eliminations were about equally divided between considerations of artistry and considerations having to do with his political, social, and religious philosophy. But very often the two types of reasons went hand in hand, so that it is impossible to assign a given case solely to one or the other category. Thus during his strongly Marxian phase, the brashness with which the young convert to socialism urged his propaganda must itself have seemed to the mature Auden to be a fault in taste and a violation of artistic standards. And the same consideration was presumably present when he left in the discard certain of his poems in lighter vein where his vivid sense for comedy led him somewhat beyond the bounds of propriety.

In some cases, as shown in the first, third, fourth, and fifth chapters, verbal alterations seem to have been made and passages cut out in order to make the text conform more to the social and religious philosophy held by the author in 1945 instead of that prevailing with him at the date of composition. In other cases, the alterations and omissions seem to have been made in order to give greater precision and imaginative effectiveness to the poem. In a number of early poems, full of reformist zeal, psychological insight, and intriguing symbolism, the main substance could be saved and made acceptable to the mature poet by the expunging of a few stanzas in which the Marxian line was too closely followed, or the references to reverend institutions and individuals were too disrespectful, or the autobiographical references too intimate. In others, as will be seen in the Supplementary Notes, his objection to the passages eliminated may very well have been on the grounds of their relative dullness or diffuseness. For while dullness and diffuseness are not generally characteristic of Auden, he does give the impression of engaging frequently in improvisation, and his work did sometimes require pruning down and tightening up to give it full effectiveness.

The same distribution of probable reasons holds for the score of poems previously published by Auden in book form (not including the five plays), but not reproduced in the 1945 collection. There were more than half a dozen important pieces in *The Orators* (1932), the 1933 *Poems*, and the 1936 *On This Island* which were eliminated obviously because they were so blatantly propagandistic and revolutionary, the picture of industrial ruin and moral degeneracy in Britain was so exaggerated, the prophecies of revolution so confident, because the doctrine of the class struggle led the young poet into so much abusive treatment of all types among the bourgeoisie, including scholars and churchmen, and the gleeful enthusiasm of the intellectual gang-leader led him to so much vivacity in his attack on the rival gang, represented by the "Cambridge ulcer." Along with this, too, there were indiscreet references to sexual deviations among businessmen, clergymen, and intellectuals in both camps.

But there were also poems of this period which Auden discarded simply, perhaps, because they seemed to him too slight or bald, too indeterminate in effect, or too impenetrably dark. The number of these is considerably increased if we take into account the seven pieces from the 1930 edition of his poems which he replaced with others in 1933 and then left them behind for good. These latter I discuss in Appendix II. And there were poems of a later date, collected in *Another Time*, belonging to the general category of "light verse," that did not survive that volume. Mr. Auden must be, in personal conversation with congenial companions, extremely witty and entertaining. His mind is notable for range and vivacity, and he has a lively comic sense which can be turned upon any subject, even subjects where to be amusing is to be skating on thin ice. He has a natural talent for ballad-like poetry treating, with airy and flippant satire, subjects as emotionally delicate and loaded as love, death, and insanity; and at one time he took kindly to the writing of "cabaret songs" for a performer who presumably knew how to carry off these subjects with sophisticated audiences. The curious thing is that the same style of fun-making could be applied by him to themes which he took with sober seriousness. This he did in the three hilarious bloody ballads in which he exploited favorite psychological theories. Mr. Auden was, no doubt, unaware of the esthetically meretricious strain in these pieces. He could not have realized how cruelly they would mortify the sensibilities of many perfectly normal readers who did not share his psychological insights, and how an evil-minded psychoanalyst might trace in them obscure blockages or conflicts in the author's subconscious. In one case some breath of suspicion must have blown upon him, and he quietly dropped this poem out of his work. But he retained the other two.

As for poems published in periodicals and anthologies but never included in Auden's book collections (Chapters 9 and 10), the considerations involved appear to have been as often as not such as concerned the artistry or the good taste of the poems in question. There were, to be sure, in the very early period, several pieces, such as the Song published in *New Verse*, "I have a handsome profile," which would fall under the double imputation of being, at one and the same time, rather heavy-handed light verse and anything but light-handed politico-social propaganda. On the other hand, his *New Verse* "Foxtrot from a Play" and "Blues" were objectionable, if at all, because the latter was too "popular" in its meters and carried a bit far its Düreresque macabre in the treatment of death, and the former a bit too "light" in its treatment of love — which term is there so comprehensive that it covers a soldier's fondness for his rifle, the susceptibility of a theater-goer to the charms of Mae West, a dog-lover's attachment to Airedales and Pekinese, a dog's compulsion to visit an old lamp-post, and the singer's preference for the darling who is his "cup of tea." And the author seems to have concluded that his *New Yorker* chorus of glamour girls, etc., was after all hardly more than a potboiler.

There were also certain magazine poems which have a particular interest as being rough drafts for later more finished compositions, furnishing ideas and imagery which could be utilized in this later work. And special considerations attach to poems which made a part of Auden's report to the folks back home on his Icelandic sojourn in *Letters from Iceland*, and again to juvenilia from his late teens, which he never took seriously enough after his twenty-first year to regard as a part of his work for exhibition. I will discuss these latter in Appendix I. Those in *Letters from Iceland* omitted from the *Collected Poetry* were not, I think, being permanently disowned.

Auden's five plays all contained songs, choruses, and other passages in verse that might be detachable and reproducible as independent poems. The charade, *Paid on Both Sides*, is in a class by itself. It was included in the 1930 and 1933 editions of his early *Poems*, and was of such a character that the poet was able to retain, with untroubled good conscience, esthetic and ideological, half a dozen of the impressive choruses. The general theme of the drama was unexceptionable in any period of his thinking: the tragic wickedness and senselessness of personal feuds and national wars of revenge. The choruses deal with ancient and universal themes: the troublous nature of human life and its futility unless a man can look up and say, "I have been vile, but I am good"; the perils and hardships encountered by the lonely seeker making a journey into strange lands. The imagery is drawn from primitive and primary human experience, and the style has a vigor and elevation derived from the skillful adaptation of Old English lyric and epic modes.

The other four plays were conceived in a very different spirit and executed in a very different style. In making his selection from them of poems to be included in the *Collected Poetry*, Auden was faced with a much more difficult and critical problem. These plays were all written for performance at the Group Theatre, an avant-garde organization, launched in 1935 under the direction of a former Diaghilev dancer and choreographer, and for an audience of leftist radicals and (it was hoped) of common people who might be attracted by their political propaganda. They were meant to be good theater, in a spectacular modernistic way, and at the same time proletarian in style, capable of being readily understood and appreciated by the man in the street. The result was that a relatively small proportion of the lyrics turned out to be worthy of the poet's ideals in 1945.

The Dance of Death is an ingenious and entertaining spectacle, with its representation of anthropological and sociological themes in terms of pantomime and solo dancing and choral song. The satire is only too obvious; but the author has such imperfect control over his convulsive mechanism of risibility that his laughter seems to fall on the just and unjust alike, and the reader is left bewildered and unconvinced. Even so the Marxian dialectic is too nakedly exhibited to please the author in his maturity. And the effort to employ the terms of common experience and the idiom of the common man jazzed up into popular song deprives the verse of poetic seriousness. In assembling the body of his poetic writing, Auden has simply ignored the existence of this play.

The Dog beneath the Skin has pretensions to a moral significance ranging far beyond the parochial limits of political ideology, and the poet can draw upon this for poems dealing broadly with love ("I Shall Be Enchanted"), and with the hero's quest

223

for truth ("The Witnesses"). But as we read these two pieces of verse in their context in the play, we realize that, along with the broader ethical meaning, they carried special connotations suited to the Marxist intention implicit in the drama as a whole. This becomes more evident when we take them in connection with the Epilogue, with its adaptation of the famous slogan ("To each his need, from each his power") which Auden did not retain in the *Collected Poetry*. One moral of the play would seem to be that even the hero's quest for absolute truth may turn out ruinous or successful according as the hero is inspired to follow the right (that is, the leftist) ideological line. And a complementary moral would seem to be that the lover fallen into devious and perverse ways may be redeemed by an ideal of Love conformable to the right (that is, the leftist) social organization. This particular turn given to the concept of love's redemption by Love may not have been intended in the earlier form of the poem from which much of the Epilogue was drawn. It is less obvious, though probably present, in "I Shall Be Enchanted" than in the Epilogue; this made the Epilogue less admissible to the canon than the other chorus, where the special intention might go unnoted once it was taken out of the context of the play. And the similar ideological turn given to the concept of the hero's quest for truth may not have been so obviously intended in "The Witnesses" when originally published as it appears in the context of the play; out of that context, it might return to its earlier, ideologically neutral character. This sort of writing in cloudy symbols lends itself readily to a considerable diversity of interpretation according to the context — according to the stage set in which the piece is placed and the diverse lighting of the stage. This is what makes it so easy for Auden to fit poems of one period with a given *Tendenz* into the fabric or body of work in another period with a radically different *Tendenz*. (Unfortunately, one must also acknowledge that this makes it possible for an earnest and candid reader to go quite wrong in his interpretation of a given piece of work. Our only check here on human fallibility in the small is the cumulative evidence of the work in the large.)

From *The Dog beneath the Skin*, Auden also had his choice among a number of choruses surveying and commenting sadly on the *condition humaine*, where the poor are born to the degradation of the slums, and the rich, among their Ming vases, find no satisfaction for their spiritual hunger, and "he tosses at night who at noonday found no truth." Indeed, it is surprising that Auden should not have given more of these choruses the stamp of his approval. Perhaps he did not find them sufficiently Audenesque in style; they were perhaps too loose in movement and too direct in statement to suit his poetical ideal and carry the Auden trademark. And some of them are too extravagantly bald in their exploitation of the psychosomatic view of physical disease as the symptom of spiritual derangement. At any rate, he chose among them the one ("The Cultural Presupposition") that, with the fewest and most evocative words, renders the passionate revulsion he felt at the sight of man's spiritual misery in the midst of his elegantly appointed Waste Land. It is here, perhaps, that the Eliot influence most happily served him. The poetic influence is Eliot, but the poem itself, for all its directness (here modeled on Eliot's), is *echt Auden*, and one of his finest.

But the sureness with which he has picked this chorus to represent the serious side of a generally cynical and often vulgar dramatic performance is matched only by the poor judgment that led him, in 1950 to reprint from the play so questionable a poem as "Prothalamion," rejected by him in '45, and the surprising obtuseness that enabled him in 1945 to palm off the jeering parody of the Vicar's Sermon as a sober and profound exposition of religious truth. The latter is the most glaring instance of the faculty he had of reading into a work conceived in an utterly different frame of mind intentions which, at some later time, better suited his emotional outlook. And this without the alteration of a word or the excision of a phrase in this hysterical and rococo discourse. It is as if he were Prospero and with the touch of his wand were turning Caliban into Ariel, or as if, with a drop from the baptismal font, he were turning the black mass into a sacrament of Holy Church.

It implies such a curious notion of the creative process, not as something organic involving living tissues with their appropriate functions, but rather as the arrangement of words in patterns, which may at one moment signify one thing and at the next moment something quite different, as different colors are thrown upon them from the spotlight machine behind the auditors. Stephen Spender has remarked on the way Auden had "of tacking lines from a rejected poem onto a new one — as though a poem were not a single experience but a mosaic held together by the consistency of an atmosphere, a rhythm or an idea common to all its parts." But in the case of this sermon, it is not a question of tacking lines on from somewhere else, but of completely ignoring, in its new context, the atmosphere, the rhythm, and the idea of the piece as it was originally conceived. It is this strange faculty of Auden's of completely forgetting what he intended in a given imaginative work, or else of willfully assigning to it an absolutely different intention, that prevents us from giving him our full confidence. "The drift of the Maker is dark." But keeping strictly to the realm of esthetic theory (though borrowing a figure from another realm), we don't see how the same elaborate work of art can be made to serve both God and Mammon.

The Ascent of F6 is a more serious and well-organized dramatic composition than *The Dog*, but it contains very little poetry that could be reproduced in the collections. There was one piece in verse from which the author could borrow two stanzas and eke them out with two new ones to make up his "Funeral Blues." And there was an excellent half-satirical, half-admonitory chorus that could be reprinted as Song No. II, "At last the secret is out, as it always must come in the end." This is one of the happiest examples of Auden's work in "light verse."

On the Frontier is the best constructed of the Auden-Isherwood dramas. But the numerous songs in which the leftist anti-war propaganda is conveyed, while they serve well their purpose in the play, are nothing more than rhymed prose, and the author rightly judged that they added nothing to the body of his poetic work.

226

Altogether from these four plays Auden left in limbo some fifty pieces of verse that might conceivably have been included in his *Collected Poetry*, or considerably more than was discarded from all the rest of his published work. And in most of this verse from the plays the inferior poetic quality was so much involved with what must have seemed to him unsound thinking that it is virtually impossible to determine in a given case whether it was the quality of the style or of the thinking that weighed most heavily with him.

Of Auden's half-dozen librettos and choral compositions, only two fell within the period when they would be available for inclusion in the collected poetry. From *Paul Bunyan* (music by Benjamin Britten) Auden chose three attractive lyrics for reproduction; but as we have seen neither he nor the composer was well enough pleased with the work as a whole to wish to see it published.

Ballad of Heroes (again with music by Britten) contained only one piece that was the sole work of Auden; and this was a mutilated version of a poem published in a magazine two years earlier. Its interest for us here lies in the radical transformation which it underwent in form and in meaning as it was reproduced in the setting of the oratorio and the later collections. It began as a pacifist manifesto — a lively and picturesque satire on war-mongering fascism, doubled with a decidedly ambivalent, and in a religious view irreverent, treatment of the Devil. He is made the champion of independent thinking and of natural impulse (or "sin"), and the one accordingly whom emancipated spirits will prefer to the hypocritical puritanism of his opposite number. This was too subtle and complicated a set of ironies for choral rendering, and the main point of the poem was lost by an apparent identification of the opposed principles, while the original pacifism was drowned in admiration for the heroic spirit of those who wage a "war to end war." In the canonical collections the original poem was restored almost in its entirety, but the Lord only knows what the reader in '45 and '50 is supposed to make of the covert impieties which it brings along with it from its unregenerate origins. The history of this poem is a curious example (in *Ballad of Heroes*) of the freedoms Auden would sometimes take with his own work, and (in the later collections) of his occasional readiness to admit to the canon work that, if it is read so as to make full sense, could hardly have met with his approval. Perhaps it was the colorfulness and ingenuity of the composition that tipped the scales in its favor, and it is just a case of the literary connoisseur gaining the ascendancy over the religious philosopher.

Of the later librettos it is enough to say here that they further illustrate the ready virtuosity of Auden in a variety of poetical genres, that they are ingenious in conception, and rise above the level of this ordinarily pale and conventional species of writing; but that, made up as they are largely of transparent allegory, and dealing largely in the charms and spells of medieval romance, they are creations of fancy rather than imagination, and are more like expert literary exercises than like poetry as judged by current critical standards. It is not likely that many pieces from these librettos will be reproduced by Auden when he comes to make up a new collection of his poetry.

We have had little occasion to refer to the three long poems that occupy more than 160 pages in the *Collected Poetry*. They were produced in the four years immediately preceding that publication. They represent the same philosophical positions that the author held in '45, and were not far enough removed in time to invite a severely objective appraisal of their poetical quality. They were reproduced virtually without alteration of any kind. Of their literary character I have spoken briefly in Chapter 17.

As for the 1950 British collection of the shorter poems, it is clear enough that, insofar as the same poems are included, the British text is based on that of the American publication of 1945. The later collection did not include long poems, and, for some reason known to publishers, it included nothing from *The Double Man*, but did give the whole text of *Paid on Both Sides*. Sixteen poems were renamed, and four poems rejected in 1945 were restored to the canon. Thus the American public has been provided, in a single volume, with an authorized version of Auden's poems, long and short, down to 1945, and the British public with an authorized version of the shorter poems, the text being identical with that of 1945 with the exceptions noted.

Throughout our study we have had frequent occasion to indicate the difficulty of making out the original intention of this and that poem; and this applies both in poems left unchanged in the collections of 1945 and 1950 and in poems appearing there in revised form. This difficulty derives in part from the oblique or symbolic method and from other features of Auden's technique; but sometimes it would seem to be inherent in the thought itself — in what I have ventured to call its ambiguity. The difficulty is, naturally, greatest in early poems representing the poet's point of view in the thirties but revised in the forties to make them conformable to his later point of view and scattered about among poems of later origin in such a way as to give the impression that they are all cut out of the same cloth.

Even more disconcerting is the case of poems (and prose compositions) from the thirties, reflecting the ideology of that period, which were reproduced in the forties without alteration, but which it is very hard to bring in line with the poet's later philosophical attitudes, even where he clearly indicates his wish that we should do so. How numerous these may be it is impossible to determine without a much more extensive study of his output than we are able to make within the limits set. They have come to our notice chiefly in the case of volumes, like *The Orators* and *The Dog beneath the Skin*, in which, while the bulk of the poetic work was discarded for obvious reasons, a considerable number of pieces were exempted from this ban, and we were naturally moved to inquire why exception was made in these particular cases.

It was thus that we came to realize that certain of these, like the Vicar's sermon, cannot by any means be brought to bear the construction put upon them in 1945 without a very great loss of their original force and color as literary creations. In most cases, as with the ode "To My Pupils" from *The Orators* ("Which Side Am I Supposed to Be On?"), the poem yields its fullest meaning if interpreted mainly as ironical in intention. This is true of "Danse Macabre," which came to our attention because of the drastic revisions made in adapting it for the *Ballad of Heroes*, but which was almost completely restored to its original form in the later collections. Between this poem and the Vicar's sermon as they appear in their original settings there is a striking parallel in the ambiguous, or (by virtue of the burlesque manner) the flippantly tolerant, attitude toward the Devil and his works, which is greatly at variance with the attitude implied in Auden's introductory note to the sermon in the *Collected Poetry*. And there is considerable reason for assuming a similar contradiction between the original intention of the *Orators* ode and that which the poem might be supposed to carry in the later collection. For a reader at all well acquainted with such pieces in their original setting, and with the philosophical attitudes of the poet at the time of writing, the most difficult feat that can be expected is to read them now from the point of view of the poet in 1945 or 1950. And if he succeeds in doing so, he is bound to find that they have in the process lost a considerable part of their original point and pungency.

Perhaps even greater ambiguity attaches to such poems from the unregenerate days that were reproduced without change than to those in which an effort was made to adjust them to new points of view by revision and expurgation. On this general point I will have something to say in the following chapter, in which I make a brief statement as to how my estimate of Auden as a poet has been affected by my findings in this study.

However, my study has no pretensions to being a general critique of Auden's poetry.* By the nature of my assignment, the main body of his poetical work is left out of account except as a guide to an understanding of the probable reasons for his revisions and eliminations. But it seems obvious that the results of this study may often be of help to writers undertaking a formal critique of Auden's work. For the limited number of poems in which his personal censorship was applied are of crucial importance to an un-

---

* For certain developments in Auden's poetic style through *The Age of Anxiety* the reader is referred to my article, "The Poems of Auden and the Prose Diathesis," in the *Virginia Quarterly Review*, July 1949, pp. 365–83.

derstanding of his poetical ideals and the process of his thinking. My own critical conclusions suggested in the following chapter are bound to be, like all literary criticism, largely subjective. For the present I continue to deal with what are, in principle, ascertainable objective facts.

On the side of Auden's social and religious philosophy, the main effect of this study is, so far as my interpretations are well grounded, to clarify somewhat the obscure problem of stages in his thinking. It becomes increasingly clear, in the light of our findings here, supplemented by a general reading of Auden, that between 1928 and 1945 there were four main stages. In the first, from (roughly) 1928 to 1936 or 1937, his ideology was strongly Marxian; the enemy of society was a decadent bourgeoisie, and the objective of right-thinking people was a just collective society, to be brought about by revolutionary reform of the social order within existing states.* In the second, from (again roughly) 1936 or 1937 to 1939, there was a transition from Marxian to what we might denominate a humanistic ideology. Under the growing threat of fascism, the enemy was now conceived of as the totalitarian state, with its ruthless suppression of individual liberties and freedom of thought. In this stage, the ideal of class struggle and revolution at home gives way before the urgent need for action against fascism on a world scale. There seems to have been a third, and again transitional, stage in Auden's thinking, during (roughly) the years 1939–41, in which the change was from a secular hu-

* It is perhaps possible to distinguish two successive phases of this first stage, as the Marxist ideology is intensified and the propagandist motive becomes more prominent. In the earlier phase, according to Mr. Replogle, there is a heavier stress on what he calls Auden's "change of heart" theory. In this earlier phase he was more insistent on the personal-psychological conversion as prerequisite to social reform. And while he never did give this up, he was more inclined in the second phase to reconcile this with the Marxian "reliance on external material change" as primary. Again, it should be noted that in what I call the third stage there was a strong residue of Marxian ideology, especially in the propagandist play, *On the Frontier*. Auden's poetry was never rigorously and consistently Marxist, though it may be characterized over a considerable period of years as socialist-revolutionary; and any classification of it by periods depends on which of the several aspects of Marxist doctrine is being featured.

manism pitted against fascism to a strictly Christian view of the
world as one in which the ideal of the Just City is regarded as
something unattainable on earth and our main endeavor should
be to draw blueprints of the City of God, to be found only in
Heaven or Eternity. The fourth stage, from (say) 1941 to the
present time is that in which the Christian view is taken for
granted, and mere political and social wrongs, though indeed subject to criticism and reformist efforts in the name of morality and
religion, are still accepted with a becoming resignation to the will
of God.

In the large view these stages are fairly well defined, but their
limits are not fixed any more than the boundaries between states
in central Africa. We have to walk warily and make allowance
for a good deal of interpenetration of ideas and attitudes from the
several periods and ideological systems. While the terms change
and emphasis shifts, there is a continuity of feeling and drive that
tends toward the assimilation of views in one stage to those in
another. And this assimilation is everywhere promoted by the
fluid connotations of symbolic language. It is harder than usual in
poetry to distinguish in Auden between his mythology and the
moral truths which it shadows, and between his ethical ideals and
the objective truths which are supposed to underlie and guarantee
them. And as his mythology changes, it is not always easy to determine how far his ethical ideals and his view of objective truth
change with them or remain substantially the same.

We have also to make allowance for the fact that, throughout
his writing career, Auden has been a propagandist for the doctrines he has taken so much to heart; and that, as Mr. Jarrell has
perspicuously shown for the period from 1930 to 1941, no matter
what doctrine it was that he espoused at the time, his instinct and
strategy were to include within its framework elements that sometimes went together better in feeling than in logic. There is
accordingly a constant hold-over into later periods of feeling-
attitudes that are logically more appropriate in the earlier, and
frequent anticipations in the earlier of feeling-attitudes and intellectual positions that are better defined in the later. The net result

of this in his poetry in all periods is an ambiguity which does not necessarily weaken the poetic effect but does make peculiarly precarious the attempt of a critic to give a clear exposition of meanings and intentions. But the poetic vision is ever, like the life process, incorrigibly beset with contradictions. And sometimes one is inclined to speak, with Mr. Spears, of the *tensions* operating at all periods between antithetical attitudes in the poetry of Auden.

The passage from stage 3 to stage 4 is the most sudden and startling of all, and a reader acquainted with what Auden published in prose at the time as well as with the poetry will agree that it can be most precisely characterized as a conversion. At least on the level of formulated rational theory. Early in 1939 the poet contributed to a sheaf of personal credos assembled by Clifton Fadiman, entitled *I Believe*, a fourteen-page statement of his views on man and his world. These views are such as would be grown in a soil of Darwinian evolutionism (taken more in the terms of Samuel Butler and Bernard Shaw than in those of strict biological science — for Auden is able to speak of the way an individual man may go on "evolving" after reaching maturity), of anthropological and sociological science, and socialist economics. The writer is mainly concerned with such matters as the physical conditions, methods of production, and cultural forms that determine the character and status of individual men; the preventable or non-preventable causes that determine the form taken by our society and our government; the "factors that limit and hinder men from developing their powers and pursuing suitable vocations"; the function of political parties; the evils of intolerance, but the need on occasion "to accept the responsibility of our convictions"; the crucial nature of the period of social change in which we live; and the duty of us all "to defend what we believe to be right, perhaps even at the cost of our lives and those of others." The author declares his belief that "the Socialists are right and the Fascists wrong in their view of society." He declares himself "fairly optimistic" in regard to the preventable nature of causes operating in society. And though he believes that "all coer-

233

cion is a moral evil," he is evidently ready to accept war as in some cases necessary in defense of what we believe to be right.

Everything here is "scientific," rational, socially reformist, pragmatic, and earnestly moral on a strictly secular level. There is not the remotest hint of sin, grace, revelation, deity, or other theological concept, or any reference to values or sanctions outside the framework of what is nowadays called "humanist" thinking.

Later in this year 1939, Auden contributed to the *Nation* a review of a book by John MacMurray, a thinker who combines the communist doctrine with a somewhat unorthodox but highly mystical form of Christian faith. While Auden finds this writer stimulating and illuminating, he feels that he has been led astray by "his determination to believe in the existence of God." Auden doesn't mind the mythology on which MacMurray depends for the construction of his system; but he evidently wishes that he did not mistake his mythology for objective truth. He would like to have him say that "God is a term for what [man] imagines [his] real nature to be. Thus man is always making God in his own image."

Here then we find the poet hankering indeed after some mythological formula for man's experience, but resolutely determined not to accept any such mythology as other than a metaphorical embellishment to socialist doctrine.

Less than two years later, in an article in the *New Republic* reviewing a book by the Protestant theologian Reinhold Niebuhr, Auden has seriously adopted original sin, revelation, the Incarnation, and other Christian dogmas as primary truths in a world of "ideas" (immortal and transcendent), infinitely more real and substantial than the shadowy formulations of science and social theory. It is true that he injudiciously undertakes to demonstrate the validity of the Christian revelation by an appeal to the science of comparative anthropology, and he tries to make his views palatable to liberals by an admission that Christians have sometimes fallen into the errors of "Platonic dualism" and "Stoic impassivity." He would have his cake and eat it too. But he cannot disguise the fact that he has outdistanced MacMurray in his "determination to believe in the existence of God," and in 1941 abandoned all the positions that he occupied in 1939.

But all this is on the formal intellectual level. On the emotional level, a substantial continuity is still to be traced. The transition from the "liberal" to the orthodox religious position has been explored, in its subtle turns of "religious logic" or of rationalization, by Mr. Spears in an article in the *Sewanee Review* and by Mr. Jarrell in an article in the *Partisan Review*. In the more sympathetic view of Mr. Spears, the term "religious logic" applies; with Mr. Jarrell it is the psychological rationalization necessary to the poet's peace of mind. Mr. Jarrell suggests how steadily the liberalism and radicalism of Auden were accompanied by a sense of guilt associated with primitivist mythology (a poet's construction), with rebellion against parental authority, and above all parental and tribal authority in sexual matters. It is beyond the scope of my undertaking here to go into the niceties of these interpretations, or make a choice between the attitudes of the two critics toward this development in the poet. It may be sufficient to outline, in my own simplified language, what I take to be the element of continuity in the poet's feeling attitudes. And here I must certainly acknowledge that I am entering the shadowy realm of conjecture. For this is "psychology," and in this realm it is notorious that amateurs rush in with the confidence of professionals and Watson thinks himself as good as Sherlock Holmes. In human psychology one is seldom free to conduct his experiments under controlled laboratory conditions and with the subjects present for observation. The best one can hope is to construct a hypothesis that seems to fit as many of the facts as may be observed from a distance.

Suppose we take for starting point three main assumptions that bulk large in Auden's poetry throughout the whole period under consideration. One is the sense of personal guilt under which all men labor; one is the assumption that individual moral choice is the *sine qua non* of significant living and must take precedence over every other consideration; one is the need which the brave spirit feels to assert his independence of constituted oppressive authority. The problem is to see how the interplay of these three principles may form a pattern strongly affecting a man's theoretical opinions on social, political, and religious questions. I do not mean to suggest that our social, political, and religious systems may not have their own sufficient logic in the intellectual realm, but merely to remind us how this or that rational system of thinking may, as conditions alter, best suit and serve men's persistent emotional needs.

First the sense of personal guilt under which, let us say, all good men labor. This weighs heavily on us, but may be made endurable so long as we can do something about it. The cure for doing wrong is doing right. But doing right in one's personal life is extremely difficult, and for a man with a persistent sense of personal guilt, there may be some relief in the thought of doing right in the public world, or reforming society. In the early thirties it was possible, let us say, to relieve one's sense of personal guilt by attacking the public guilt of capitalism, which was held responsible for the social and material breakdown of the times. This was a very common experience of earnest men everywhere.

But this in the end proved to be a discouraging program. It did not look as if progress were being made in the West in the direction of a socialist organization of society; and reports from the East did not suggest that the Soviet form of socialism was satisfying the moral requirements of the socialist ideal. Fortunately for those of Auden's party, Hitler and Franco came on the scene in time to give a new direction to their reformist zeal. Fascism, being totalitarian, left no room for the individual moral choice which was at the core of their doctrine. And totalitarianism was the very incarnation of that oppressive authority against which the brave spirit felt moved to assert his independence. This had been equally true of Soviet communism all along, but had hardly been recognized as a fact by zealous socialists. Fascism was now Enemy No. 1, and the struggle against fascism was the area where one's sense of personal guilt could best be alleviated by an attack upon public guilt.

There was no time in which Auden's political program and his ideological position were less confused than that in which he made his visit to China and wrote his poems urging a world crusade against fascism in the name of "human justice." This could take the form of pure humanism, in which there need be no reference to authorities and standards of conduct outside humanity itself, and the sense of guilt might be completely absorbed in the exercise of the will in the task of "constructing a human justice." And now, for once, the intellectual could feel in harmony with his fellow citizens, in opposition to oppressive authority, in the active campaign for social justice, even if it led to catastrophic war.

But the intellectual still hoped to head off war. And when it came he did not like it. The motives of the nations who went to war against Hitler were not all as pure as those of Auden's humanistic liberals. England and France were fighting for their lives and property against a rival power more than they were fighting to construct a human justice as these poets conceived it. The war when it came was supported as much by mere crass egoism as it was by a noble altruism. The world war was not a pretty sight, and as it developed it must have been for Auden, as for thousands of earnest men throughout the world, a death blow to all his sanguine hopes for justice coming in with a radical reorganization of society. All his supports were crumbling under him, and he was left, like so much of the world, with no hope for justice on earth, but the strong returning sense of our universal and aboriginal guilt.

Guilt now in his vocabulary becomes sin. And sin is somehow more bearable than guilt. For guilt is man's offense against himself, his human code of right and wrong, and to get rid of it requires a greater effort than most men are capable of. The mass of men, as religion recognizes, will never be capable of it. Liberalism had proved entirely ineffectual in preventing the crimes against humanity that provoked the war and the crimes against humanity which its prosecution involved. By 1941, when he wrote his article on "The Means of Grace" for the *New Republic*, Auden was convinced of the bankruptcy of liberalism as a means of saving humanity from its oppressive sense of guilt. It was fascism and the world war that brought Auden to this realization. As he says in this article: "It has taken Hitler to show us that liberalism is not self-supporting" — that is, that it needs the support of powers quite outside of man.

Now, strictly speaking, neither guilt nor sin are terms proper to liberalism. Liberalism does not think in these terms. Liberalism thinks in terms of what is wrong with the world and what can be done to make it right. And it is a short-sighted and impatient liberalism, unacquainted with history, that expects the world to be set right within a man's lifetime. But the poetic liberalism of Auden always required the support of the notion of guilt, taken directly from current psychology and indirectly from primitive religion. In primitive religion guilt is the feeling of fright one has at having broken tribal tabus or gone against the will of the ancestors who had established the tribal code. In current psychology guilt is also associated with rebellion against parental authority, especially in sexual matters.

In the final stage of his progress, the concept of guilt is insufficient to the poet's need to face the desolating realization that all his hopes for mankind have been illusory. He can no longer be satisfied with a picturesque poetic mythology drawn from fairy tale and saga. Still less can he be satisfied with the patient determination of humanistic thinkers throughout history to make what slow progress is possible in the constructing of a "human justice," inspired by the widely held ideals of social decency and personal goodness. He has been so utterly disillusioned with regard to men's capacity for goodness, and has grown so weary of his role as champion of the human ideal, that he requires the religious concept of sin to bring him a certain tranquillity in the acceptance of life. For sin is disobedience to some postulated Absolute Being altogether beyond and separate from men, and in orthodox Christianity it is predicated on the assumption that men are inveterately subject to such disobedience by every condition of their birth and living. The denial of this truth is, for the orthodox, the first and greatest of all sins, and the recognition of it the first and greatest of all virtues. And the religious man, though sinful, has the supreme comfort of feeling that he is possessed of this prime virtue. He has also the comfort of feeling that he is living in immediate filial relationship to the Absolute Being, the Wholly Other, a relationship made uneasy, to be sure, by the sense of his own sinfulness, but warm with intimacy and assurance of grace.

And this brings us to still another element of continuity in Auden's thought throughout his career. Mr. Jarrell has much to say of the loneliness to which every man is condemned as this is featured by Auden in all periods of his writing. This loneliness, so far as human relationships are concerned, is felt as much by the poet in his latest as in his earlier stages. But now, in his close contact with the Absolute Being, his sense of loneliness is greatly lightened.

And still another possible item of continuity in discontinuity. The poet's loneliness must always have been with him a cause of satisfaction as well as of sorrow. For the acute consciousness of his separation from others distinguishes the superior man from those whose notions of love and companionship are not sufficiently elevated to make them aware of their essential loneliness. Auden was leader of a school of writers as much as anything else because he typified their sense that they were exiles in a world of commonplace people wanting in intellectual and spiritual liveness and insight. This want of liveness and insight was particularly marked in those who wielded influence and authority in the world, and rebellion against authority in the intellectual, political, and spiritual realms was the mark of a superior mind.

With his religious conversion, it might seem that the poet had given up his greatest claim to superiority. And this might be more than seeming, as he put on the sober habit of religious humility. But this effect does not necessarily follow. For his religious conversion did carry with it a new order of superiority, in separating him from that very party of progressive liberals among whom he had been a distinguished leader. It was they who prided themselves on their separateness from the ordinary run of unperceptive middle-class people. And now he takes his stand apart from, and

THE MAKING OF THE AUDEN CANON

over against, those who were most notable for their superiority, and whose prestige was greatest among those to whom he addressed his poetry. He was thus more alone, more of an exile, than ever.

But he does not insist on this gray eminence. For he is confident that many will be going over along with him. As he says in the *New Republic* article: "Cultured people, to whom, until recently, theological terms were far more shocking than any of the four-letter words, are now in such danger and have seen so many of their absolute assumptions destroyed, that they may even overcome this final prudery." And he is ready to recommend to them a cure for their bewilderment and insecurity in the form of a theological treatise by the famous Protestant writer Reinhold Niebuhr, whose doctrine of sin and grace he proceeds to outline for them. He undertakes to show them that this doctrine need not offend their liberalism and that its absolute assumptions are well grounded in historical revelations which may be "examined by the methods of comparative anthropology." And he suggests that civilized man is justified in making his absolute assumptions by the urgent need he has to find firm support for his ethical ideals.

In referring to the absolute assumptions of liberals, Auden seems to me to assume too much. For the true liberal assumes nothing as *truth*, being satisfied to work for the realization of his human *ideals*. Absolute assumptions about truth have been the joy and the bane of man's thinking ever since he developed the power of generalization. And the most persistent is the assumption that whatever a man conceives of as necessary to his spiritual comfort is an objective fact in the nature of the universe. Poets have been as prone to this as other men, and they have the special professional need of mythological constructions to give wings to their imagination. Mr. Spears has noted this in the case of Auden, whose whole career, he says, "may be described as a search for beliefs, both for himself and as 'metaphors for poetry.'"

But in tracing the course of Auden's thought there are other points to be noted that add to the complexities of the problem.

One must take into account the synthetic and somewhat fanciful psychological formula employed by him through a considerable course of years — a formula compounded out of suggestions from many professional and amateur psychological writers, but mingled and served up according to a recipe of his own invention. It is here that we are most forcefully reminded that we have to do with a poet and not a scientist or philosopher guided by the rules of logic and controlled in his conclusions by empirical evidence. This poet reminds us more of that brilliant novelist D. H. Lawrence, with his native insights and his eccentric theories of the "solar plexus," etc. Auden's complicated and somewhat obscure psychological theory of Eros, guilt, death wish, etc., is less prominent in the very early and the very late periods, but is regnant throughout the second and third. The problems it raises are much too complicated and difficult to be thoroughly dealt with here, even if one had the technical training to justify one in passing critical judgments; and it would take a close examination of the whole body of his poetry to provide an adequate explication of his meaning in the innumerable passages in which this formula appears.

And then, finally, the nature of my undertaking has not given occasion to deal adequately with that emphasis on moral discipline in the individual which characterizes Auden's work throughout. If we tend to overlook this in our reading of him, it is simply that it goes along with so many other distracting and appealing features of his literary personality — the zestful pride he took as a young man in being a rebel against stodginess and convention, his conscious sophistication and showmanship, his undercutting wit and irony, his penchant for satire directed against even those institutions associated with the training and discipline of character, and above all the restless play of an imagination that will not be confined within the limits of any parochial discipline.

As for the poems published in the present decade, if, in spite of their subtlety and refinement, their quiet charm and sober correctness of taste, they fail to captivate us like those we read in the thirties, it is partly that, with the author's submission to authority in Church and State, so much of the wind has gone out of his sails. He is still the champion of the individual against the pressures of mass opinion and political dogma. He has come to the age when men born in an earlier stage of civilization are made uneasy and irritable by the novelties and gross vitalities of a new time; they look back with nostalgia to the good old days, and lay about them with gentlemanly irony directed against the vulgarization and standardization of modern life. One feels that he still reserves the right of a good Protestant to make his private interpretation of doctrines which he accepts, and take with a grain of salt the statutory prescriptions of legislators and governors which he acknowledges as legally binding. But he is no longer the fighting rebel against authority in church and government and the classical schools of art. His imagination is tamer in the sense that *tame* is an antonym to *wild*. And he can hardly expect to shock and beguile and bespell as he did in the days when he wrote "To throw away the key and walk away," or "Hearing of harvests rotting in the valleys," or when he wrote "Spain 1937," or even when he wrote "September 1, 1939."

In making up the canon of his poetical works, Auden eliminated a very considerable body of inferior poems, and of poems reflecting ideological and philosophical views on which he had turned his back; and by revisions and expurgations in a considerable body of other poems he made them reasonably acceptable to him at a time when he was concerned that his work should be as edifying spiritually as it was imaginatively arresting. In certain other cases he reprinted without alteration poems and prose pieces which in their original setting represented attitudes which must later have come under his reprobation, relying apparently on their appearance in more reputable company to invest them with an odor of sanctity which was not theirs to begin with. By printing them mainly in alphabetical order, according to their opening lines, without regard for chronological sequence, subject matter, and philosophy, he made it very difficult for his readers to interpret individual poems in terms of their original conception. This results in a great deal of gratuitous obscurity and ambiguity, which tends to spread like a haze over the whole course of his writing. And while, with a willing suspension of critical urgency, this haze of ambiguity may make his earlier poetry more readily assimilable to the body of work produced when the poet had come to his philosophical maturity, it has the effect of leaching out from many of the early poems a good part of their colorfulness, pungency, and point.

His alternative would have been to range his poems in chronological order and leave them, as far as was consistent with his artistic standards, just as they were originally written. We should then be able to read them in their original context and to follow the course of an interesting mind in its progress through successive periods in the pursuit of truth. This manner of presentation would have done better justice to many fine poems as intelligible and organic creations of poetic art. It would have involved the candid admission on the author's part that, by his present lights, he had occasionally been subject to error and confusion. But such candor would only have reflected credit on the poet, and it could not in the end have been a disservice to the truth as he later came to see it.

ℭ20

W. H. Auden: The Question of Identity

OCCASIONALLY I have been asked by friends acquainted with the nature of this study how my findings here affect my estimate of Auden's poetic work. And I might be expected to make at least a brief statement on this point.

A close examination of his work in general, and of his dealings with it in making up the canon of 1945–50, has confirmed my original high estimate of his imaginative powers as applied in this or that poem or series of poems taken individually. Auden impresses me still as the most gifted of the poets who have been so often bracketed with him as constituting a school of radical writers. And among contemporary poets in the English language he stands very high for the daring originality and brilliancy of his imaginative and linguistic effects.

And when it comes to subject matter and thought, he has the added distinction of being perhaps the most representative of poets in his time writing in the English language. He has seen a good deal of the world and witnessed history in the making. He has been very much aware of the main contemporary currents of thought in political theory, science and psychology, the fine arts and literature, philosophy and religion. He has been a prodigious reader, and remarkable for the ease and suggestiveness with which he has made use of his reading for the nourishment of his creative faculties. He has written notable poems on Voltaire and Pascal, on Freud and Yeats and Brueghel. He knows as much of Darwinism as can be learned from Samuel Butler, Bernard Shaw, and Gerald Heard; as much of socialism as can be learned from the

Communist Manifesto; as much of psychology as can be learned from Groddeck, John Layard, and Jung's *Integration of the Personality*. In "New Year Letter" his allusions to poets and philosophers are in terms of confident familiarity; and he can be epigrammatic on the subject of Blake, Catullus, and Rilke, of Rimbaud, Baudelaire, and Kipling; on Descartes, Berkeley, Aristotle, Rousseau, and Hegel. He has discovered St. Augustine, Kierkegaard, and Reinhold Niebuhr. In physical science one takes for granted that he has read Eddington and Jeans, and, still better, his list of Modern Sources in the notes includes Hyman Levy's *Modern Science* and serious metaphysical treatises by Collingwood and Whitehead. No poet of our time has covered more ground, or ground more favorable to the growth of speculations suited to the felt needs of the time. He is to poetry what Aldous Huxley is to prose. But he is not to be mistaken for a Julian Huxley, a William James, a Santayana, or an Einstein. Like Tennyson he has endeavored to make himself acquainted with the philosophical thinking of his time, and he has been much more confident and dogmatic than the great Victorian in drawing conclusions.

All of this has a distinct bearing on the philosophic passion which may give added force and ponderability to the imaginative creations of a poet. Many great poets have had considerable learning beyond the limits of belles-lettres — witness Dante, Chaucer, Donne, Milton, Goethe, Coleridge, Shelley, St. John Perse. It is a marked weakness of most poetry since Tennyson that it has been so out of touch with the serious thought of our time. And in spite of the invincibly literary strain in Auden that leads him so often to "fall for" uncritical thinking in the realm of theory, it is a great distinction in him that he stands out among modern poets by his earnest effort to be an educated modern thinker.

But in any attempt to place his work as a whole in a scale of poetic "greatness," one is faced with the very difficult problem posed by the role of spiritual prophet assumed by him or thrust upon him by his enthusiastic followers and interpreters. And here we are obliged to take note of certain features of his mentality and poetic character that do not go any too well with his function as a prophet. In the long run, in writing with these pretensions, it is not possible to make a sharp separation between the imaginative and the intellectual faculties. The way a poet thinks is bound to have some effect on the images that he conceives and on the form and texture of the work in which these images are assembled and combined.

When I speak of the poetic character, I have in mind the character assumed by a poet in presenting his thoughts to his audience; and in this particular case I have in mind the way the poet conceives of himself as a performer. A prophet, if he is self-conscious enough to conceive of himself at all as performer, thinks solely of the powers at his command for communicating his spiritual message. He is simply a carrier of the truth that is in him. But it is recognized by Auden's most sympathetic admirers that he conceives of himself as one bound to dazzle and amuse. His poetic function, in our sophisticated age, requires him to wear masks and assume roles; and these vary greatly from poem to poem and from stage to stage of his career.

No one has shown greater virtuosity in assimilating this and that style from his predecessors. Dazzling certainly and hauntingly impressive were several of the choruses in *Paid on Both Sides* inspired by Anglo-Saxon models; dazzling and amusing in the manner of Edward Lear many passages in *The Age of Anxiety* with, this time, their *parody* use of Anglo-Saxon meters, epithets, and alliteration. And parody is much employed to relieve the solemnity of his religious poems, "The Sea and the Mirror" and "For the Time Being." One could not ask for anything more feelingly "incantatory" than his use of the Italian sestina in "Paysage Moralisé," with its teasingly provocative recurrent line-end symbols. No poet ever packed more associative feeling and thought into the images of valleys, mountains, islands, cities, water, and into that mere abstraction, sorrow.

Auden's use of imagery from the boys' game of secret agents and conspirators gives a pleasing air of mystery to many of his revolutionary poems and poems featuring heroic pilgrimages "beyond the frontier." His style in his teen-age period is brightened by many a device from Eliot and Robinson, and in later poems he has produced effects suggestive of Eliot and Hopkins. In "A Communist to Others" he makes good use of Burns's tail-rhyme stanza for satirical effects in the spirit of Burns. In his "light verse" period he wrote amusing cabaret songs, and in his propagandist plays with Isherwood, saucy lyrics that would pass for "proletarian."

Whatever modes he took over from earlier writers were most perfectly assimilated to his own purposes in the more discursively reflective poetry of 1937–40, in which prose tonalities tend to dominate; and it is in such poems as "Journey to Iceland," "At the Grave of Henry James," "In Memory of Sigmund Freud," "Spain 1937," and "September 1, 1939," that he is most perfectly himself and least the performer. These poems are not devoid of irony and sophisticated refinements of thought; but there is little suggestion of the satirical mask and the assumed theatrical role. They are earnest, direct, and manly in their rendering of the poet's sentiments. It is true that in his meditations "At the Grave of Henry James" he makes great play with James's mannerisms, his frequent use of French words, his curiously figurative language, and his elaborate periphrastic periods and locutions. But this is done in the kindliest spirit of a devoted disciple mimicking the style of a revered master. It is more by way of compliment than of lampoon, and it serves to reduce the emotional heat of a poem that is in essence a confession of sins both esthetic and spiritual.

In all periods of his writing, it is made interesting and provocative by the use of familiar idioms and items from familiar experience, and by the air of mystification which makes it all so intriguing and exciting. It is when you come to figuring out the precise intention in terms of prose discourse that you run into real trouble. For here it is that you have to reckon with the chameleon quality of the poet's mind. At first the effect of this quality might seem most bewildering, because most occult and disguised, when the poems of a given period are taken by themselves. One is more aware of the changing colors, and can make more allowance for the fact of change, in a general view, as one follows the development and sequence of doctrinal ideas through distinct periods with their distinguishable ideologies and philosophical positions. But here too the mask and the role are operative in creating ambiguity. For a time this very ambiguity may serve as a solvent for the contradictions or incongruities among the several overlapping positions, as new points of view begin to invade the old. But gradually, if we insist on knowing where the poet stands at a given moment, we grow more and more uneasy.

It is true that, by discreet revisions and eliminations in the poems of the thirties, and by throwing the poems of all periods together in a heap without regard to their temporal sequence, the author does his best to iron out the contradictions and incongruities. And here perhaps the ordinary reader, who does his reading perforce in one of the later collections, will do well to settle down cozily in his deck chair, give up trying to take his bearings, and submit to the sleepy charm, as distinct outlines are blurred in the general haziness that envelopes the landscape. But for anyone with access to the earlier volumes, the uneasiness becomes still more acute as he compares the original texts with those of 1945 and 1950, where so many relatively unambiguous poems are translated into the terms of Auden's later thinking, only to find themselves rather shockingly out of place. And at this point we are obliged to conclude that the poet, with the best of intentions, is virtually misrepresenting the thought which actually informed the earlier writing.

One of the least ambiguous of Auden's works is the set of poems, "In Time of War," together with the verse "Commentary" which accompanied them, as they were written in 1938 and published early in 1939 in Auden and Isherwood's *Journey to a War*. His thoughts on history and the world situation, inspired by his visit to China during the Japanese invasion, took shape as a vision of mankind at length summoning its collective will to the struggle against fascism, and determined, in a spirit of secular humanism, to "construct at last a human justice" upon earth. But this did not carry the specifically religious implications that would satisfy Auden in 1945, and the Commentary was accordingly revised in such a way as to give his thought a very different turn from what it had originally, and such as would lead one to read into the whole set of poems intentions which were almost certainly not present in 1938. There can be no objection on esthetic grounds to an author's discarding whole poems which in his maturity he disapproves of either for their sentiments or their style. But when it comes to altering the wording here and there so as to alter the meaning radically, when it comes to the cutting out of considerable passages which are offensive for ideological or philosophical reasons, the poet overlooks the presumably organic nature of artistic creation. And he must be assuming a low level of critical discrimination on the part of his readers if he supposes that the poem thus expurgated will not in the end betray the tenor of its thought as originally conceived.

Even more dismaying was the transformation made in the satirically intended Vicar's Sermon in *The Dog beneath the Skin* when it was solemnly served up among other edifying dishes in the *Collected Poetry*. The fault in artistry here is in supposing that a piece written in this style, to expose the employment of ecclesiastical rhetoric for morally questionable ends, can, without the slightest change, be made to serve for serious spiritual edification. I suppose the reason why this prodigious sleight of hand has gone unnoticed is that serious readers of "Depravity: A Sermon" were not acquainted with the play in which it first made its appearance. Or more likely, there have been no devout readers of Auden's poetry who have taken this piece of prose seriously enough, or read it with close enough attention, to have realized its absurdity.

In the case of the Vicar's sermon, Auden in reprinting told us in a prefatory note just how he wished the piece to be understood. For the most part, with such questionable work where it is reproduced with little or no revision, he simply leaves it to its new setting to suggest an interpretation conformable to the sounder views of his maturity. And in the case of poems like "Danse Macabre" and "Which Side Am I Supposed to Be On?" (the early ode "To My Pupils"), the reader must ignore most of the ironical implications that gave the original poem so much of its vivacity or land in a mess of well-nigh unresolvable perplexities. When it comes to Auden's "light verse," it is more in the reader's feelings and his taste than in his mind that the ambiguities cause distress. He must adjust himself in poems like "Prothalamion" to the bewildering ambivalence of the poet's feelings about "love." In jolly ballads like "Victor" and "Miss Gee," even if he grants for the sake of argument the scientific validity of Auden's psychosomatic theory, the reader's revulsion against the gratuitous cruelty of the poet's attitude toward suffering and insanity prevents him from falling in wholeheartedly with the comic (the "clinical") view of human nature. With a writer whose ironic shafts are directed so indiscriminately upon every target in view, the reader is left too often in uneasy doubt which side he is actually supposed to be on.

We are here concerned with what is sometimes called the integrity of a work of art. I am thinking of this use of the word by Matthiessen in his admirable pioneering critique of Eliot. The integrity of a work of art derives, in the last analysis, from the integrity or integrality of the artistic conception. And this in turn involves the integrity of the poet's mental process, since it is impossible to separate entirely the forms taken by the poet's imagination from the way he thinks.

In using the term integrity, or better integrality (a more cumbersome but rather more precise word in this context), I am not making it a synonym for honesty or even sincerity, in the ordinary sense of that word. I am not suggesting that, in writing, or in rewriting his poems, Auden was motived by an intent to deceive his readers or even himself. Through all his writings there runs, I feel, a core of moral earnestness, a wish to be right with himself and with whatever principle of ethical significance there may be in the world. That a man should change his opinions, or shift his position in regard to great issues, with more light and more mature understanding, is a highly honorable proceeding and reflects credit on the human intelligence and our capacity for learning and improving ourselves. And that a man should have the candor to publish to the world such changes of opinion and position is again highly honorable and to be admired. In our time there are innumerable writers and artists and men in every calling who have followed a course parallel to Auden's.

And how, one may say, can we question the right of an author to be his own judge as to the intent of a piece of writing, or to make it over so as to give it a new direction? What I have suggested is that such a making over of a work of literary art is not to be accomplished by cutting out a few offensive passages, or by merely hanging the work in a different gallery in different company; and that it is vain to suppose that now it means something essentially different from what it did. Again, it is surely any writer's privilege to drop by the way poems which seem to him to be inartistic or to carry meanings that seem to him unworthy. But when he retains other poems of the same period and inspiration which carry much the same meanings, but so mingled with other quite different meanings as to invest the whole with a disquieting air of ambiguity, the question of integrity, or simple consistency, is acutely raised.

Consistency is perhaps the less misleading term, suggesting as it does an analogy with other works of art in which the material consistency of the medium is of prime importance. Such media are the potter's clay and the cook's cake-mix. Consistency may go with a considerable number of diverse ingredients; and the most seductive flavors in culinary confections are secured by the combination of many substances as seemingly incompatible as oil and vinegar, or sugar and spice. And here we are reminded of the emphasis recently laid on paradox and tension as strengthening features of poetry, and of Robert Penn Warren's view that, if one is to avoid shallowness and sentimental flatness, the final positives of a poem must be "earned" in their struggle with the negatives that are so prominent in our ordinary thinking and experience. Paradox and tension are certainly prominent features of Auden's poetry, but this analogy would be misleading if applied to the special feature I have in mind. There can be no question about the strengthening effect for poetry of tensions set up between things which actually coexist in all our experience, such as light and dark, bitter and sweet, or the realistic and the idealistic view of human nature. What I have in mind in the poetry of Auden is opposites which cannot well coexist logically or practically, like incompatible meanings of the same word in the same context, or conflicting lines of conduct in a given situation recommended in the same breath.

We must agree that in Auden's most ambiguous work the combination of ingredients is almost invariably piquant and intriguing. And the critical problem is simply whether the effect of the single poem, or still more, the effect of his poetry as a whole, has that final consistency or integrity which in the end satisfies us and gives us the feeling that, as Wordsworth would say, we have been tendered "feeding pleasures."

I will not contend that this sort of satisfaction depends on what we consider the "soundness" of the ideas or insights that inform the poetry. Certainly I would not assert that the logical soundness of Marxian ideology or the Christian faith or Freudian psychology determines the degree of satisfaction to be had in a poem inspired by these systems of thought. When it comes to the scientific theorizing of amateur psychiatrists, or the metaphysical thinking of a Kierkegaard, we enter more debatable territory, as we are likely to do whenever an element of the eccentric or uncritical is present. For in such cases the thinking, however brilliant and provocative, lends itself to a kind of sophistication that does not favor artistic consistency in the work informed by it. The same thing may be true of general concepts such as "love," when they are made to cover too many incongruous or incompatible elements. This they often seem to do in Auden when his peculiar brand of psychiatry gets mixed up with the social doctrine of "disciplined love," and these two, unequally yoked together, begin to be combined with, or pass over into, the concept of the divine Agape. It is conceivable that all three of these might be made to fuse in the mind of a Plato or in the art of a Dante; but we are not satisfied that this miracle has been worked by Auden.

In considering Auden as a poet representative of his time, what

I have called his chameleon quality might be counted to him for a merit. For our time, like any other, like Donne's or Tennyson's, has been notable for the variety and complexity of its intellectual crosscurrents and conflicting emotional attitudes; we have hardly begun yet to sort out the ideas and attitudes which, in simplifying historical perspective, may come to be thought of as dominant. And it may be considered an advantage to find between the covers of one book a maximum reflection of the characteristic movements of the time. But that is a consideration more important for the student of *Kulturgeschichte* than for the votary of the arts. Or at any rate what we prize in literary art is not confusion but richness in the representation.

In a work of art, as in a man, we are best satisfied when we are confidently aware of a wholeness, or integrality, that underlies all the diverse and even conflicting elements. And we are most satisfied when there is a consistent thread running through the whole course of a man's life or the whole body of an artist's work.

In the case of Auden, it is our doubt on this point that makes us hesitant to class him with writers in whom we have this sense of wholeness or integrity. We do not take in his work the confident satisfaction that we do in the work of a Voltaire, a Swift, a Molière, a Wordsworth, a Keats, or a Browning. Or to take examples from the poets of our own time, we do not feel in his work the integrity that we feel in poets of lesser gifts — in Spender, or Marianne Moore, or in Robinson Jeffers; or in poets of comparable or greater gifts — Wallace Stevens, or Dylan Thomas, or Frost, or Eliot. Through a man's work we are reaching out to the man. And if it is true that the style is the man, we feel with these that we are making contact with at least as much of the man as shows in his work, and that we know sufficiently with whom we are dealing. With Auden we are not sure of this.

We know that he is a very gifted actor and mimic; and he has beguiled many an hour with his impersonations. But we cannot give ourselves up to him without certain reservations. Isherwood noted how as a young man his character changed with his hat.

And we are never sure from moment to moment which of his many hats he will next be wearing.

It is, in the last analysis, a question of identity, and other things being equal, our fullest admiration goes to the poet who on this point never leaves us in doubt.

SUPPLEMENTARY NOTES

Supplementary Notes

Note to Chapter 3: Verbal Revisions

FOR readers interested in poetic craftsmanship as exhibited in quite minor retouchings given by the poet to published work when he comes back to it later, I will add a few instances of such revision beyond those given in Chapters 1 and 3. For the convenience of anyone wishing to go farther in this subject I also will list near the end of this note other poems than those discussed in which I have found minor verbal revisions.

"Journey to Iceland" is one of Auden's finest poems, unusually charged with the emotion felt in the contemplation of life in the large by a spirit eager for perfection brought face to face with the ineradicable imperfections of human nature. It was written against the dark background of fascism threatening Europe. Both Auden and MacNeice went to Iceland, it would seem, seeking relief from the pressures of European politics, hoping to find there an "island" untouched by the spiritual sickness of the times, or at least to find temporary escape in the saga world from the desolating pressures of European politics. What MacNeice found, in his "Eclogue from Iceland," was the spirit of Grettir bidding them "go back to where you belong," bidding them make what little gesture they could against the hatreds and vulgarities of their world. That was their duty and their only chance. What Auden found, in "Journey to Iceland," was a small replica of the same vulgarities and hatreds from which they were seeking to escape, the same loneliness, discouragements, and for defense and cure, nothing but the writer's art. Where "tears fall in all the rivers," and the driver "in a blinding snowstorm starts upon his deadly journey," nothing remains to the writer but to "run howling to his art."

Auden begins with an account of the traveler's "limited hope" of finding escape on this island cut off from the world by the pitiless ocean. He lists the "natural marvels" of the landscape, the historical places for the tourist's observation, the dead heroes in whom the mind may rest from its spiteful dreams, and the deserts where a lover, pale with too much passion, may at length "feel pure." But he finds that Iceland is simply "the natural setting for the jealousies of a province." He finds men asking the same desperate questions about justice and happiness. He comes to the conclusion that "our time has no favourite suburb," that the promise of youth is "only a promise"; and he reaches his final image of the driver starting out in the blinding snowstorm.

That was three years before the outbreak of the second great war. Nine years later, when the war had gone on for five years, one can imagine Auden preparing the copy for his collected poetry, and the need he felt to take particular pains with the text of this poem. At any rate, it does show many more revisions, and more minute alterations, than usual.

In 1945 "Journey to Iceland" had already appeared five times in print. The earliest version appeared in the *Listener* for October 7, 1936; the second in *Poetry* for January 1937; the third in *Letters from Iceland*, published during the year 1937 by Faber and Faber in London (in August) and by Random House in New York; the fourth version in *Selected Poems*, Faber and Faber, May 1938; and the fifth in *Some Poems*, Faber and Faber 1940. In most respects the texts of these five early versions are identical except for minute variations in punctuation. In several cases *Poetry* has minor variations in wording, of which the most striking is "marvels of nature" for "natural marvels" in the fourth stanza. *Poetry* misprinted "bog" for "bag" in stanza 5, and the *Listener* misprinted "row" for "vow" in stanza 9. The text of *Collected Shorter Poems* is identical with that of 1945.

The most extensive of all the revisions in 1945 consisted in the cutting out of the eleventh stanza of the original, in which Auden describes Iceland as a "mendicant shadow" of the European world; in Iceland people wear the same flashy suits, the Minister of Commerce is insane, and the huts are blessed with jazz and with "the beauty's set cosmopolitan smile." Here, as so often with Auden, the omission of the passage is a distinct improvement in the tone of the poem, but deprives us of a helpful gloss on the poet's intention. For these images of current European vulgarity are out of key with the rest; but they were part and parcel of the writer's thought.

In most of the other verbal revisions, a critical reader is inclined to question whether the poet's first inspirations were not the better. Thus in stanza 3, where the coordinating conjunction "and" is replaced by the subordinating "as." The "and" is more informal and "poetic" than the "as," with its suggestion of fussy precision. The same thing holds for the replacement of the definite article "the" by the indefinite articles "a" and "an." Instead of "the horse-shoe ravine" we now have "a horse-shoe ravine"; instead of "the issue of steam from a cleft," we have "an issue of steam from the cleft." Apparently the author, in the interest of accuracy, wishes to specify that there was *one* horse-shoe ravine and *one* issue of steam. But this sort of precision is prosy; and more natural even in prose is the use of "the" in this context. "The horse-shoe ravine," whether there is one or many, is the sort of thing pointed out to the tourist as a natural marvel. And so in the tenth stanza, where the slow-moving blood "asks all your questions," replaced in 1945 by "all *our* questions." The pronoun "your" is equivalent to "one's," and is at least equally natural with the more limiting "ours." In the next to the last stanza the first line began with the conjunction "for." "For our time has no favourite suburb." This followed immediately on the omitted stanza, in which Iceland was represented as infected with the urban vulgarities of jazz and the "set cosmopolitan smile." Evidently the poet thought the logical connection implied by "for" was not clear, and he substituted the expletive "no." The latter is more emphatic, more the language of "public speech," and much less Audenesque (at least in the thirties). In the fifth stanza, for "the *rock* where / An outlaw dreaded the dark," we now read "the fort." Perhaps the fort is historically more correct, but the rock of the original version is more evocative. It is as if this poet, as he grew older, had become distrustful of his instinct, and was inclined to super-compensate for his former neglect of grammatical precision. One wonders if he had fallen under the influence of some literal-minded friend, or some stylebook editor.

But perhaps the most interesting of the revisions are those in the seventh stanza, beginning,

> For Europe is absent. This is an island and therefore
> Unreal.

In 1945 he replaces "unreal" with "a refuge." The meaning is essentially the same; but the earlier phrasing is more philosophical and the latter more precise and perhaps more readily understood by the man in the street. Auden often uses the island image to suggest the way in which the sentimentalist resorts to illusions to escape the pressures of "reality." Longfellow, under the influence of German metaphysics, tells us that "life is real, life is earnest." And Auden, trying to get away from illusory "transcendentals," warns us against the dangers of isolation (or island-living). Well, unreality is man's refuge against unpleasant reality. To say that Iceland is an island and therefore unreal is imaginatively more impressive than to say it is an island and therefore a refuge; but the latter is more exact or explicit in terms of prose discourse. Personally I feel that Auden's first instinct was the better.

The stanza then continues:

> Unreal. And the steadfast affections of its dead may be bought
> By those whose dreams accuse them of being
> Spitefully alive.

I will not take the time to undertake an explication of the meaning of this rather difficult passage, but merely record that for "And the steadfast affections of its dead," Auden substituted "where the fast affections of its dead." This, on the whole, must be judged to be an improvement.

The upshot of this discussion is to suggest, first, the great pains Auden would sometimes take to polish up a poem in which he was deeply interested; and, second, how uncertain his judgment was, at this transitional stage of his writing as he passed from the earlier apolyptic style to his later more discursive manner. At times his later more conformist attitudes betrayed him into alterations not in keeping with his earlier inspiration.

In a number of poems from a few years later his revisions were more extensive and more surely such as to improve the effect. In all there were six of the sonnets in the sequence "In Time of War" to which Auden gave particularly careful attention at the time he prepared copy for *Journey to a War*. They were all reproduced without alteration in 1945 and 1950 except for a misprint in 1950 (in XIII, "mourning's" for "morning's"). One of these (XVIII) we have discussed in Chapter 3. Three of them, made up in part of lines salvaged from two discarded sonnets, will be discussed in the note to Chapters 6 and 10. There remain XII and XXI to be considered.

Sonnet XII, "And the age ended, and the last deliverer died," was written before the others of this sequence, before Auden went to China, and was published in *New Verse* in the June–July number of 1936. In this poem three separate lines were substantially revised in 1945. In the fifth line, "No, not again" (an obvious filler) was replaced by the more meaningful "They slept in peace." In the ninth line, "Only the sculptors and musicians were half-mad" reads in the revision, "Only the sculptors and the poets." Poets were better representatives of the ideology of the age than musicians; and from antiquity poets have had a reputation for madness. In line 13, in the original, the invisible powers without remorse "struck down the son, indifferent to the mother's curse." In the revised version they "struck down the sons who strayed into their course." Thus by a single stroke the author eliminated a rather melodramatic and rhetorical touch, smacking of Thomas Gray or Samuel Johnson, and tightened up the meaning of the poem. It may be noted that this poem originally bore the title "The Economic Man." In the modern world it is the economic man who takes the place of the old warrior hero in battling the dragon. When Auden fitted the poem in with the other China sonnets, the title was dropped; and now one lacks the special clue to its original intention.

Sonnet XXI was first published, with four others, in the *New Republic* for December 7, 1938, as well as in the *British Statesman and Nation* (July 2), the *Living Age* (September), and in the anthology *New Writing*, for autumn 1938. In *Journey to a War*, certain misprints in the *New Republic* version were corrected. The first line in the original reads, "Man does not die and never is completed"; in the revision, "The life of man is never quite completed," much truer as a statement of fact, and a more accurate version of what was meant. This is also an improvement on the variant form which appears in *New Writing* (autumn 1938, p. 4), "The course of man is never quite completed." In the third line, in the *New Republic*, "But, as an artist feels his goodness gone," "power" takes the place of "goodness" as the marking trait of an artist.

"Exiles" was the title originally given to this poem; and it makes a good illustration of one of the two senses in which this image is occasionally used by Auden, as pointed out in Chapter 5. Exiles are those daring spirits whose vision does not jibe with that of their fellows because it goes beyond theirs, and who must be alien in their own land or (like Joyce) deliberately leave home to maintain the independence of their thought. But the term is also applied to those defeated ones, like the characters in *The Age of Anxiety*, who are "lost in a world they never understood." It is of them it is said that "loss is their shadow-wife," and that "anxiety receives them like a grand hotel." (These uses of the term have been admirably discriminated by Richard Hoggart in his *Auden: An Introductory Study*, Chatto and Windus, and Yale

University Press, 1951.) But here again the title had to be dispensed with to conform to the general plan for the sequence. And, in any case, Auden had already included a poem entitled "The Exiles" in the first part of the 1945 collection.

In "The Cultural Presupposition," which was originally a chorus in *The Dog beneath the Skin,* four easily dispensable lines were dropped and a new line substituted for one of these, with the general effect of clarifying the thought. "In Memory of W. B. Yeats" appeared first in the *New Republic* for March 8, 1939, and the *London Mercury,* April 1939; it was reprinted in *Another Time* and finally in *Collected Poetry.* In all but the *New Republic* version the texts are identical. In the *New Republic* the very interesting second section of ten lines is missing, except that the opening line, "You were silly like us; your gift survived it all," is replaced by "He was silly like us; His gift survived it all." This line also takes the place of the final lines of the first section, "O all the instruments agree / The day of his death was a dark cold day." It looks as if Auden offered the *New Republic* a truncated version, or else an earlier version to which were added later the precious new lines. Or could it be that the limitations of space in that periodical compelled him or the editors to cut the poem down to the required length?

Poems, other than those discussed, in which I have noted minor verbal revisions are the following: "A Bride in the 30's," "A Summer Night 1933," "Autumn 1940" (variations in *New Year Letter*), "Brussels in Winter," "Dover 1937," "Epithalamion," "Gare du Midi," "Herman Melville," "Luther," "Perhaps," "Spring 1940" (variations in *New Year Letter*), "The Bonfires," "The Capital," "The Climbers," "The Composer," "The Ship," "The Witnesses," "Through the Looking-Glass," "To You Simply"; and, among the Songs and Other Musical Pieces, Nos. XIX, XX, XXIV, XXVI, XXIX, XXXV. Further data on these poems will be found in the Appendix Check List of Poems in *Collected Poetry.*

The text of *New Year Letter* (Faber and Faber, 1941) is in the main identical with that of *The Double Man* (Random House, copyright 1941); but the paging indicates that the two books were not printed from the same plates. There were variations in the notes to "New Year Letter" (apparently corrections and additions in *Double Man*); and the British volume does not include the list of Modern Sources. There are variations in the Prologue and Epilogue, "Spring 1940" and "Autumn 1940." In *New Year Letter,* the sonnets of "The Quest" are numbered but have no titles, whereas in *The Double Man* they have titles but are not numbered. The text of the poems in these two volumes and 1945 is identical with that published in the *New Republic* save for the correction of an obvious misprint in "The Hero" (XVI), and the substitution of "The Pilgrim" for "The Traveler" as title for No. IV, "The Traveler" having already been used by Auden for another poem. In the whole of the poem "New Year Letter" the only significant variations were in the title (*New Republic*, "Letter to Elizabeth Mayer": *New Year Letter*, "Letter"; *Double Man* and *Collected Poetry*, "New Year Letter") and the correction of a German phrase in Part III, line 1468 (in 1945 Auden left out the line numbers present in *New Year Letter* and *The Double Man*).

With regard to punctuation, variations from version to version are found in a very large proportion of all poems studied. It is almost sufficient to say that the early Auden was inclined to leave out marks of punctuation wherever humanly possible, and that the later Auden was inclined to restore them wherever it seemed proper to himself or his editors. In Song No. XXVI from *Letters from Iceland* and the *New Statesman and Nation*, "O who can ever gaze his fill," an interesting distinction was made in the earlier versions between the cheerful parties to this debate and the cheerless one, Death. In the longer utterances of the cheerful parties, the punctuation is normal; in the utterances of Death, in italics, there is virtually no punctuation even where it would be required in any prose writing and most poetry. Death is not interested in such ephemeral but humanly important matters as commas and semicolons. But in 1945 and 1950, each separate statement of the gloomy fellow is duly indicated by one of these marks; and the effectiveness of the poem is reduced by one degree.

The ends of lines in particular, Auden seemed to feel, could be left to their own natural pauses. Early and late, he was especially cavalier in his use of the period, ordinarily employed to mark the end of a grammatical sentence. This is particularly marked, even so late as 1945 and 1950, where the end of a long sentence, which is also the end of a stanza, is not infrequently left with no punctuation mark of any kind, to the bewilderment of a reader looking for guidance. Instances will be found in "A Bride in the '30's," "Pascal," "A Summer Night 1933," "Through the Looking-Glass," "At the Grave of Henry James," "Which Side Am I Supposed to Be On," "Casino," and other poems. Sometimes the period is omitted in the later collections where it was present in the original; sometimes it is omitted both in the original and in the later versions. Sometimes, the other way round, a period is placed at the end of a stanza though the stanza has not yet come to its predicate, as in "The Grave of Henry James." Auden doubtless considers that the presence or absence of a predicate is a purely arbitrary requirement for a sentence; psychologically, or in terms of vocal rendering, a sentence ends when you have come to the end of what you feel to be a thought unit and drop your voice; a new sentence begins where you make a new start.

The early Auden was impatient with anything that suggested convention and prescription; and he may also have been not unwilling to startle and rouse his reader by novelties of procedure. In this, of course, he was in the movement with his modernistic contemporaries, and not very radical in comparison with the others. If his punctuation later appears much more conventional, one is not certain whether this is a reflection of his growing conventionality of thought, or simply means that he did not wish to carry on a perpetual running fight with editors and style books.

Note to Chapter 5: Elimination of Stanzas

AMONG poems in which considerable passages were eliminated in the later collections probably for reasons having nothing to do with Auden's political or religious opinions, are "Danse Macabre" and "Heavy Date," both of them included in *Another Time* in their entirety. We have seen in Chapter 16 how more than half of "Danse Macabre" was cut out in adapting it as a lyric to be sung in *Ballad for Heroes*, and how two stanzas of the original poem were dropped in the collections of 1945 and 1950. In the discarded passage were listed the numerous disguises that the Devil may take on when seeking to lead men astray. These details serve no good purpose in developing the main theme of the poem; their interest is very minor, and they are there simply for the fun of it. In finally discarding them, Auden was simply unloading surplus baggage.

Similar considerations may have prevailed in the cutting out of six longish stanzas from "Heavy Date," which was in *Another Time* No. I of the second part, comprising "Lighter Poems." This is probably on the whole the least inspired composition ever made public by a poet whose imagination seldom failed to give us something piquant and stimulating. The writer is sitting at his window on a dull Sunday morning while waiting for his "darling" to come to their rendezvous, and (to kill time) reflecting on the differing quality of love as conceived by people of different occupations, and then on the very special love felt by himself and his friend. He refers to sociological findings on the subject of love by Malinowski, Rivers, and Ruth Benedict. He concedes that, while "Love requires an Object," "almost anything will do." As a child he was in love with a pumping engine, which he then thought "every bit as beautiful as you." He concludes that for them it is "mutual need" that is their one "sine qua non."

All this is "light" enough. But, not content with these coherently philosophical reflections, the author also indulges in sheer free association of ideas, frankly "writing / Down whatever nonsense / Comes into my head." And so we have "a bull dog by a trombone / On a grassy plain," a steam roller in an orange grove, and other images admittedly unexplainable by any operation of the conscious mind, and unrelated to his general theme, faintly suggesting that the author had recently visited an exhibition of paintings by Salvador Dali. And there are rambling references to the death of Zola, "murdered by a stove" — as the author might have seen him in a current moving picture — and to the difficulty of carrying St. Francis' love of the lower animals to the point of harboring love for a louse. Such is the subject matter of four rejected stanzas. Still another has reference to the author's compulsion to dream like any other intellectual of the "Middle Classes," and in another the poet says to his darling he'd "love to go on / Telling how I love you," but wisely decides that "would be silly."

Altogether the rejected passages are such as any writer with a critical sense would be sure to cut out of his poem when, in time, he came to it cold. The only thing one doesn't understand is why this whole poem did not go into the discard along with the rejected stanzas.

Note to Chapters 6 and 10: More Discarded Poems

THERE were more than half a dozen poems published in periodicals and the early collections but not reproduced in 1945 and 1950, for the discussion of which no convenient place could be found in the main body of this study. In this note I will comment briefly on such of these as have come to my notice.

No. IX of the *Poems* 1933 is a lyric known by its first line, "It's no use raising a shout." This is a lively ballad, in pungent vernacular, addressed by a disillusioned lover to his (or more likely her) opposite number, declaring that their affair is positively over. Each stanza ends with the refrain,

> Here am I, here are you:
> But what does it mean? What are we going to do?

This poem was republished, along with the entire contents of the earlier volume, in Auden's *Poems*, 1934 and 1935. It was popular with Auden's readers, and one can see no reason why it should have been denied admission to the canon. One can only guess that somehow it seemed to the poet to be too much in the vein of "light verse." It is precisely on this account that it is prized by anthologists. It is included by Oscar Williams in his "Little Treasury of Light Verse," appended to *A Little Treasury of Modern Poetry*, along with four other "lighter" poems by Auden — "Foxtrot from a Play," "Refugee Blues," "As I Walked Out One Evening," and "The Unknown Citizen" — the last three published in *Another Time*, and all retained in *Collected Poetry*.

A possible reason for discarding this poem, aside from its lightness, is suggested by the interpretation of it given by Mr. Jarrell in his *Southern Review* article already referred to. Mr. Jarrell was writing four or five years before the publication of the *Collected Poetry*, and could not have anticipated the severity with which Auden was to judge much of his early work; but he does bring into the open elements in this poem which the later Auden would probably not approve. He notes the characteristic fusion in it of evolutionary and Marxist strains. The "I" of the poem, he suggests, is presented as "a lay-figure of late capitalism," and as such, he is also the product of an evolutionary process that is destined to eliminate him altogether. "The strategic value in Auden's joining of Marxism and evolution," Mr. Jarrell concludes, "his constant shifting of terms from one sphere to the other, is this: the reader will tend to accept the desired political and economic changes (and the form of these) as themselves inevitable, something it is as ludicrous or pathetic to resist as evolution."

I doubt if many readers then or now would penetrate the meaning of this esoteric symbolism; and I don't feel certain that the images noted carried for Auden the intention indicated. But this interpretation *does* bring the poem into line with Auden's theories in the thirties, and it does make sense out of several items that must otherwise remain very dark and arbitrary (such as, "In my veins there is a wish, / And a memory of fish"). And it is clear enough that in 1945 Mr. Auden did not still regard these political and economic changes as inevitable, and still less wish to recommend submission to them. It is not likely that Mr. Auden missed Jarrell's article that concerned him so closely. This is even less likely since it was published in the same periodical that in the summer of 1939 had most hospitably welcomed the British poet by devoting eight spacious pages to four of his most serious poems, including his "Herman Melville" and his "Pascal." It seems just possible that Mr. Jarrell's explication of his early song had brought back to Auden's mind the more or less hidden implications of its imagery and determined him to eliminate it from his authorized gospel.

Among the rejected poems from *On This Island* were Nos. XXII, 1, "Night covers up the rigid land," and XVIII, "The Sun shines down on the ships at sea." The first of these is one of two songs written for the composer Benjamin Britten. It is a slight thing, in which a deserted lover nurses his wounded pride. It might well have been included among Auden's Songs and Other Musical Pieces, and there is no way of knowing why he did not consider it good enough to be given a place there. But this is not a matter on which any critic is likely to pick a quarrel with the poet.

No. XVIII is a kind of song or ballad, which has greater interest in relation to the *Weltanschauung* of the youthful Auden. It is part of a poem which appeared in the *New Oxford Outlook*, 1933, entitled "To a Young Man on His Twenty-First Birthday." The part reprinted in *On This Island* shows the young man much impressed with the futility or noxiousness of most people's occupations. Nobody has time enough to do anything important or forward-looking. The teacher sets his examinations, the journalist writes his "falsifications," the poet recites to Lady Diana, the judge enforces "the obsolete law." The climax is reached with the banker making a loan for the war, and "the expert designing his deadly long-range gun," not because he wants to, but . . . "What can I do? It's my bread and butter." This is, as it stands, a neat and effective piece of satire, but perhaps too direct, too entirely lacking in the "oblique" (the symbolic) approach, to suit Auden's ideal and genius for poetry.

This later version was an improvement over the original; it is very greatly reduced in length and otherwise altered—new matter added, and matter from the original so shifted about that it is virtually a new poem. Only the two opening stanzas and the closing stanza are identical with the original. Many lines of the middle stanzas are retained, though coming in a different order, and with occasional new lines substituted for the old. Many items in the original have considerable interest in themselves, but tend to distract attention from the main line of the poem. Some were hardly

267

more than fillers and of trifling quality. Thus the lines: "If I stop to think, it makes me feel squiffy, / Shocking I know, but it's very diffy."

One particularly interesting stanza in the anthology version, beginning "Creatures of air and darkness, from this hour," was saved up by Auden and later used to eke out a chorus in *The Dog beneath the Skin*, page 33. This stanza is in a different verse form from the earlier parts of the chorus; but Auden adds another stanza in this new verse form to give it greater carrying power.

Here we have an excellent example of Auden's bravery in cutting away superfluous matter to reduce a sprawling composition to more suitable form, and at the same time his thrifty salvaging of discarded verse for service in a different context.

Among rejected poems from *Another Time* was the sonnet on A. E. Housman. This poem begins ostensibly as an apology for Housman and what he was, under the guise of explaining how he got that way. For *tout comprendre c'est tout pardonner*. But the irony is evident from the very start: "No one, not even Cambridge was to blame." The poem is a double-barreled attack on a distinguished poet of an earlier school, who was, as Auden says, "the leading classic of his generation." It is first of all Auden's contribution to the fight for recognition by his own radical school of writing. But the animus was almost more against Cambridge than against Housman's style of writing. Cambridge, as we have seen, was synonymous, for Our party, with the conservative gang against whom the Oxford radicals directed their darts in the enthusiasm of their war-making. But, Auden writes here, not even Cambridge was to blame for the crusted scholastic pedantry that characterized the Cambridge don and author of *A Shropshire Lad*. When Auden collected his poems in 1945, the literary and ideological Indian wars of the early thirties were long over. Housman was, after all, a fellow poet, and a poet to whom some real deference was due. And he was dead. *De mortuis nil nisi bonum!* Auden had no recourse but to bury the hatchet quietly, and no reason for digging it up for the *Shorter Poems* in 1950. (In time, I suppose, it can be restored to his works with no invidious reflections upon anybody.)

Among poems published in periodicals and never reproduced in book form were two bits of verse which appeared in the *Adelphi* during 1931. The first, in the June number, consisted of two "Case Histories." Each of these was a sort of miniature anecdote or epigram in four lines without rhyme. One recorded the case of a son who, since his mother had wanted to be a missionary in

Africa, must have his novel printed in Paris. Clever sons must make a gesture of reaction against over-pious mothers. In the other the lady who had praised the writer's German was unable to see the point of his remark when he said his parents died before he was born. Her answer was: "But that is impossible." Literal-minded people will take one literally. In December appeared three "Cautionary Rhymes," their title perhaps suggested by Hilaire Belloc's *Cautionary Tales,* mentioned by Auden in his first "Letter to Lord Byron." These tiny poems were rhymed and epigrammatic, but more wise than funny. The third, however, has the familiar Auden combination of the funny and the horrific. It declares that if you deny freedom to new life,

> You'll find a cancer in your breast
> Or a burglar in your flat.

Whether or not Auden had forgotten this poem, the psychological notion that repressions can produce cancers was the germ of the ballad of "Miss Gee" discussed in Chapter 8. Auden's way of salvaging ideas or phrases from discarded poems for use in others that he kept will be further illustrated in the following paragraphs.

Two other poems not reprinted after their first appearance in magazines serve the purpose of quarries where stone could be cut for later building. They were both published in the *New Republic* for December 7, 1938. They were evidently preliminary sketches made in China and intended to form part of the sonnet sequence "In Time of War." One was entitled "Press Conference," and emphasizes the evasiveness of officials who are always so "glad to give you information."

> O lies are noble but each glib evasion
> Seems only to confirm the Yellow River crossed.

The notion of the noble lie was used by Auden in Sonnet XIII of his sequence: "All princes must employ the Fairly-Noble unifying Lie." In "Press Conference" he goes on with references to the fall of Teruel and the Austrian Anschluss. He asks if there are truly human, just, or strong men, and answers his own question in the negative — "not in this room, this world. Our small star warms to birth." This image he uses, with some adjustment, in Sonnet XIII:

> our star has warmed to birth
> A race of promise that has never proved its worth.

And then in the final tercet of the earlier poem, he strikes off a passage of two lines which he reproduces entire in XIII, referring to the prodigious but wrong-headed Chinese —

> This passive flower-like people who for so long
> In the eighteen provinces have constructed the earth.

"Press Conference" is an interesting piece of on-the-spot reporting, and not unworthy of inclusion in Auden's published work. But he made the wise choice of transferring some of its more effective touches to a poem of a higher order of imaginative power; in this latter, he starts out bravely to make a song in praise of life "as it blossoms out in a jar or a face," but ruefully admits before he has done that "history opposes its grief to our buoyant song."

In the same number of the *New Republic* appears another rejected sonnet entitled "Air Raid." And here again Auden suppresses the on-the-spot reporting in favor of the wider-ranging commentary of Sonnet XIV. In "Air Raid," "our rays investigate the throbbing sky," revealing the Japanese bombers and "the little natures that can make us cry"; in Sonnet XIV, "the sky throbs like a feverish forehead," and "the groping searchlights suddenly reveal / The little natures that will make us cry." In "Air Raid" it is the Japanese pilots who "execute the will / Of the intelligent and evil till they die." In XIV it is, more broadly, for us earth-dwellers, the earth that "obeys / The intelligent and evil till they die." Here again Auden has discarded an interesting first draft for a finished work of wider scope and vision. In XV he goes on with the subject of the Japanese bombers, so insulated from normal humanity that "they can only see / The breathing city as a target which / Requires their skill." They are a sad example of how possible it is for a people to choose a fate perversely and "turn away from freedom."

APPENDIXES

⟪I

Auden's Juvenilia

IT IS always of great interest to consider the productions of a gifted poet written in early youth and left behind him as juvenilia. We may applaud him for his taste and wisdom in judging them unworthy of inclusion in his collected volumes of poetry. But with writers as highly endowed as Auden, we are likely to find work that would be the making of many a minor poet.

In Auden's case we are peculiarly fortunate in that he had almost from the beginning a friend who knew his worth and preserved the manuscripts of very early work which the author himself might have relegated to the wastebasket. Such was Christopher Isherwood who, in "Some Notes on Auden's Early Poetry" in *New Verse*, November 1937, gives us two poems which must have been written, as I reckon, as early as the poet's eighteenth year. These are "The Carter's Funeral" and "Allendale." According to Isherwood they were entirely imitative of Hardy, Edward Thomas, and Frost. They are both written in ballad-like stanzas neatly rhymed and metered. The first one sings the death of a humble carter who is called "one of the masters of things." I suppose the Hardy influence is traceable in the bird who "looks peak-faced on, / Looks and sings." "Allendale" anticipates a favorite theme of Auden in the thirties, with its silent smelting-mill, eloquent of "decaying industries." There is here no social ideology, nor any formed philosophy. But the chimney points skyward as if it were asking, "What lies there?" while "we" take what comfort we can in our dreams, "asking no reason."

In his autobiographical novel, *Lions and Shadows*, Isherwood tells us how his friend "Hugh Weston," about Christmas 1925, sent him a big envelope full of poems in his own handwriting. Of these he prints "four which I now think the best — chiefly because they most successfully resemble their originals." Mr. Isherwood was very careful, in his note "To the Reader," not to claim absolute "truth" for the contents of this book. The characters are all, he says, "caricatures." But it is pretty well agreed that Hugh Weston bears an extremely close resemblance to Auden as he was known to Isherwood; and I see no reason for doubting that these four poems as they stand are the work of Auden.

Isherwood may be right in finding these poems important chiefly because they are so imitative (again of Hardy, Thomas, and Frost). They are not the Auden of *Poems* 1930. But each one would stand on its own merits in, say, a Georgian anthology. And in their feeling-tone and subject matter, along with their distinct points of difference from the later work, they do anticipate it in certain definite ways. The first two have subjects naturally interesting to the boy who for years planned to be a mining engineer, and which continued through the thirties to occupy the poet's imagination. The first is on "The Traction Engine." Like so much of his later machinery this one is long out of commission, "its engine rusted fast, its boiler mossed, unfired." But there is no hint of any ideological application of this fact. The writer's sentiment is all devout admiration for the disused machine, which "seems well to deserve the love we reserve / For animate things." The next presents "The Engine House" with its roaring water-powered machinery testifying to "the wild joy those waters felt / In falling."

The other two are poems of nature as symbol and promoter of human moods. "Rain" evokes the peace that follows a warm shower and heralding lark-song; with the lark-song, the poet will "know the meaning of lust again." Meantime he contents himself with a mood that makes him "one with horses and with workmen." "The Rookery" describes the nests "the rooks had made in some past century." But the rooks "have gone, have gone," said the dumb world. "We said no word; / But in the silence each one's thought was heard." This might indeed be a bit "in the school of" Frost. And it surely corresponds to something genuinely a part of Auden's sensibility. But from 1930, Auden was too deeply committed to the moral and political movements of his time to indulge himself in these indefinable "thoughts that do often lie too deep for . . ."

This is not all that we have from Auden in his teens. It is fortunate that American university libraries here and there have secured copies of *Oxford Poetry* dating from 1926–28, in which may be found work of Day Lewis, Stephen Spender, Louis MacNeice, and other poets who have since become famous. Here we have several more poems of Auden that he has not dignified by inclusion in later volumes, even in his earliest *Poems*. These were,

I assume, slightly later than those discussed above. They are still not the Auden who had found himself. He had not yet identified, sorted out, and assembled the peculiar features of his imaginative world, nor enlisted under any banner except that of the muse. But while these poems do not have the controlled direction that is given by consciousness of a mission, they are perhaps for that very reason more exuberant and uninhibited. The poet is here savoring life richly through every sense, and through every faculty of thought and feeling.

He is, to be sure, rather heavily literary and over-determined by influences from books and the arts. In one single poem ("Thomas Epilogises"), not unusually long, he has references to Rembrandt, Mozart, Handel; to Hamlet's Ophelia, Ulysses and the sirens, Job and his three preachy friends, Nebuchadnezzar in the grass, the Apocalypse, and doubting Thomas; to Swift's Brobdingnag and Beowulf's Grendel (whom he confuses with "Grendel's dam," referring to "her dripping back"). He has Job scraping himself with "blunted occam razors,/He sharpened once to shave himself." He introduces Greek and German words (*Weltschmerz* and *Wanderlust*, in the latter conscientiously giving the "u" an uncalled-for umlaut for full measure). He does not fail to introduce into the same landscape, glimpsed from a train window, gasometers, gallipygous nymphs, and pterodactyls. His "mutual love" has reached its first eutectic. His epigraph to this poem is from Gertrude Stein, and his "sunken acreage of basement kitchens" seems to show him going one better than the Eliot of the "Preludes." In "Cinders," from the same number, we have references to Plato's Symposium and the Platonic year, to Leibnitz's monads, to Browning's "Childe Roland," to Jesebel, Troytown, Babylon, and Ezekiel ("Can these bones live?"). In another from 1928, "In Due Season," we have fair Cressid and Jacob wrestling with an angel.

Frost and Eliot were not the only American poets of whom Auden had taken note. Isherwood mentions Weston's warm admiration for Robinson, whose "austerity" he prized. Isherwood and Weston "nearly had a quarrel over"

> The forehead and the little ears
> Have gone where Saturn keeps the years.

Isherwood thought this was unintentionally funny, but Weston particularly liked it. Auden's "The Letter" (in the 1926 *Oxford Poetry*) strongly reminds one of Robinson. Auden shows that he can handle with deftness the sort of ballad stanza with eight four-accent lines neatly rhyming that Robinson was so fond of, as in "For a Dead Lady," "The Master," and "The Field of Glory." One notes in particular the fastidious, grammatically involved sentences, with their curious qualifying clauses, interruptions, and neat circular articulations of thought like verbal vortices. Thus in the final stanza,

> He knows not, though perhaps he will,
> Of much remaining to be done,

or again, further down in the same sentence,

> And he knows even less than we
> However casual may be
> The comment that our shoulders make.

We do not have here the studiously negligent syntax, the mysterious disconnections of thought, with links dropped out, that characterize Auden's poetry in the thirties.

Another early poem that distinctly echoes Robinson's manner is "Portrait," included by L. A. G. Strong in his anthology, *The Best Poems of 1926*. This poem shows how well young Auden had absorbed, not merely "To a Dead Lady," but "Richard Cory," "The Master," "Eros Turannos," and perhaps "The Field of Glory." The "forehead and the little ears" and "the breast where roses could not live," etc., are matched in "Portrait" by "the lips so apt for deeds of passion," "the hair to stifle a man's breath," etc. Most striking is Auden's use of the "point of view" technique so much employed by Robinson: "We people on the pavement looked at him"; "And we who delve in beauty's lore"; "For we were not as other men: / 'Twas ours to soar and his to see." Above all, the townsfolk trying to tell the story which they are incapable of understanding: "We tell you, tapping on our brows, / The story as it should be . . ." In Auden, "we who watch / Horizons to redress the wrong / See only Götterdämmer-ung" ("The Man against the Sky"?).

> Not one of us, except in dreams,
> Can alter by a word it seems
> The story that is written.

Even the dreams may be an echo of the visions in Robinson, and the cadence of the ballad stanza ending is almost exactly the same; in Robinson:

> We'll have no kindly veil between
> Her visions and those we have seen —

> As if we guessed what hers have been,
>   Or what they are or would be.

Auden's "story" is different from Robinson's and his sophistication of a different and lesser order.

But to return for a moment to the poems in the Oxford anthologies, in these poems from 1926, 1927, and 1928 there is a pervading strain of old-mannish disillusion, cynicism, and self-conscious intellectual detachment; as is natural, considering the author's age and condition (twentyish and an Oxford wit) and the moment in our literary history (postwar and pre-depression). In their 1926 Preface, two of the authors (Charles Plumb and W. H. Auden) remark on the necessity for poetry to "face the circumstances of its time." "If," they say, "it is a natural preference to inhabit a room with casements opening on Fairyland, one at least of them should open upon the Waste Land." Rex Warner, in his verse "Manifesto" (1928), declares that he lives "snail-like in an egoistic shell," that he is always crying out for the moon, and riding to break a lance against the world

> And challenge it
>   To match my wit
> With situation and with circumstance.

Auden (in "Cinders") tells how "the crew of us" in a college room "expound our neat cigar philosophies," aware of "God above, as harmless as you please." God is "the keeper of a Paradise for fools, / A dear Arch-monad in horn spectacles."

These four poems of Auden are more than anything else about "love," or — more accurately — about the urgencies of the flesh, which in youthful celibates are everywhere known to be strong, and not least in those whose imaginations are fired by Keats and Ovid, and whose energies are not all exhausted in the football field. Their love, writes young Auden, is "as pure as the Symposium" — which, according to our prevailing standards, was not any too pure. They are willing, like other men, to

> Breathe, propagate, and with a sour face
> Do our eugenic duty by the race.

At times they pay their respects to "nicer things" — such as the beauties of nature, turning to lyrics when "tired of lechery"; but even while in the lyric mood they are likely to see "a phallic symbol in a cypress tree." They are eclectic enough to meet Desmond "behind the fives court every Sunday night," and at the same time let themselves be pursued all summer by Isobel "with her leaping breasts." They have their moments of surcease, when "love [is] put away at evenfall / Shamefacedly behind the stable wall."

We all know that "lechery" has been a dominant theme of poetry from the beginning of literary time. But seldom, since the days when in all the arts the cult of fertility was followed as a religious obligation, has this subject been served up to us more frankly, save in purposely pornographic writing. The note of satire cannot altogether mask the zestfulness with which it is done, nor overcome the sense of pathos which attaches to the evocation of youth burning in his Nessus shirt. But, to speak the plain truth, there is something refreshing about the honest candor with which this subject is handled by the young Oxford poet. Along with the pride of innovation and intellectual daring goes a drive toward truth not always found in the Muse's followers, for which the 1920's offered a favoring climate.

The poem of Auden's in the 1927 *Oxford Poetry* entitled "Extract" is the only one of these earliest pieces included in the 1928 Spender volume of Auden's *Poems*. It is there identifiable by the opening line, "Consider if you will how lovers stand," and has undergone some slight revisions from the *Oxford Poetry* version, where the first line reads, "Consider, if you will, how lovers lie." Mr. Isherwood, realizing how impossible it must be for most readers to have a sight of the Spender volume, has reproduced this poem in his *New Verse* article. It represents a transitional stage between the earliest poems and those of the 1930 volume. It is in iambic pentameters without rhyme, and it is bristling with "unpoetic" expressions like "sporadic heartburn" and "music stultified across the water." The scientific metaphor characteristic of that stage of Auden's writing appears in the reference to "clinicallyminded" lovers, to lovers who have "ligatured the ends of a farewell," and to the "glabrous suction of good-bye" (this last in the earlier version). The author is still interested in deviationist forms of love; and these lovers take a "last look back" upon the "dazzling cities of the plain where lust / Threatened a sinister rod." A new kind of critical irony is found in the turning of the frustrated lovers to scientific interests, "content if they can say 'because.' " But there is no suggestion here of the later ideology.*

* In Chapter 9 we have seen how a phrase from the final line reappears in a distinctly ideological piece included in the 1930 *Poems* as No. III, and in *Collected Poetry* under the title "Venus Will Now Say a Few Words."

ℭ II

Poems in the 1930 Volume Replaced by Others in 1933

OF THE twenty-seven poems in the 1928 volume, five survived the author's critical scrutiny till 1933 and appear in the second edition of the *Poems* as published by Faber and Faber in that year; and all of these were admitted to the canon in 1945.* There were five poems from the 1928 volume that appeared in the 1930 *Poems* but were replaced in 1933 by other, presumably later poems; and 1930 included two other poems not in either 1928 or 1933 (No. II, "Which of you waking early and watching daybreak," and No. VI, "To have found a place for nowhere"). Altogether seven poems from 1930 were discarded and replaced in 1933. The first edition of the published *Poems* offered thirty pieces in addition to the whole of *Paid on Both Sides*; and for some reason, either the poet or the publishers wished to include exactly the same number of poems in the second edition. Hence every new poem admitted required the elimination of one of the earlier pieces. I think we can say without hesitation that in every case the new poem was distinctly superior to the one it replaced. And we may plausibly assume from internal evidence that the canceled poems represented a somewhat earlier date of composition. They are, however, of very great interest as for the most part showing Auden in an experimental stage that led directly into the manner of writing that characterizes most of the work included in the 1933 volume and much of that in the 1936 *On This Island*.

* They are "To throw away the key and walk away," which became a chorus in *Paid on Both Sides*, and is given the title "The Walking Tour" in 1945; "From the very first coming down" ("The Love Letter"); "Who stands, the crux left of the watershed" ("The Watershed"); "Control of the passes was, he saw, the key" ("The Secret Agent"); and "Taller to-day, we remember similar evenings" ("As Well As Can Be Expected").

This is not true of the first of these displaced poems, No. II, which made way for the incomparable "Chorus from a Play," "Doom is dark and deeper than any sea-dingle" ("Something is Bound to Happen"). The latter is one of the most distinctive and characteristic of all Auden's poems. The piece it replaced, "Which of you waking early and watching daybreak," would hardly be recognizable as Auden's if we did not have the evidence of this publication. It is not so much experimental in new modes of expression, as an able exercise in nineteenth-century modes. It is a longish meditative poem written in fluid, straightforward-moving blank verse lines in stanzaic groups of varying length. In one place an Arnoldian Homeric simile ("As a boy lately come up from country to town . . . So is the fate of the insolent mind") takes up twenty lines of a single stanza. The whole makes a sort of exultant hymn in honor of the earth and its abounding life as a man conceives of it as he goes to work at daybreak full of anticipations of "success, / A fresh rendezvous or unexpected inheritance." It is not mainly satirical, as this passage might suggest, but radiates the feeling of peace and promise inspired by the new day. This reminds the poet of "the first day when truth divided/Light from the original and incoherent darkness." There is a sense of a man's personal oneness with nature that might make you think of George Meredith or Walt Whitman. That earth, "the mother of all life," is "always with him and will sustain him," is often felt by him, as when "caught in a storm on fells / And sheltering with horses behind a dripping wall." (This image, in almost the same words, is used in "Rain," one of the early poems reproduced by Isherwood in his *New Verse* notes.) One detail that does distinctly remind one of the later Auden is the reference to "the insolent mind" that has "homicidal phantasies / Of itself as the divine punisher of the world" (cf. "Victor"), and to the "aphasia and general paralysis of the insane." But very unlike Auden, at any rate in tone and feeling, is the concluding passage about "truth's assurance of life – that darkness shall die," and death's "promise to man . . . of security upon earth and life in heaven." This is, to be sure, the dream of old men, free from all anxieties and even from animal desire, sitting peacefully in their rock gardens and blessing the new life before they die. But this tones in perfectly with the general tenor of the piece, reminding one more of Whitman than of any poet of our day; there is even the Whitmanesque promise to man "pushed on like grass-blade into undiscovered air."

Most of all distinguishing Auden's manner here from his poetry of the thirties and forties is the simple plainness of the effusive style, with its direct statements instead of symbolic indirections or (as in the later poetry) the James-like involution of figure and syntax.

The other six rejected poems in their experimental modernism are much more like those that take their place. The main difference is that in the new poems the new style is successfully handled, and even when the connection of the images is somewhat vague the desired effect is secured, whereas in the earlier ones the obscurities of reference are too dense, the several parts of the poem fail to connect, and the intended effect does not come off. Thus in No. VI, "To have found a place for nowhere," the most persistent reading fails to make us sure whether the subject is soldiers returned to their homes, either living or as "revenants," or something altogether different. In the new poem, on the other hand, "Between attention and attention" (now "Make Up Your Mind"), while the technique is daringly modernistic and "oblique," we are in no doubt that what we have to do with is the ordinary run of people so worn down by material and social pressures and attrition, so lacking in personal drive and direction, that they are left without distinct faces, or any grace, and are occupied with nothing more significant than "registering / Acreage, mileage."

The old No. IX ("The crowing of the cock") has apparently this same theme clumsily and ineffectually developed, and is replaced by the extremely effective monologue "It's no use raising a shout." This latter poem we have discussed in the Notes, but without much success in guessing at the reasons why Auden discarded it in 1945. No. XIII ("Bones wrenched, weak whimper, lids wrinkled, first dazzle known") would seem to have a related theme, tracing the gradual effacement of personal identity as life goes on and the continuous reduction of the sense of value in human experience until one arrives at "life stripped to girders, monochrome." But the theme bogs down in the end in undecipherable metaphors. It is replaced by the lively satirical song about a woman without recognizable character, "What's in your mind, my dove, my coney," reproduced in 1945 as Song No. XXXVIII. This latter is not one of Auden's most successful poems, but it has a much sharper definition than the piece it replaces.

No. XXIII seems to have a religious theme. At least it introduces a soul conscious of sin, the cross, and the Saviour ("approaching, utterly generous, came on / For years expected, born only for me"). And it concludes with the prophetic declaration "these bones shall live" and an obscure reference to Biblical characters ("Adam's brow" and "the wounded heel"). Along with these go still more obscure references perhaps to love, "the delicious lie." But it is hard to place this in the picture along with the religious images and with others from nature. This number was replaced by "The Bonfires" ("Look there! the sunk road winding"). This latter poem is certainly not remarkable for clarity of intention. But it has the sharpness and imaginative definition of the best poems of this period. Each crisp stanza brings its provocative and intriguing images — "the cock's alarm / In the strange valley," "hedgehog's gradual foot, / Or fish's fathom," "The sound behind our back of glacier's calving." The images all seem to have their relation to the ideological struggle in which the poet is now "engaged." "Glacier's calving" is perhaps a symbol for the violent social displacements of his time with the birth of new ideas; and the images from fish and hedgehog suggest the evolutionary process, now in its social phase. The cock's alarm is probably a reminder of the Biblical cock-crow and the challenge to Peter's loyalty. There is no doubt that this poem is to be preferred to the one whose place it took.

Nos. XXV and XXVII are both poems having to do with love. The first ("Suppose they met, the inevitable procedure") introduces lovers whose meeting blots out the rubbishy experiences of the day, but who, since they feared "that doddering Jehovah whom they mocked," never took advantage of the unlocked doors to sleep together. So far all seems clear; but then are intruded several seemingly unrelated episodes of drenched fishermen dragging their boat up on the beach, of the survivor of some combat dropping as the bayonets close in, of (I think) a childbirth, and of a thousand dancers transformed to tiger lilies, and finally of what appears to be a reference to the inscription over the gate to Dante's hell. It is quite impossible to get these disparate items into any sort of pattern. It is as if the poet had been trying his hand at some dadaist or surrealist method of free association. All that remains for the most diligent reader is some notion of lovers who were damned because they did not have the courage to defy some authority which they did not acknowledge as binding. In 1933 this poem was replaced by the highly impressive "Better Not" ("Who will endure / Heat of day and winter danger"). There is probably some parallelism of theme between this and the earlier poem. But here we have definitely the challenge to the generous spirit of brave adventuring not taken up, for "no one goes / Further than railhead and the ends of piers." The dreary meaninglessness of such lives is symbolized by a typical Auden landscape of rusting rails, signals down, and ships long high and dry, with unused maps lying about in them. The stultifying spirit of prohibition is symbolized by "the rotting stack / Where gaitered gamekeeper with dog and gun / Will shout 'Turn back.' " This is one of Auden's most brilliant imaginative projections of the revulsion he felt in those days from the negative morality of submission to prescribed codes, his demand for personal freedom of choice and for courage in following the natural dictates of the heart. It is a vast improvement over the confused poem it replaces. But it is not easy to see how in 1945 he could have admitted it to the canon; he must somehow have given it a quite new interpretation conformable to his new religious philosophy.

No. XXVII, "No trenchant parting this," is a much more intelligible composition than XXV. It is first a characterization of the spirit in which two lovers break off their relation; and then a picture of the way one of them, who has been swimming, throws back the hair from his forehead and smiles, a smile that signifies the end to the joy they have had. One cannot help thinking of the way the man in Eliot's "La Figlia que Piange" leaves the girl, "Some way incomparably light and deft . . . / Simple and faithless as a smile and shake of the hand." It is, in the latter half, a rather effective poem. But it cannot in any way compare with the one that took its place, "What Do You Think?" ("To ask the hard question is simple"), which has much in common with it in conception, and which also makes one think of "La Figlia che Piange." There is much here too about the manner in which these two were together, just how they listened and spoke, "The eyes looking / At the hands helping." There is, too, as in Eliot, the continuing resonance of their meeting in the memory; and the question is raised whether love can remember "the question and the answer," and whether it can recover "What has been dark and rich and warm all over." There are fine supporting touches from nature. And altogether we have here a good example of how the poet by deeper dwelling on his subject can, from a fumbling start, arrive at a perfect embodiment of his poetic idea.

C III

Check List of Poems in the *Collected Poetry*

THE following abbreviations are used: CP for the *Collected Poetry* 1945; CSP for the *Collected Shorter Poems* 1950; OTI for *On This Island* (the American edition of *Look, Stranger!*, 1936) 1937; *Paid* for *Paid on Both Sides* (in *Poems* 1930 and 1933, etc.); *Journey* for *Journey to a War* 1939; AT for *Another Time* 1940; DM for *The Double Man* 1941; NYL for *New Year Letter* 1941 (the British edition of *The Double Man*). *Poems* 1930 refers to poems included in both editions of this volume; *Poems* 1933 to those included only in the second edition. But in the case of poems from *Paid*, page references are to the more readily accessible 1933 edition of *Poems*.

In each case the items are given in the following order: the title in CP, the beginning page, the first line, the page number in CSP, title in CSP if changed from CP, the place of earlier publication in an Auden volume, then in periodical or anthology earlier than Auden book collection, with the earlier title if any or different from CP, brief notations as to revisions, and finally publication in *Poems* 1934, *Selected Poems* 1938, and/or *Some Poems* 1940. Unless otherwise specified, it is understood that revisions noted as made in an earlier Auden volume were retained in CP and CSP.

Where a poem is indicated as from *Paid*, special reference is not made to CSP, to *Poems* 1934, or to *Some Poems* 1940, it being understood that this charade was included entire in all these volumes. Nor is reference made to the *Criterion*, in which this work appeared in January 1930, pp. 268–90.

In the case of Part I: Poems, the titles are given in italics, the first lines in roman type; in Part III, Songs and Other Musical Pieces, the first lines, serving as titles, are given in italics; in Part V, "The Quest," the individual titles are given in italics, as in CP and DM, and the first lines in roman type, and the numbers given in NYL but not in CP or DM, are given in parenthesis.

Asterisks are attached to poems as in CP and CSP, where a footnote states: "The poems marked by asterisks are published for the first time in book form." This is obviously more true for CP than for CSP.

PART I: POEMS

A Bride in the '30's, 36, Easily, my dear, easily you move your head. CSP
51. OTI XXI. The *Listener,* 20 Feb. 1935, p. 317 (vol. 13.1), same title.
Half a dozen verbal alterations and much variation in punctuation in CP.
Also included in *Selected Poems* and *Some Poems.*

Adolescence, 23, By landscape reminded once of his mother's figure. CSP
41. Prologue to *The Orators.* Also in *Selected Poems.*

Aera sub Lege, 117, Hidden law does not deny. Notes to "NYL," DM 113.

*A Healthy Spot, 134, They're nice – one would never dream of going
over. CSP 144.

All Over Again, 83, Not from this life, not from this life is any. *Paid* in
Poems 1933, 12.

Always in Trouble, 24, Can speak of trouble, pressure on men. *Paid* in
Poems 1933, 12.

Another Time, 41, For us like any other fugitive. CSP 57. AT I, xxx.

*Are You There? 35, Each lover has some theory of his own. CSP 50,
"Alone."

As He Is, 179, Wrapped in a yielding air, beside. CSP 187. AT I i, first
line title.

As Well As Can Be Expected, 113, Taller today, we remember similar evenings. CSP 122, "Taller To-day." *Poems 1930* XXVI.

A Summer Night 1933 (to Geoffrey Hoyland), 96, Out on the lawn I lie
in bed. CSP 110. OTI II. The *Listener,* March 1934, 421. Four stanzas cut
out in CP, and other minor revisions. Also in *Selected Poems* and *Some
Poems.*

As We Like It, 25, Certainly our city with its byres of poverty down to.
CSP 41, "Our City." OTI XXXI. "Epilogue." Two stanzas cut out in
CP and other minor revisions. Also in *Selected Poems.*

*Atlantis, 20, Being set on the idea. CSP 37.

At the Grave of Henry James, 126, The snow, less intransigent than their
marble. CSP 137. *Partisan Review,* July–August 1941. Slight verbal alterations and five stanzas omitted in CP.

Autumn 1940, 101, Returning each morning from a timeless world. Epilogue to NYL and DM. The *Nation,* Dec. 7, 1940, 563. Textual variations in NYL.

Better Not, 176, Who will endure. CSP 184. *Poems 1933,* XXV.

Blessed Event, 103, Round the three actors in any Blessed Event. Notes to
"NYL," DM 159.

Brussels in Winter, 151, Wandering the cold streets tangled like old string.
CSP 160. AT I x. *New Writing,* Spring 1939, 1. Slight revisions in AT.

*But I Can't, 135, Time will say nothing but I told you so. CSP 146, "If I
Could Tell You."

*Canzone, 161, When shall we learn, what should be clear as day. CSP 169.
Partisan Review, September–October 1943, 389.

Casino, 91, Only the hands are living, to the wheel attracted. CSP 106.
OTI XXV.

*Christmas 1940, 118, The journals give the quantities of wrong. CSP 130.
CSP corrects a misprint.

Consider, 27, Consider this and in our time. CSP 43. *Poems 1930* XXIX.

Crisis, 169, Where do They come from? Those whom we so much dread.
CSP 177. AT I xxiv. *Atlantic Monthly,* September 1939, 358.

Danse Macabre, 59, It's farewell to the drawing-room's civilized cry. CSP 77. AT I viii. The *Listener*, 17 Feb. 1937, 304 (vol. 17.1), "Song for the New Year." Two stanzas cut out in CP.

Do Be Careful, 151, Upon this line between adventure. CSP 159, "Between Adventure." *Poems* 1930 VII.

Dover 1937, 111, Steep roads, a tunnel through the downs are the approaches. CSP 121. AT I xxviii, "Dover." *New Verse*, November 1937, 2, "Dover." Slight verbal revision in AT.

Edward Lear, 76, Left by his friend to breakfast alone on the white. CSP 93. AT I vii, same title.

Epitaph on a Tyrant, 99, Perfection, of a kind, was what he was after. CSP 112. AT II vi, same title. *New Statesman and Nation*, Jan. 21, 1939, 81.

Epithalamion (For Guiseppe Antonio Borgese and Elizabeth Mann, Nov. 31, 1939), 171, While explosives blow to dust. CSP 179. AT III vi, same title.

Family Ghosts, 132, The strings' excitement, the applauding drum. CSP 143. *Poems* 1930 XX.

Few and Simple, 161, Whenever you are thought, the mind. CSP 169.

For the Last Time, 56, In gorgeous robes befitting the occasion. Notes to "NYL," in DM 132.

Gare du Midi, 9, A nondescript express is in from the South. CSP 25. AT I xxv, same title. *New Writing*, Spring 1939, 2, same title. Slight revisions in AT.

Happy Ending, 125, The silly fool, the silly fool. CSP 137. *Poems* 1930 XIX.

Have a Good Time, 155, "We have brought you," they said, "a map of the country." CSP 163. "Journal of an Airman," *The Orators* 46.

Heavy Date, 105, Sharp and silent in the. CSP 115. AT II i. Six stanzas cut out in CP.

Hell, 51, Hell is neither here nor there. CP 67. AT I xii.

Herman Melville (for Lincoln Kirstein), 146, Towards the end he sailed into an extraordinary mildness. CSP 154. AT I xiii. *Southern Review*, Autumn 1939, 367 (vol. 5.2). Some lines cut out and other revisions in AT.

His Excellency, 17, As it is, plenty. CSP 31. OTI XII. Correction of misprint in CP.

Hongkong 1938, 62, Its leading characters are wise and witty. CSP 79. *Journey* 23, "Hongkong."

In Father's Footsteps, 95, Our hunting fathers told the story. CSP 109, "Our Hunting Fathers." OTI III. The *Listener*, 30 May 1934, 911, "Poem." Also in *Selected Poems*.

In Memory of Ernst Toller (d. May 1939), 124, The shining neutral summer has a voice. CSP 136. AT III iii, same title.

In Memory of Sigmund Freud (d. Sept. 1939), 163, When there are so many we shall have to mourn. CSP 171. AT III v, same title.

In Memory of W. B. Yeats (d. Jan. 1939), 48, He disappeared in the dead of winter. CSP 64. AT III ii, same title. *London Mercury*, April 1939, 579. *New Republic*, Mar. 8, 1939, 123. Ten lines cut out of *New Republic*, or supplied later.

In Sickness and in Health (For Maurice and Gwen Mandelbaum), 29, Dear, all benevolence of fingering lips. CSP 45.

In War Time (For Caroline Newton), 3, Abruptly mounting her ramshackle wheel. CSP 19.

I Shall Be Enchanted, 39, Enter with him. CSP 55, "Legend." *The Dog beneath the Skin*, 26. Slight revisions in CP.

It's So Dull Here, 144, To settle in this village of the heart. CSP 154. OTI XXIII. *New Verse*, June 1934, 12, "Poem." Extensive revisions in OTI.

It's Too Much, 131, The Spring unsettles sleeping partnerships. *Paid* in *Poems* 1933, 21.

January 1, 1931, 153, Watching in three planes from a window overlooking the courtyard. CSP 161. *The Orators*, Ode No. I. Much revision in CP.

Journey to Iceland, 7, And the traveller hopes: "Let me be far from any." CSP 23. *Letters from Iceland*, 25, "Journey to Iceland: A Letter to Christopher Isherwood, Esq." The *Listener*, 7 Oct. 1936 (vol. 16.2). *Poetry*, January 1937, 179. Revisions in both *Letters from Iceland* and CP. Also in *Selected Poems* and *Some Poems*.

Kairos and Logos, 11, Around them boomed the rhetoric of time. CSP 25. *Southern Review*, Spring 1941, 729 (vol. 6.4).

Law Like Love, 74, Law, say the gardeners, is the sun. CSP 91. AT I ii.

Leap before You Look, 123. The sense of danger must not disappear. CSP 135.

Let History Be My Judge, 156, We made all possible preparations. CSP 165. *Poems* 1930, XII.

Like Us, 123, These had stopped seeking. CSP 134. Extract from Ode IV of *The Orators*, 100.

Luther, 179, With conscience cocked to listen to the thunder. Notes to "NYL" in DM 125. The *Christian Century*, Oct. 2, 1940, 1208. Verbal revisions in DM.

Macao, 18, A weed from Catholic Europe, it took root. CSP 35. *Journey* 22.

Make Up Your Mind, 22, Between attention and attention. CSP 40, "Easy Knowledge." *Poems* 1933 VI.

Many Happy Returns (for John Rettger), 68, Johnny, since today is. CSP 84.

Matthew Arnold, 54, His gift knew what he was — a dark disordered city. CSP 73. AT I xxvii, same title. The *Listener*, 14 Sept. 1939, 508, and *The Nation*, Sept. 30, 1939, 350.

Meiosis, 79, Love had him fast but though he fought for breath. CSP 96. OTI XXIX. The fifth one of four sonnets in *New Verse*, Oct. 1933, 16. Slight verbal revision in OTI.

Missing, 43, From scars where kestrels hover. CSP 58. *Poems* 1930 XXIV.

Montaigne, 98, Outside his library window he could see. Notes to "NYL" in DM 126.

Mundus et Infans (for Arthur and Angelyn Stevens), 72, Kicking his mother until she let go of his soul. CSP 89.

Musée des Beaux Arts, 3, About suffering they were never wrong. CSP 19. AT I xxi, same title. *New Writing*, Spring 1939, 2, "Palais des Beaux Arts." Slight corrections in AT.

1929, 62, It was Easter as I walked in the public gardens. CSP 79. *Poems* 1930 XVI. Sixteen lines cut out in the 1933 edition. Also in *Some Poems*.

Nobody Understands Me, 72, Just as his dream foretold, he met them all. CSP 88. OTI XI.

Not All the Candidates Pass, 83, Now from my window-sill I watch the night. CSP 99. OTI X. *New Country* (ed. Michael Roberts) 1933, 205.

This is Part II of "A Happy New Year" (to Gerald Heard). Three stanzas cut out in OTI, and two more in CP. Other minor revisions.

Orpheus, 158, What does the song hope for? And the moved hands. CSP 166, misprint in the first line. AT I xix, same title. *London Mercury*, June 1937, 118.

Our Bias, 118, The hour-glass whispers to the lion's paw. CSP 130. AT I xv.

Oxford, 80, Nature is so near; the rooks in the college garden. CSP 96. AT I v, same title. The *Listener*, 9 Feb. 1938, 323 (vol. 19.1). Considerable revision and one stanza dropped in AT.

Pascal, 86, O had his mother, near her time, been praying. CSP 101. AT I xvi, same title. *Southern Review*, Autumn 1939, 370 (vol. 5.2) *Life and Letters Today*, January 1940.

Paysage Moralisé, 47, Hearing of harvests rotting in the valleys. CSP 63. OTI VII. The *Criterion*, July 1933, 606. Also in *Selected Poems*.

Perhaps, 89, O Love, the interest itself in thoughtless Heaven. CSP 104. OTI I, "Prologue." *New Country*, 1933, 193, "Prologue." *New Statesman and Nation*, July 16, 1932, 69, "Poem." Minor revisions in OTI and CP. Also in *Selected Poems* and *Some Poems*.

Petition, 110, Sir, no man's enemy, forgiving all. CSP 120. *Poems* 1930 XXX. Also in *Some Poems*.

Please Make Yourself at Home, 82, Not as that dream Napoleon, rumour's dread and centre. CSP 98, "Like a Vocation." AT I xxiii. *Southern Review*, Autumn 1939, 366 (vol. 5.2), "The Territory of the Heart."

Pur, 134, This lunar beauty. CSP 145, "Like a Dream." *Poems* 1930 XVII.

Remember, 144, Tonight the many come to mind. *Paid* in *Poems* 1933, 33.

Rimbaud, 121, The nights, the railway-arches, the bad sky. CSP 133. AT I xi, same title. *New Writing*, Spring 1939, 3.

Schoolchildren, 52, Here are all the captivities; the cells are as real. CSP 68. AT I iv, same title. The *Listener*, 21 July 1937, 130, "Hegel and the Schoolchildren."

September 1, 1939, 57, I sit in one of the dives. CSP 74, "1st September, 1939." AT III iv, same title. *New Republic*, Oct. 18, 1939, 297, "September: 1939." Eighth stanza cut out in CP.

Shut Your Eyes and Open Your Mouth, 104, Sentries against inner and outer. CSP 114. *Poems* 1930 XIV.

Something Is Bound to Happen, 34, Doom is dark and deeper than any sea-dingle. CSP 49, "The Wanderer." *Poems* 1933 II. *New Signatures* (ed. Michael Roberts) 30, "Chorus from a Play." Also in *Selected Poems* and *Some Poems*.

Spain 1937, 181, Yesterday all the past. The language of size. CSP 189. AT III i, same title.

Spring 1940, 93, O season of repetition and return. Prologue to NYL and DM 11. Textual variations in NYL.

Such Nice People, 92, On Sunday Walks. CSP 107. *Poems* 1930 XXI.

The Bonfires, 77, Look there! The sunk road winding. CSP 93. *Poems* 1933 XXIII. Some revision in CP.

The Capital, 100, Quarter of pleasures where the rich are always waiting. CSP 113. AT I xiv, same title. *New Writing*, Spring 1939, 1. Revisions in AT.

The Climbers, 41, Fleeing the short-haired mad executives. CSP 56. OTI XX. *New Oxford Outlook*, November 1933, 153, "Poem." Revisions in CP.

APPENDIXES

The Composer, 5, All the others translate: the painter sketches. CSP 21. AT I xxii, same title. *New Writing*, Spring 1939, 4. Verbal revisions in AT.

The Creatures, 133, They are our past and our future: the poles between which our desire unceasingly is discharged. CSP 144. AT I iii, same title.

The Cultural Presupposition, 46, Happy the hare at morning, for she cannot read. CSP 62, "Culture." From *The Dog beneath the Skin* 91. Several lines cut out in CP.

The Decoys, 122, There are some birds in these valleys. CSP 134. "Journal of an Airman" in *The Orators*, 70, no title.

The Diaspora, 55, How he survived them he could never understand. Notes to "NYL" in DM 90.

The Exiles, 158, What siren zooming is sounding our coming. CSP 166. Ode III in *The Orators*. Four stanzas cut out in CP. Also in *Selected Poems*.

The Labyrinth, 9, Anthropos apteros for days. Notes to "NYL" in DM 154.

The Lesson, 116, The first time that I dreamed, we were in flight. CSP 128.

The Love Letter, 44, From the very first coming down. CSP 60. *Poems* 1930 V. This is also in *Poems* 1928.

The Model, 45, Generally, reading palms or handwriting or faces. CSP 61.

The Novelist, 39, Encased in talent like a uniform. CSP 54. AT I xx, same title. *New Writing*, Spring 1939, 4.

The Prophets, 99, Perhaps I always knew what they were saying. CSP 112. AT I ix. *Southern Review*, Autumn 1939, 369 (vol. 5.2).

The Questioner Who Sits So Sly, 177, Will you turn a deaf ear. CSP 185. *Poems* 1930 I.

The Riddle, 149, Underneath the leaves of life. CSP 157. AT I xxxi. *New Republic*, July 26, 1939, 331, "The Leaves of Life."

The Secret Agent, 29, Control of the passes was, he saw, the key. CSP 44. *Poems* 1930 XV. Also in *Poems* 1928.

The Ship, 132, The streets are brightly lit; our city is kept clean. CSP 142. *Journey* 20. The *Listener*, 18 Aug. 1938, 343 (vol. 20.1). *New Republic*, Dec. 7, 1938, 130. Minor revision in *Journey*.

The Sphinx, 33, Did it once issue from the carver's hand. CSP 49, *Journey* 19. Also in *Some Poems*.

The Traveller, 55, Holding the distance up before his face. CSP 73. *Journey* 21. *New Statesman and Nation*, Aug. 27, 1938, 314.

The Unknown Citizen, 142, He was found by the Bureau of Statistics to be. CSP 152. AT II vii, same title. The *Listener*, 3 Aug. 1939, 215.

The Voyage, 168, Where does the journey look which the watcher upon the quay. CSP 176. *Journey* 17.

The Walking Tour, 145, To throw away the key and walk away. *Paid* in *Poems* 1930, 28.

The Watershed, 175, Who stands, the crux left of the watershed. CSP 183. *Poems* 1930 XI. Also in *Poems* 1928 VI.

The Witnesses, 185, Young men late in the night. CSP 194. *The Dog beneath the Skin* 13, beginning "The young men in Pressan to-night." The *Listener*, 12 July 1933. The second half of this poem, in six-line stanzas, beginning "You are the town and we are the clock," is taken from Part III of a much longer poem, "The Witnesses," to be found in Alida Monro, *Recent Poetry 1923–1933*, Poetry Bookshop, Dec. 1933, and in

289

Janet Adam Smith, *Poems of Tomorrow*, Chatto and Windus, 1935. One stanza was omitted and other revisions made in *The Dog beneath the Skin*.

This One, 19, Before this loved one. CSP 36. *Poems* 1930 XVIII.

Through the Looking-Glass, 113, The earth turns over; our side feels the cold. CSP 126. OTI IX. *New Verse*, February 1934, 6, "Poem." Minor revisions in CP. Also in *Selected Poems* and *Some Poems*.

To E. M. Forster, 53, Here, though the bombs are real and dangerous. CSP 72. Dedicatory poem to *Journey*.

Too Dear, Too Vague, 78, Love by ambition. CSP 94. *Poems* 1930 X.

*To You Simply, 42, For what as easy. CSP 57. *New Signatures*, 1932, 32, "Poem." Two lines cut out and other minor revisions in CP.

True Enough, 54, His aging nature is the same. Notes to "NYL" in DM 93.

Two's Company, 5, Again in conversations. CSP 21, "Never Stronger." *Poems* 1930 VIII.

Venus Will Now Say a Few Words, 109, Since you are going to begin today. CSP 118. *Poems* 1930 III. Also in *Selected Poems*.

Voltaire at Ferney, 6, Almost happy now, he looked at his estate. CSP 22. AT I xvii, same title. The *Listener*, 9 Mar. 1939, 53. *Poetry*, June 1939, 119. One stanza omitted and other minor revisions in CP.

We All Make Mistakes, 152, Watch any day his nonchalant pauses, see. CSP 160, "A Free One." *Poems* 1930 IV. Also in *Selected Poems* and *Some Poems*.

We're Late, 26, Clocks cannot tell our time of day. Notes to "NYL" in DM 75.

What Do You Think? 141, To ask the hard question is simple. CSP 151, "The Hard Question." *Poems* 1933 XXVII. The *Criterion*, July 1933, 608. Also in *Selected Poems*.

What's the Matter? 143, To lie flat on the back with the knees flexed. CSP 153. OTI XIX.

When the Devil Drives, 147, Under boughs between our tentative endearments how should we hear. CSP 156. *Poems* 1930 XXVIII.

Which Side Am I Supposed to Be On? 136, Though aware of our rank and alert to obey orders. CSP 147. Ode V in *The Orators* (To My Pupils). *New Signatures*, 1932, 23, "Ode." Also in *Selected Poems*.

Who's Who, 17, A shilling life will give you all the facts. CSP 31. OTI XIII. Also in *Selected Poems* and *Some Poems*.

Year after Year, 140, Though he believe it, no man is strong. *Paid* in *Poems* 1933, 37.

PART II: LETTER TO A WOUND

Letter to a Wound (prose), 191. *The Orators*, Book I, "The Initiates," IV, "Letter to a Wound," 35.

PART III: SONGS AND OTHER MUSICAL PIECES

I. *As I walked out one evening*, 197. CSP 227. AT I xxvi. *New Statesman and Nation*, Jan. 15, 1938, 81, "Song."

II. *At last the secret is out, as it always must come in the end*, 199. CSP 229. The *Ascent of F6*, 116.

**III. *Carry her over the water*, 199. CSP 229. *Paul Bunyan*.

IV. *Dear, though the night is gone*, 200. CSP 230. OTI XXVIII. *New Verse*, April–May 1936, 12, "The Dream."

*V. *Eyes look into the well*, 201. CSP 231.

VI. *Fish in the unruffled lakes*, 201. CSP 231. OTI XXVII. The *Listener*, 15 April 1936, 732 (vol. 15.2), "Poem." Also in *Some Poems*.

*VII. *"Gold in the North," came the blizzard to say*, 202. CSP 232. *Paul Bunyan*.

*VIII. *Song for St. Cecilia's Day*, 203. In a garden shady this holy lady. CSP 233.

*IX. *Jumbled in the common box*, 206. CSP 235. The *Nation*, March 29, 1941, 382, "Song."

*X. *Lady, weeping at the crossroads*, 207. CSP 236.

XI. *Lay your sleeping head, my love*, 208. CSP 238. AT I xviii, *New Writing*, Spring 1937, 122, "Poem."

XII. (Tune: St. James' Infirmary) *Let me tell you a little story*, 209. CSP 239. AT II ii 1, "Miss Gee." *New Writing*, Fall 1937, 161. Minor revisions and considerable expansion in AT.

XIII. *Let the florid music praise*, 213. CSP 243. OTI IV.

XIV. *Look, stranger, on this island now*, 214. CSP 243. OTI V. The *Listener*, 18 Dec. 1935, 1110 (vol. 142), "Seaside." One stanza omitted in OTI. Also in *Selected Poems* and *Some Poems*.

XV. *May with its light behaving*, 214. CSP 244. OTI XVI. The *Listener*, 15 May 1935, "Poem." Also in *Selected Poems* and *Some Poems*.

*XVI. *My second thoughts condemn*, 215. CSP 245.

XVII. *Not, Father, further do prolong*, 216. CSP 246. Ode VI in *The Orators*. Revisions in CP.

XVIII. *Now the leaves are falling fast*, 217. CSP 247. OTI VIII. *New Statesman and Nation*, 14 March 1936, 392. Also in *Selected Poems* and *Some Poems*.

XIX. *Now through night's caressing grip*, 218. CSP 247. *The Dog beneath the Skin*, 115. Also in *Selected Poems* and *Some Poems*.

XX. – *"O for doors to be open and an invite with gilded edges,"* 219. CSP 248. OTI XXIV. The *Spectator*, May 31, 1935, 917, "In the Square." Textual revisions in CP. Also in *Selected Poems* and *Some Poems*.

XXI. *O lurcher-loving collier, black as night*, 220. CSP 249. AT II iv, "Madrigal." *New Verse*, Summer 1938, 5, "From the Film 'Coal-Face.'" Also in *Selected Poems* and *Some Poems*.

XXII. *O the valley in the summer where I and my John*, 220. CSP 250. AT II iii 1, "Johnny" in "Cabaret Songs for Miss Hedli Anderson."

XXIII. *Over the heather the wet wind blows*, 221. CSP 251. AT II v, "Roman Wall Blues."

XXIV. *O what is that sound which so thrills the ear*, 222. CSP 251. OTI VI. *New Verse*, December 1934, 4, "Ballad." Very slight revisions in OTI.

XXV. *"O where are you going?" said reader to rider*, 223. CSP 253. Epilogue to *The Orators*. Also in *Selected Poems* and *Some Poems*.

XXVI. *"O who can ever gaze his fill,"* 224. CSP 253. From "Letter to William Coldstream, Esq." in *Letters from Iceland*, 227. *New Statesman and Nation*, 16 January 1937, 81, "Song." Minor revisions in *Letters from Iceland* and in CP. Also in *Selected Poems*.

XXVII. *O who can ever praise enough*, 226. CSP 255. From "Letter to E. M. Auden," in *Letters from Iceland*, 142. *Poetry*, January 1937, 182.

XXVIII. *Say this city has ten million souls*, 227. CSP 256. AT II viii, "Refugee Blues."

XXIX. *Seen when night is silent*, 228. CSP 258. *The Dog beneath the Skin*, 65 (Song of the 1st Mad Lady). Many phrases from II of "Five poems" in *New Verse*, October 1933, 15. Verbal alterations in CP.

XXX. *Stop all the clocks, cut off the telephone*, 228. CSP 258. AT II iii, 3, "Funeral Blues." *The Ascent of F6*, 112. Two stanzas substituted in AT for the last three stanzas in *The Ascent*.

XXXI. *That night when joy began*, 229. CSP 259. OTI XXVI. Misprint in CSP or correction of misprint in CP.

*XXXII. *The single creature leads a partial life*, 230. CSP 259. *Paul Bunyan*.

XXXIII. *The summer quickens all*, 230. Paid in *Poems* 1933, 32.

*XXXIV. *Though determined Nature can*, 231. CSP 260 (XXXIII).

XXXV. *Underneath the abject willow*, 232. CSP 261 (XXXIV). OTI XXII, 2, being the second of "Two Songs" (for Benjamin Britten). Also in *Selected Poems*. CP has one line altered from OTI and *Selected Poems*.

XXXVI. (Tune: Frankie and Johnny) *Victor was a little baby*, 233. CSP 262 (XXXV). AT II ii 3, "Victor." *New Writing*, February 1937, 194, "Victor." Important revisions and eliminations in AT.

XXXVII. *Warm are the still and lucky miles*, 238. CSP 267 (XXXVI). AT I xxix, "Song."

XXXVIII. *What's in your mind, my dove, my coney*, 239. CSP 268 (XXXVII) *Poems* 1933 XIII. Also in *Selected Poems*.

PART IV: DEPRAVITY: A SERMON

Depravity: A Sermon (prose), 243–47. This is the Vicar's Sermon in *The Dog beneath the Skin*, 162–69.

PART V: THE QUEST: A SONNET SEQUENCE

The Quest: A Sonnet Sequence, 251–62. NYL 163–82; DM 165–84. *New Republic*, Nov. 25, 1940, 716–19. In the *New Republic* the sonnets have both numbers and titles; in NYL, numbers but no titles; in DM and CP, titles but no numbers. In all versions the sonnets are in the same order.

(I) *The Door*, Out of it steps the future of the poor.

(II) *The Preparations*, All had been ordered weeks before the start.

(III) *The Crossroads*, The friends who met here and embraced are gone.

(IV) *The Pilgrim*, No window of his suburb lights that bedroom where. In *New Republic* and DM the title is "The Traveler."

(V) *The City*, In villages from which their childhoods came.

(VI) *The First Temptation*, Ashamed to be the darling of his grief.

(VII) *The Second Temptation*, The library annoyed him with its look.

(VIII) *The Third Temptation*, He watched with all his organs of concern. Published in *Poetry*, October 1940, p. 9, under the title "Poem," with several variations in punctuation and spelling.

(IX) *The Tower*, This is an architecture for the odd.

(X) *The Presumptuous*, They noticed that virginity was needed.

(XI) *The Average*, His peasant parents killed themselves with toil.

(XII) *Vocation*, Incredulous, he stared at the amused.

(XIII) *The Useful*, The over-logical fell for the witch.

(XIV) *The Way*, Fresh addenda are published every day. Slight variations in punctuation.

292

(XV) *The Lucky*, Suppose he'd listened to the erudite committee.
(XVI) *The Hero*, He parried every question that they hurled. Obvious misprint in DM.
(XVII) *Adventure*, Others had swerved off to the left before.
(XVIII) *The Adventurers*, Spinning upon their central thirst like tops.
(XIX) *The Waters*, Poet, oracle and wit.
(XX) *Garden*, Within these gates all opening begins.

PART VI: NEW YEAR LETTER

New Year Letter (January 1, 1940) (To Elizabeth Mayer) Under the familiar weight, 265–316. NYL, "Letter," 17–75. DM 15–71. The *Atlantic Monthly*, January and February 1941, 56–63, 185–93, "Letter to Elizabeth Mayer" (January 1, 1940). Among the four texts there are many minor variations. The three book versions agree in correcting the German in line 1468, CP p. 309. The CP version is more nearly identical with that of DM. In line 1001, "But why and when and where and how?" corresponds in these versions with "But where to serve and when and how?" in NYL. Line 1030–31 precede 1032–33 in these versions and follow them in NYL. Proper names, frequently given in capitals in CP and DM, are in the same cases given in italics in NYL and in lower-case roman letters in the *Atlantic*. Many words and phrases from Latin, Greek, and French, given in italics in CP and DM, are printed roman in NYL and the *Atlantic*. NYL and DM agree in numbering the lines in the margin, and the number of lines is the same. None of the variations noted involve any significant differences in meaning.
[Notes to the poem "New Year Letter" (prose and verse). These are not reproduced in CP or CSP; but many of incidental poems are reprinted in CP, Part I, and are referred to in this Check List. Between the text of the notes in NYL and DM there are a few minor variations and (apparently) corrections made in DM; and the list of Modern Sources (DM 161–62) is not included in NYL.]

PART VII: IN TIME OF WAR

A Sonnet Sequence with a verse commentary

In Time of War: Sonnet Sequence, 319–34. *Journey to a War*, 259–85.
I. So from the years the gifts were showered: each. CSP 271.
II. They wondered why the fruit had been forbidden. CSP 271.
III. Only a smell had feelings to make known. CSP 272.
IV. He stayed: and was imprisoned in possession. CSP 272.
V. His generous bearing was a new invention. CSP 273.
VI. He watched the stars and noted birds in flight. CSP 273.
VII. He was their servant – some say he was blind. CSP 274.
VIII. He turned his field into a meeting-place. CSP 275.
IX. They died and entered the closed life like nuns. CSP 275.
X. As a young child the wisest could adore him. CSP 276.
XI. He looked in all His wisdom from the throne. CSP 276. Also in *Some Poems*.
XII. And the age ended, and the last deliverer died. CSP 277. *New Verse*, June–July 1936, 8, "The Economic Man." Considerable revision in *Journey*. Also in *Some Poems*.

XIII. Certainly praise: let the song mount again and again. CSP 277. Misprint in CSP. Passages in this poem taken from a discarded poem, "Press Conference," in *New Republic*, Sept. 7, 1938, 130.

XIV. Yes, we are going to suffer, now; the sky. CSP 278. Passages from this poem taken from a discarded poem, "Air Raid" in *New Republic*, Dec. 7, 1938, 130.

XV. Engines bear them through the air: they're free. CSP 279. This poem is a continuation of the theme of XIV and "Air Raid."

XVI. Here war is simple like a monument. CSP 279.

XVII. They are and suffer: that is all they do. CSP 280.

XVIII. Far from the heart of culture he was used. CSP 280. *New Statesman and Nation*, July 2, 1938, 14; *New Republic*, Dec. 7, 1938, 130; the *Living Age*, September 1938, 24: in all of the periodicals the title is "Chinese Soldier." The third stanza greatly altered in *Journey*.

XIX. But in the evening the oppression lifted. CSP 281.

XX. They carry terror with them like a purse. CSP 281.

XXI. The life of man is never quite completed. CSP 282. *New Republic*, Dec. 7, 1938, 130, "Exiles." *New Writing*, Autumn 1938, 4, "Exiles." In *Journey* revisions and corrections.

XXII. Simple like all dream wishes, they employ. CSP 283. Misprint in CSP.

XXIII. When all the apparatus of report. CSP 283.

XXIV. No, not their names. It was the others who built. CSP 284.

XXV. Nothing is given: we must find our law. CSP 284.

XXVI. Always far from the centre of our names. CSP 285.

XXVII. Wandering lost upon the mountains of our choice. CSP 285. The *Listener*, 3 Nov. 1938, 943, "Sonnet." Several verbal revisions in *Journey*. *Commentary*, 337–47, Season inherits legally from dying season, CSP 286–96; *Journey* 289–301. Two stanzas omitted and much revision in CP. *Some Poems*, 79–80, has the last stanzas beginning "Night falls on China," identical with *Journey*. CSP appears to be in all respects identical with CP.

PART VIII: THE SEA AND THE MIRROR
A Commentary on Shakespeare's "The Tempest"
(To James and Tania Stern)

The Sea and the Mirror, 351–404. For the *Time Being*, 3–59. I have observed no variations except slight differences in spelling, and the substitution of I, II, III for Chapter I, Chapter II, Chapter III, in CP. Alonso's speech to Ferdinand, 366–69, appeared in the *Partisan Review*, September–October 1943, 386–88, "Alonzo to Ferdinand." Slight revision and correction of misprint in CP.

PART IX: FOR THE TIME BEING
A Christmas Oratorio
(In Memoriam Constance Rosalie Auden 1870–1941)

For the Time Being, 407–66. First published in the volume *For the Time Being*, New York: Random House, copyright 1944. I have observed no variations whatever except typographical: the separate sections of the poems, such as "Advent," are in CP indicated by roman numerals (I, II, etc.) instead of being spelled out (ONE, TWO, etc.).

CIV

Poems of Auden Not Reprinted in the *Collected Poetry*

1. Very early poems reproduced by Isherwood in "Some Notes on Auden's Early Poetry" in *New Verse*, November 1937, 4–9:
The Carter's Funeral, Sixty odd years of poaching and drink.
Allendale, The smelting-mill stack is crumbling, no smoke is alive there.
2. Very early poems reproduced by Isherwood in *Lions and Shadows*:
The Traction Engine, 186
The Engine House, 186
Rain, 187
The Rookery, 187
3. Poems in Spender's hand-printed volume, *Poems* 1928, not reprinted in *Poems* 1930:
I. (a) The sprinkler on the lawn.
  (b) We saw in Spring.
  (c) This peace can last no longer than the storm.
  (d) 'Buzzards' I heard you say.
  (e) Consider if you will how lovers stand (given with slight variations by Isherwood in *New Verse*).
  (f) Amoeba in the running water.
  (g) Upon the ridge the mill-sails glow.
II. I chose this lean country.
V. On the frontier at dawn getting down.
IX. Because the sap fell away.
X. The mind to body spoke the whole night through.
XII. The four sat on in the bare room.
XIII. To-night when a full storm surrounds the house.
XIV. Night strives with darkness, right with wrong.
XVII. The spring will come.
XVIII. The summer quickens grass.
XIX. Some say that handsome raider still at large.
4. Poems in *Poems* 1930 not continued in the 1933 edition:
II. Which of you waking early and watching daybreak.
VI. To have found a place for nowhere.
VII. The crowing of the cock.
XIII. Bones wrenched, weak whimper, lids wrinkled, first dazzle known.

XXIII. Nor was that final, for about that time.
XXV. Suppose they met, the inevitable procedure.
XXVII. No trenchant parting this.
5. Poem in L. A. G. Strong, *The Best Poems of 1926*, New York, 1926.
Portrait, The lips so apt for deeds of passion, 9.
6. Poems in *Oxford Poetry*:
Thomas Epilogizes (1926), Inexorable Rembrandt rays, which stab.
The Letter (1926), He reads and finds the meaning plain.
Cinders (1926), Four walls are drawn tight round the crew of us.
Extract (1927), Consider, if you will, how lovers lie (see also above under 3).
In Due Season (1928), In Spring we waited. Princes felt.
7. Poems in *The Orators* not reprinted in CP:
From "Journal of an Airman":
After the death of their proud master, 44.
Well, Milder, if that's the way you're feeling, 49.
Last day but ten, 58.
Beethameer, Beethameer, bully of Britain, 65.
I'm afraid it sounds more like a fairy story, 66.
The draw was at five. Did you see the result? 73.
From the Six Odes:
II. (To Gabriel Carritt, Captain of Sedbergh School XV, Spring, 1927)
Walk on air do we? And how!
IV. (To John Warner, Son of Rex and Frances Warner) Roar Gloucestershire, do yourself proud.
8. Poems in *Poems 1933* not reprinted in CP:
IX. It's no use raising a shout. Also in *Poems 1934*.
XX. Get there if you can and see the land you once were proud to own. Also in *Poems 1934*.
9. Poems in *On This Island* not reprinted in CP:
XIV. Brothers, who when the sirens roar. Michael Roberts, ed., *New Country*, Hogarth Press 1933, "A Communist to Others."
XV. The chimneys are smoking, the crocus is out in the border. *New Country*, 1933, "Poem," 214–16, Me, March, you do with your movements master and rock. (Restored in 1950 as "Two Worlds.")
XVII. Here on the cropped grass of the narrow ridge I stand. *New Oxford Outlook*, November 1933, 148, "The Malverns." (Restored in CSP as "The Malverns.") Also in *Selected Poems* and *Some Poems*.
XVIII. The sun shines down on the ships at sea. (Greatly reduced from "To a Young Man on His Twenty-First Birthday," in *New Oxford Outlook*, 1933.)
XXII, 1. First of Two Songs (for Benjamin Britten), Night covers up the rigid land.
XXX. (To Christopher Isherwood), August for the people and their favourite islands. *New Verse*, October–November 1935, 7, "To a Writer on His Birthday." (Restored in CSP, 32 as "Birthday Poem.") Also in *Selected Poems* and *Some Poems*.
10. Poems in *Letters from Iceland* not reprinted in CP:
Last Will and Testament (Auden and Louis MacNeice), We, Wystan Hugh Auden and Louis MacNeice.
Letter to Lord Byron (Parts I–V), Excuse, my Lord, the liberty I take.
Detective Story, For who is ever quite without his landscape.

Letter to William Coldstream, Esq., "But Landscape," cries the Literary Supplement. (This poem includes a lyric reprinted in CP as Song XXVI.)
11. Poems in *Another Time* not reprinted in CP:
A. E. Housman, No one, not even Cambridge, was to blame.
James Honeyman, James Honeyman was a silent child ("Three Ballads").
O Tell Me the Truth about Love ("Four Cabaret Songs for Miss Hedli Anderson").
Calypso, Driver, drive faster and make a good run ("Four Cabaret Songs").
12. Poems in *New Year Letter* and *The Double Man* not reprinted in CP: It might seem both pedantic and invidious to list the thirty-odd scraps of verse interspersed among the prose notes to "New Year Letter," which served somewhat the same purpose for that poem as Eliot's famous notes for *The Waste Land.* They are for the most part nuggets of rhymed thought set down by Auden in his notebook and transferred to the printed volume. Many of them are mere quatrains — not lacking in wit — and will doubtless be collected in time in some appendix to Auden's poetical works. Anyone wishing not to have missed anything from Auden's hand can easily look them up in either the American or the British publication, one of which is to be found in many public libraries. But we may well assume that the nine of them reproduced in CP (listed in Chapter 18 and in our Check List) are those best worth preserving and exhibiting.
13. Poems in periodicals and anthologies since 1930 not reprinted in any of Auden's book collections:
Case-Histories. The Adelphi, June 1931, 198.
Cautionary Rhymes. The Adelphi, December 1931, 181.
Song, I have a handsome profile. *New Verse,* January 1933, 3.
Interview, Having abdicated with comparative ease. *Cambridge Left,* Summer 1933, 5.
A Happy New Year, Part I (to Gerald Heard), *New Country* (Michael Roberts, ed.), Hogarth Press, 1933.
Five Poems. New Verse, October 1933, 14–17.
 I. Sleep on beside me though I wake for you.
 II. I see it often since you've been away.
 III. At the far end of the enormous room.
 IV. The latest ferrule now has tapped the curb.
 [V. Love had him fast: but though he caught his breath. This became XXIX of *On This Island* and "Meiosis" in CP.]
Poem, The fruit in which your parents hid you, boy. *New Verse,* July 1933.
Speech from a Play, . . . you too are patients. *New Verse,* February 1935, 10.
Foxtrot from a Play, The soldier loves his rifle. *New Verse,* April–May 1936, 12.
Blues (for Hedli Anderson). Ladies and Gentlemen, sitting here. *New Verse,* May 1937, 4.
Poem, Under the fronds of life, beside. *New Writing* (John Lehmann, ed.), Fall 1937, 170.
Air Raid, Our rays investigate the throbbing sky. *New Republic,* Dec. 7, 1938, 130.

Press Conference, Officials are always glad to give you information. *New Republic*, Dec. 7, 1938, 130.

The Glamour Boys and Girls Have Grievances Too, You've no idea how dull it is. The *New Yorker*, Aug. 24, 1940, 20.

14. Poems in the five dramatic compositions not reprinted in CP:

It seems hardly worth while listing here the fifty-odd pieces of detachable verse in Auden's dramatic compositions not reprinted in the *Collected Poetry* further than I have done in Chapters 12–15 and in the Check List. Readers wishing to be thorough in their reading will have little difficulty in finding these five plays in university libraries or the public libraries of the larger American cities. *Paid on Both Sides* was reproduced entire not merely in the *Poems* 1930 (1933), but also in *Poems*, Random House 1934, Faber and Faber 1934 and 1935, in *Some Poems*, 1940, and in *Collected Shorter Poems* 1950. *The Dance of Death* was reproduced entire in the 1934 (1935) *Poems*; and the three Auden-Isherwood plays are even more readily accessible. I will, however, list certain pieces from the plays that were printed in periodicals or early collections but discarded in CP.

From *The Dog beneath the Skin*.

Chorus, The Summer holds: upon its glittering lake, 11–13. *Selected Poems*, 65–67. *Some Poems*, 31– 33.

Chorus, You with shooting-sticks and cases for field-glasses, 54–56. *Selected Poems*, 72–74.

Semi-Chorus, Love, loath to enter, 179. *Selected Poems*, 76. This is a small fragment of a piece entitled "Poem," from *New Oxford Outlook*, May 1934, 82–84. Even from this portion some lines have been cut out in *The Dog*.

From *The Ascent of F6*.

Song of Mrs. Ransom, Michael, you shall be renowned, 54. *Selected Poems*, 79.

Speech of Mrs. A, Death like his is rich and splendid, 88–89. *Selected Poems*, 80.

Chorus and Mrs. R., Acts of injustice done, 117–18. *Some Poems*, 39.

15. Lyrics in the opera, *Paul Bunyan*, music by Benjamin Britten. This opera was copyrighted but not published. The manuscript of Auden's libretto, in the Columbia University Library, I have not seen, and I cannot identify any poems from this work other than the three named by Auden in the copyright acknowledgment in CP and referred to in Chapter 16.

16. Poems omitted in CP but restored in CSP:

Prothalamion, You who return to-night to a narrow bed, 192. This is made up from choruses in *The Dog beneath the Skin*, 140–41, 143.

Two Worlds, The chimneys are smoking, the crocus is out in the border, 123. (See above, section 9.) Extensive revisions in OTI.

The Malverns, Here on the cropped grass of the narrow ridge I stand. (See above, section 9.) One eleven-line stanza cut out in OTI; seven three-line stanzas cut out in CSP.

Birthday Poem (to Christopher Isherwood), August for the people and their favourite islands, 32. (See above, section 9.) Slight revision in CSP in stanza 8.

17. The earliest listed poem of Auden's, beginning, "It is a lovely sight and good," appeared in *Public Schools Verse, 1923–1924*, Heinemann 1924. This I have not seen.

BIBLIOGRAPHICAL NOTE
AND INDEX

Bibliographical Note

VOLUMES BY AUDEN INCLUDING POETRY

Poems. W. H. Auden. S.H.S. (Hand printed at Oxford by Stephen Spender; probably fewer than 45 copies).

Poems. London: Faber and Faber, September 1930.

The Orators: An English Study. London: Faber and Faber, 1932.

Poems. London: Faber and Faber, November 1933. (This is the second edition of the 1930 *Poems*; seven poems in 1930 edition replaced by others in 1933.)

The Dance of Death. London: Faber and Faber, November 1933 and October 1935.

Poems. London: Faber and Faber, 1934 and October 1935; New York: Random House, copyright 1934. (This includes the contents of *Poems* 1933, including *Paid on Both Sides,* and of *The Orators* and *The Dance of Death.*)

The Dog beneath the Skin, or Where Is Francis? A play in three acts, by W. H. Auden and Christopher Isherwood. London: Faber and Faber, May 1935; New York: Random House 1935. (My references are to the Faber and Faber volume.)

The Ascent of F6, A tragedy in two acts, by Auden and Isherwood. London: Faber and Faber, September 1936. New York: Random House, copyright 1937. (My references are to the Random House volume.)

On This Island. New York: Random House, 1937. Issued in England under the title *Look, Stranger!* London: Faber and Faber, October 1936. (My references are to the Random House volume, but I use the date of first publication, 1936.)

Spain. London: Faber and Faber, 1937 (twelve pages).

Letters from Iceland, by Auden and Louis MacNeice. London: Faber and Faber, July 1937; New York: Random House, copyright 1937. (My references are to the Random House volume.)

On the Frontier, A Melodrama in Three Acts, by Auden and Isherwood. London: Faber and Faber, October 1938; New York: Random House, copyright 1938. (My references are to the Random House volume.)

Selected Poems. London: Faber and Faber, 1938.

Journey to a War, by Auden and Isherwood. London: Faber and Faber,

March 1939; New York: Random House, copyright 1939. (My references
are to the Random House volume.)

Another Time. London: Faber and Faber, June 1940. New York: Random
House, copyright 1940. (My references are to the Random House volume.
In all essentials the texts seem to be identical.)

Some Poems. London: Faber and Faber, 1940, fourth impression 1944. (In-
cludes *Paid on Both Sides,* and a selection of lyrics from *Poems* 1933, *The
Orators, The Dog beneath the Skin, The Ascent of F6, Look, Stranger!,
Letters from Iceland,* and *Journey to a War.*)

The Double Man. New York: Random House, copyright 1941. (This is almost identical in contents and text with *New Year Letter,* London: Faber
and Faber, May 1941. There are slight variations in text and even in contents, mainly in the notes to "New Year Letter." The London volume
presumably appeared earlier than the New York one. My references are
in general to the Random House volume.)

For the Time Being. New York: Random House, copyright 1944; London:
Faber and Faber, March 1945. (Includes "The Sea and the Mirror" and
"For the Time Being.")

The Collected Poetry of W. H. Auden. New York: Random House, copyright 1945; London: Faber and Faber, 1948.

The Age of Anxiety, A Baroque Eclogue. New York: Random House;
London: Faber and Faber, 1948.

Collected Shorter Poems 1930–1944. London: Faber and Faber, Ltd., 1950.

Nones. New York: Random House, copyright 1951; London: Faber and
Faber, 1952.

Mountains. London: Faber and Faber, 1954.

The Shield of Achilles. New York: Random House, 1955; London: Faber
and Faber, 1955.

The Old Man's Road. New York: Voyages Press, 1956.

OTHER PUBLICATIONS INCLUDING POETRY BY AUDEN

Ernst Toller, *No More Peace! A Thoughtful Comedy,* translated by Edward Crankshaw, music by Herbert Murrill, lyrics translated and adapted
by W. H. Auden. New York and Toronto: Farrar and Rinehart, copyright 1937.

Ballad of Heroes, for tenor or soprano solo, chorus, and orchestra, by W. H.
Auden and Randall Swingler, composer Benjamin Britten. London:
Boosey and Hawkes, 1939.

Paul Bunyan, an opera, music by Benjamin Britten, with libretto by Auden.
London: copyright by Hawkes and Son, 1941. Withdrawn before publica-
tion. Auden's manuscript of the libretto is in the Columbia University
Library.

The Rake's Progress, opera in three acts, music by Igor Strawinsky, libretto
by Auden and Chester Kallman. Copyright 1949, 1950, 1951, by Boosey
and Hawkes, libretto printed in U.S.A.

"Delia or a Masque of Night: Libretto for a One Act Opera," by Auden
and Chester Kallman, in *Botteghe Oscure* XII (1953), 164–210.

The Magic Flute: An Opera in Two Acts, by Mozart, libretto by Auden
and Chester Kallman, after the German libretto of Schikaneder and Giesecke. New York: Random House, 1956.

AUDEN BIBLIOGRAPHIES

"Writings by W. H. Auden," in *New Verse*, Nos. 26–27, November 1937, pp. 32–46. (A list of his published volumes and of many individual poems in periodicals and anthologies (26 items), of articles in books (10), and miscellaneous prose (10).)

"A W. H. Auden Bibliography 1924–1955," compiled by Joseph P. Clancy, in *Thought* (Fordham University Quarterly), XXX, Summer 1955, pp. 260–70. (This very useful bibliography includes books by Auden, poetry, drama, prose; uncollected materials — juvenilia, essays, and reviews (more than 100 items), introductions to books; critical books and articles on Auden (100 items); and victrola recordings.)

BOOKS AND ARTICLES CONCERNED WITH AUDEN REFERRED TO IN THE TEXT

W. H. Auden. *Making, Knowing and Judging.* Oxford: Clarendon Press, 1956. (This is Auden's inaugural lecture as professor of poetry delivered at Oxford on June 11, 1956. In slightly abbreviated form it appears as "The Making and Judging of Poetry," *Atlantic Monthly*, January, 1957, pp. 44–52. It is a valuable source of information about Auden's beginnings as a poet and his present views on the nature and function of poetry.)

Richard Hoggart. *Auden: An Introductory Essay.* London: Chatto and Windus, 1951; New Haven: Yale University Press, 1951. (My references are to the Chatto and Windus volume.)

Christopher Isherwood. *Lions and Shadows.* London: Hogarth Press, 1943; Norfolk, Conn.: New Directions, 1947.

Christopher Isherwood. "Some Notes on Auden's Early Poetry," *New Verse*, November 1937, pp. 4–9.

Randall Jarrell. "Changes of Attitude and Rhetoric in Auden's Poetry," *Southern Review*, Autumn 1941, pp. 326–49.

Randall Jarrell. "From Freud to Paul: The Stages of Auden's Ideology," *Partisan Review*, Fall 1945, pp. 437–57.

John Lehmann. *The Whispering Gallery: Autobiography I.* New York: Longmans, Green and Co., 1955.

Justin M. Replogle. "The Auden Canon: the 1930's Poetry of W. H. Auden, C. Day Lewis, and Stephen Spender." Doctor's dissertation, University of Wisconsin, 1956. This very useful study is unpublished, but may be consulted in microfilm.

Delmore Schwartz, "The Two Audens," *Kenyon Review*, Winter 1939, 35–45.

James G. Southworth, *Sowing the Spring; Studies in British Poets from Hopkins to MacNeice.* Oxford: Basil Blackwell, 1940. "Wystan Hugh Auden," 128–47.

Monroe K. Spears. "Late Auden: The Satirist as Lunatic Clergyman," *Sewanee Review*, Winter 1951, 50–74.

Monroe K. Spears. "The Dominant Symbols of Auden's Poetry," *Sewanee Review*, Summer 1951, 392–425.

Stephen Spender. "W. H. Auden and his Poetry," *Atlantic Monthly*, July 1953, 74–79.

Index

I. Names and Subjects

ond versions of poems not retained, 66, 69, 70, 73, 162; of passages in second versions restored in 1945, 199
Eliot, T. S., 41, 60, 74, 115, 116, 121, 139, 143, 148, 169, 182, 207, 208, 225, 247, 250, 253, 275, 283
Emerson, Ralph Waldo, 23
Engels, Friedrich, 26, 130
Eros, 57; and Agape, 18, 30–1, 51, 58, 157, 217; creative, 18, 19; and death-wish, 50; Freudian, 18, 30, 51, 174; and guilt, 241; Paidagogos, 63
Escapism, 72, 115, 151, 169
Ethical absolutes, 31–5
Ethics and religion. *See* Christianity, etc., City of God, Deity, Discipline of character, Eros, Ethical absolutes, Freeing men's minds, Heroic quests, Higher consciousness, Moral earnestness, Personified life force
Evolutionism, 23, 34, 36. *See also* Darwinian evolutionism

Fabianism, 115
Fadiman, Clifton, 233
Fascism, 6, 8, 21, 38, 61, 70, 72, 88, 137, 179, 186, XVI, 233, 236, 248
Fear, 72, 75, 87, 91; and greed, 39
Fernandez, Ramon, 143
Francis of Assisi, Saint, 265
Franco, Francisco, 137, 236
Freeing men's minds, 78, 85
Freud, Sigmund, 44, 46, 115, 127, 244
Freudian and pseudo-Freudian, 17, 30, 46, 51, 102–5, 163, 174, 252
Frost, Robert, 253, 273, 274, 275

Gay, Maisie, 121
Genghis Khan, 6
Gide, André, 48
Giesecke or Gieseke, Karl Ludwig, 190, 302
Gilbert, Sir William Schwenck, and Sullivan, Sir Arthur, 155, 174
Goethe, Johann Wolfgang von, 245
Goya, Lucientes, 139
Gradualism, 115
Gray, Thomas, 261
Grigson, Geoffrey, 137
Groddeck, George, and Groddeckian psychology, 44, 46, 83–4, 93, 121, 130–4, 245

Group theatre, 223
Guilt, 235–7

Handel, George Friedrich, 275
Hardy, Thomas, 273, 274
Heard, Gerald, 23, 36, 118, 119, 137, 244
Hegel, Georg Wilhelm Friedrich, 6, 245
Hemingway, Ernest, 94
Henry the Fifth, King, 176
Heroic quests and pilgrimages, 88, 96, 97, 158–61, 224
Hesiod, 128
Higher Consciousness, 23, 118
Hitler, Adolph, 35, 50, 94, 95, 192, 197, 198, 236, 238
Hobbes, Thomas, 6
Hogarth, William, 203
Hoggart, Richard, 32, 52, 81, 82, 261, 303
Holliday, Terence, 194
Hoover, Herbert, 94, 95
Hopkins, Gerard Manley, 70, 112, 247
Horace, 98, 143
Horder, Sir Thomas, 120
Houdini, Harry, 179
Housman, A. E., 268
Humanism, humanist, etc., 7, 8, 59, 128, 163, 187, 231, 237, 248
Huxley, Aldous, 245
Huxley, Julian, 245

Isherwood, Christopher, 5, 10, 37, 65, 69, 90, 98, 103–4, 114, 124, 143, 148, 150, 155, 166, 167, 185, 187, 189, 197, 215, 226, 247, 248, 273–4, 278, 301, 303

James, Henry, 59–61, 83, 207, 247, 281
James, William, 245
Jarrell, Randall, 32, 33, 99, 218, 232, 235, 239, 266, 267, 303
Jeans, Sir James, 94, 245
Jeffers, Robinson, 167, 253
Johnson, Samuel, 261
Jones, Ernest, 121
Joyce, James, 52, 115, 116, 261
Jung, Carl Gustav, 127, 245
Juvenal, 74
Juvenilia, 67, 93, Appendixes I and II

Kafka, Franz, 46, 207

II. Auden's Poems and Volumes Containing Poems

Of poems in the Check-List, only those are given here to which reference is made in the main text. Published volumes are italicized, and only those pages are listed where reference is made to the volume as a whole. For individual poems in *Collected Poetry* Part I titles are given, followed by variant titles in *Collected Shorter Poems*; in Part III, first lines with the number. Poems not reprinted in *Collected Poetry* are starred; for these, titles are given if present in the original form, otherwise first lines, and reference is made to earlier volumes of Auden's in which they appeared.

A Bride in the 30's, 262, 263, 285
*Acts of injustice done (*Ascent of F6*), 183, 298
*Address for a Prize-Day (*Orators*, prose), 17–20, 85
Adolescence, 95, 96, 285
*A. E. Housman (*Another Time*), 268, 297
Aera sub Lege, 210, 285
*After the death of their proud master (*Orators*), 82, 296
*A Happy New Year (Part I), 54, 112, 117–21, 297
*Air Raid, 42, 270, 297
*Allendale, 273, 295
All Over Again, 145, 285
Always in trouble, 33, 145, 285
*Always the following wind of history (Paid on Both Sides, *Poems* 1930), 145, 212.
Another Time, 22, 99, 100, 106, 127, 142, 201, 210, 221, 266, 297, 302
Are You There? (Alone), 213, 285
*Argument (*Orators*, prose), 16, 33, 77
As I walked out one evening (Song I), 266, 290
A Summer Night 1933, 46–7, 262, 263, 285
As We Like It, 19, 45–6, 213, 285
As Well As Can Be Expected, 212, 279, 285
At last the secret is out, as it always must come in the end (Song II), 184–5, 226, 290
At the Grave of Henry James, 55, 59–63, 212, 247, 263–4, 285
*August for the people and their favourite islands (*On This Island*; in 1950, Birthday Poem), 74–6, 82, 215, 296, 298
Autumn 1940, 22, 97, 210, 262, 285

Ballad of Heroes, 21, 191, 198–200, 227–8, 264, 302
*Because I'm come it does not mean to hold (Paid, *Poems* 1930), 146–7
*Beethameer, Beethameer, bully of Britain (*Orators*), 84, 296
Better Not, 282–3, 285
*Blues: Ladies and gentlemen sitting here, 125, 222, 297
*Bones wrenched, weak whimper, lids wrinkled, first dazzle known (*Poems* 1930 only), 281, 295
*Brothers, who when the sirens roar (*On This Island*; original title, A Communist to Others), 23, 54, 67–70, 119, 247, 296
Brussels in Winter, 262, 285
But I Can't (If I Could Tell You), 213, 285

*Calypso (*Another Time*), 101–2, 297